LAWRENCE KASANOFF

MALIBU BLONDE

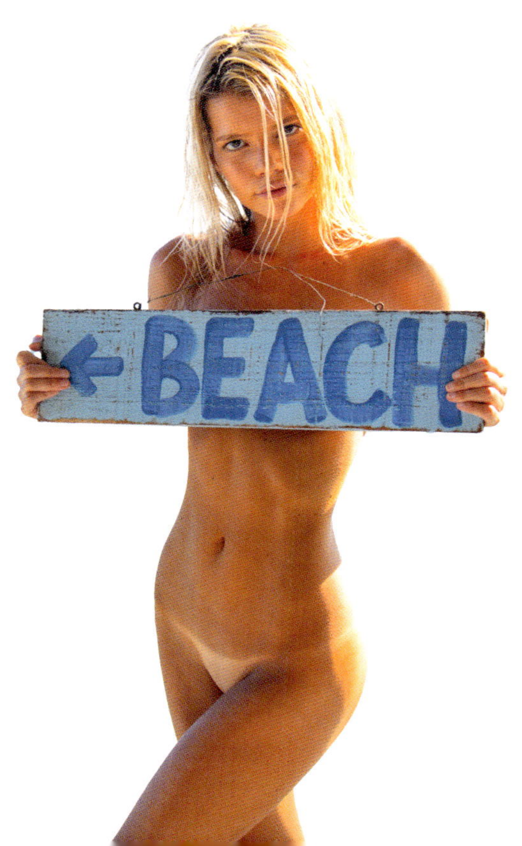

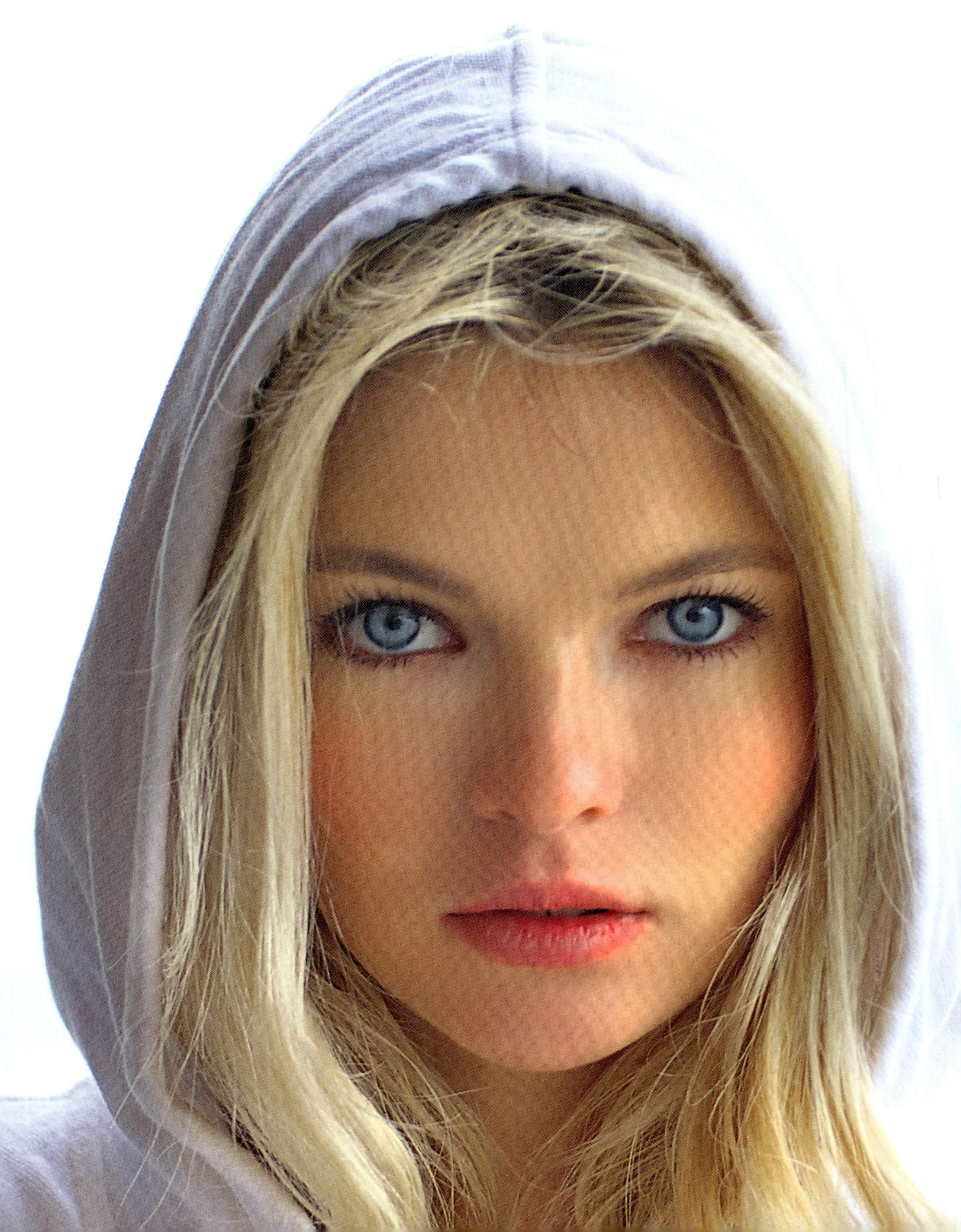

LAWRENCE KASANOFF

MALIBU BLONDE

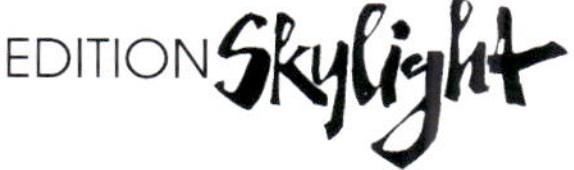

FOR MALIBU

I've lived in LA my whole adult life. About 10 years ago, I moved to Malibu for what I thought would be a few months. I never left. Why? Just a few dozen miles from Los Angeles, Malibu often feels like a totally different world. This is where you can share your breakfast with dolphins and seals, or watch surfers ride the perfect wave. But it is more than that. Malibu evokes a feeling of a simpler, happier, freer time. Go anywhere in the world and mention Malibu, and people associate it with images of that time: blonde women frolicking on the beach – young, pretty, happy, without a care in the world; old red Mustang convertibles; puppy dogs chasing footballs; Beach Boys music; movie stars; surfing and fun, fun, fun. Malibu is iconic. It is the Shangri-La of endless summer. I wanted to capture that energy of innocent, playful, free spirited sexy fun in this book, and share it. (Fun is wildly underrated these days.) My goal is to make people smile. And why limit smiles to people? So, all the money I make from this book and the images in it, will be donated to endangered animal charities (see last page, or go to www.malibublonde.com for more info). Maybe we can get animals to be happier, too. I want to thank first and foremost all the models, who volunteered their time in the hopes of helping animals. Special Thanks to: Marina Masowietsky, for casting so many of the models; Nina Borghi, Rebecca Wolcott and Julio Morin for organizing and coordinating so much of this, not to mention putting up with me; Jim George and Sean Derek, for their creative advice and everlasting support; and of course, Manfred Olms and the team at Edition Skylight, for their support, creative vision and great spirit. Have fun!

Lawrence Kasanoff

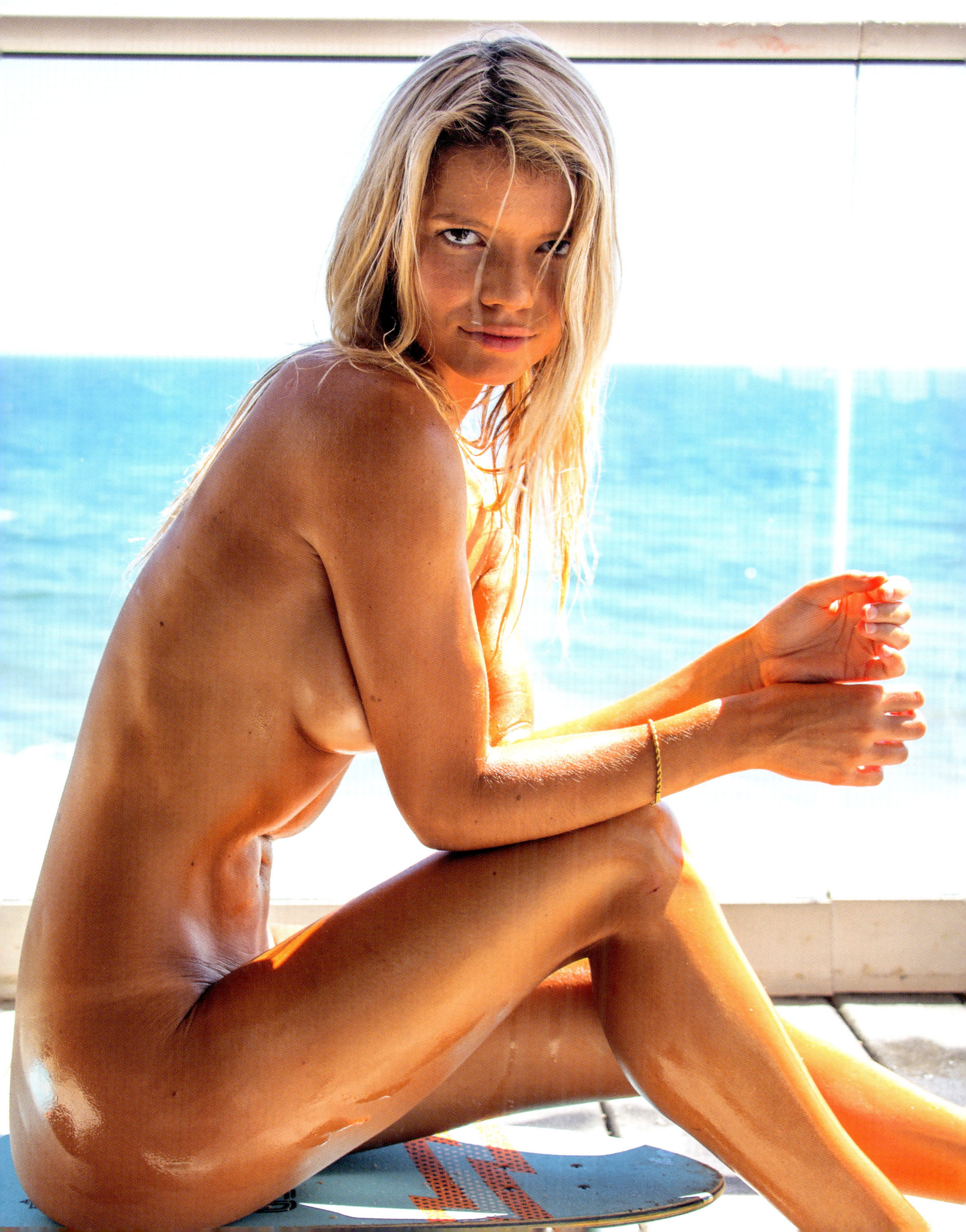

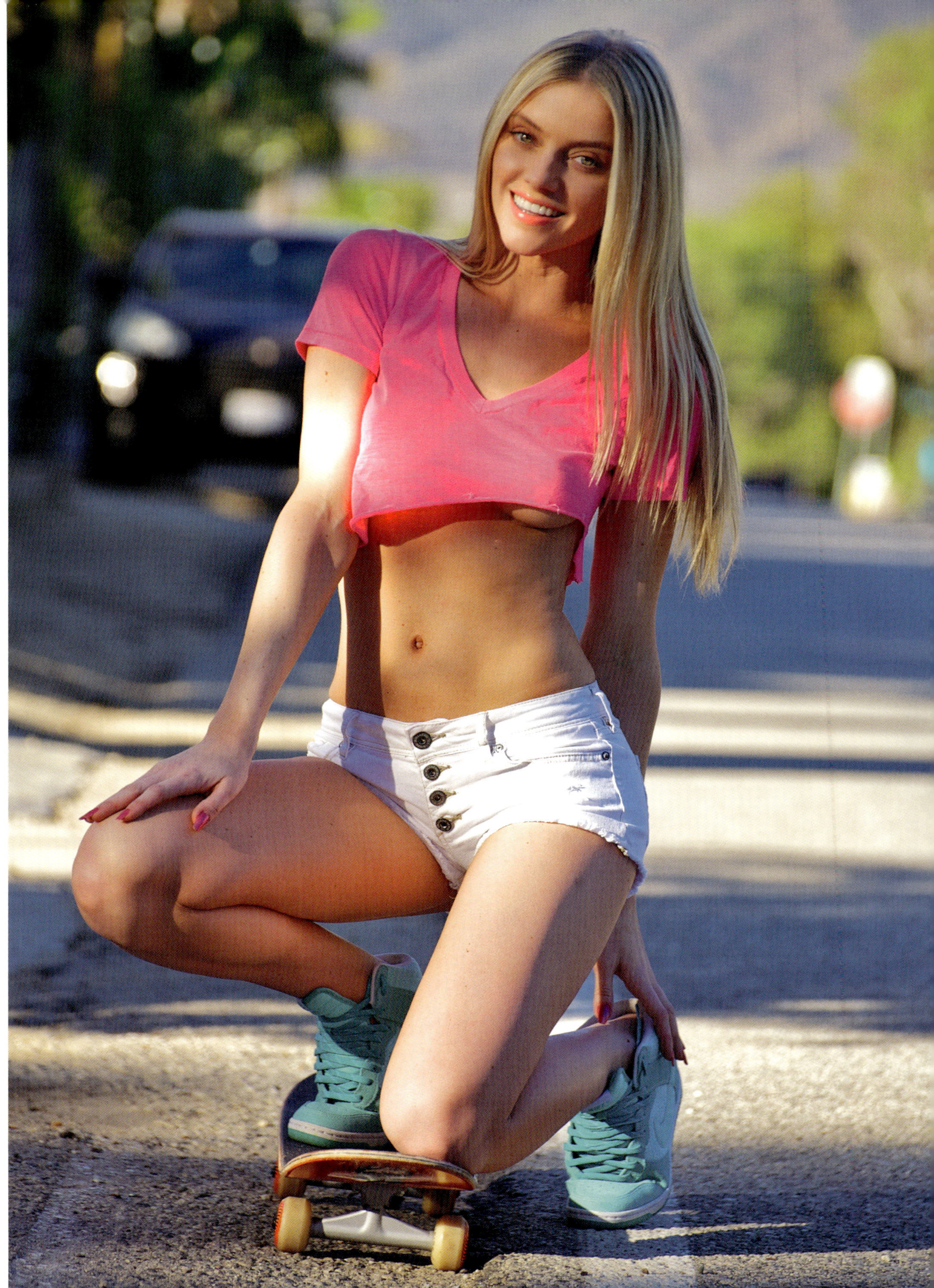

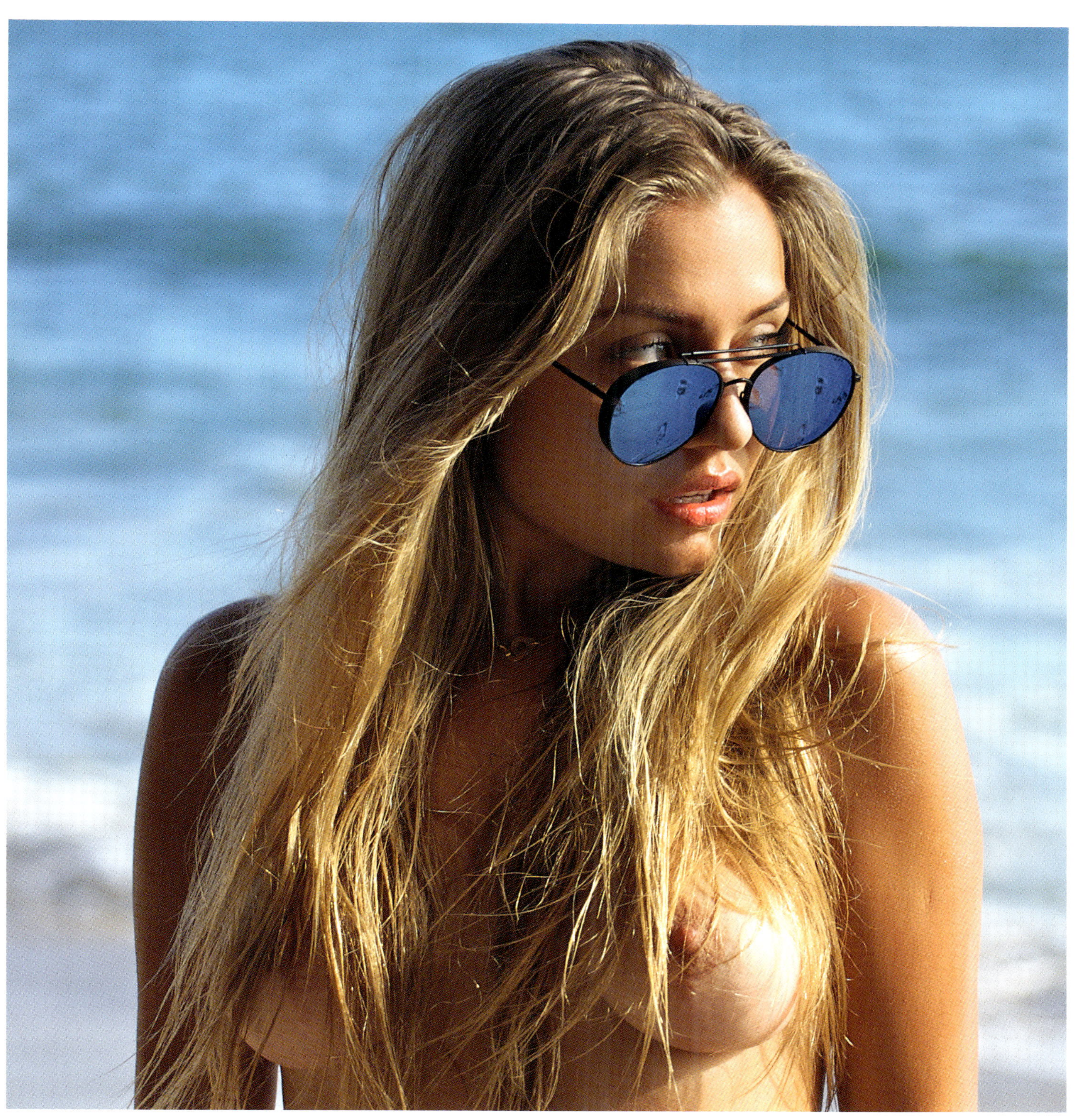

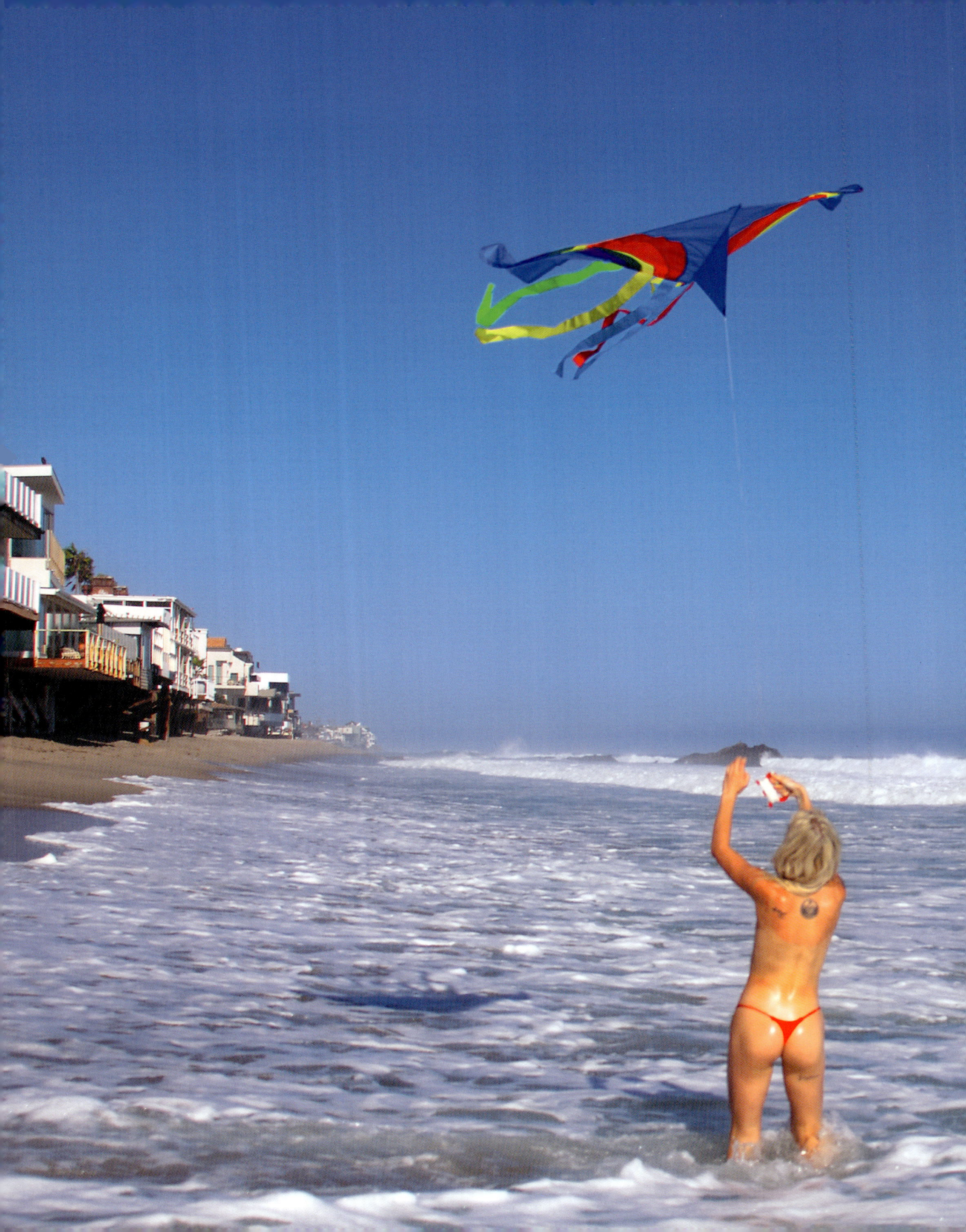

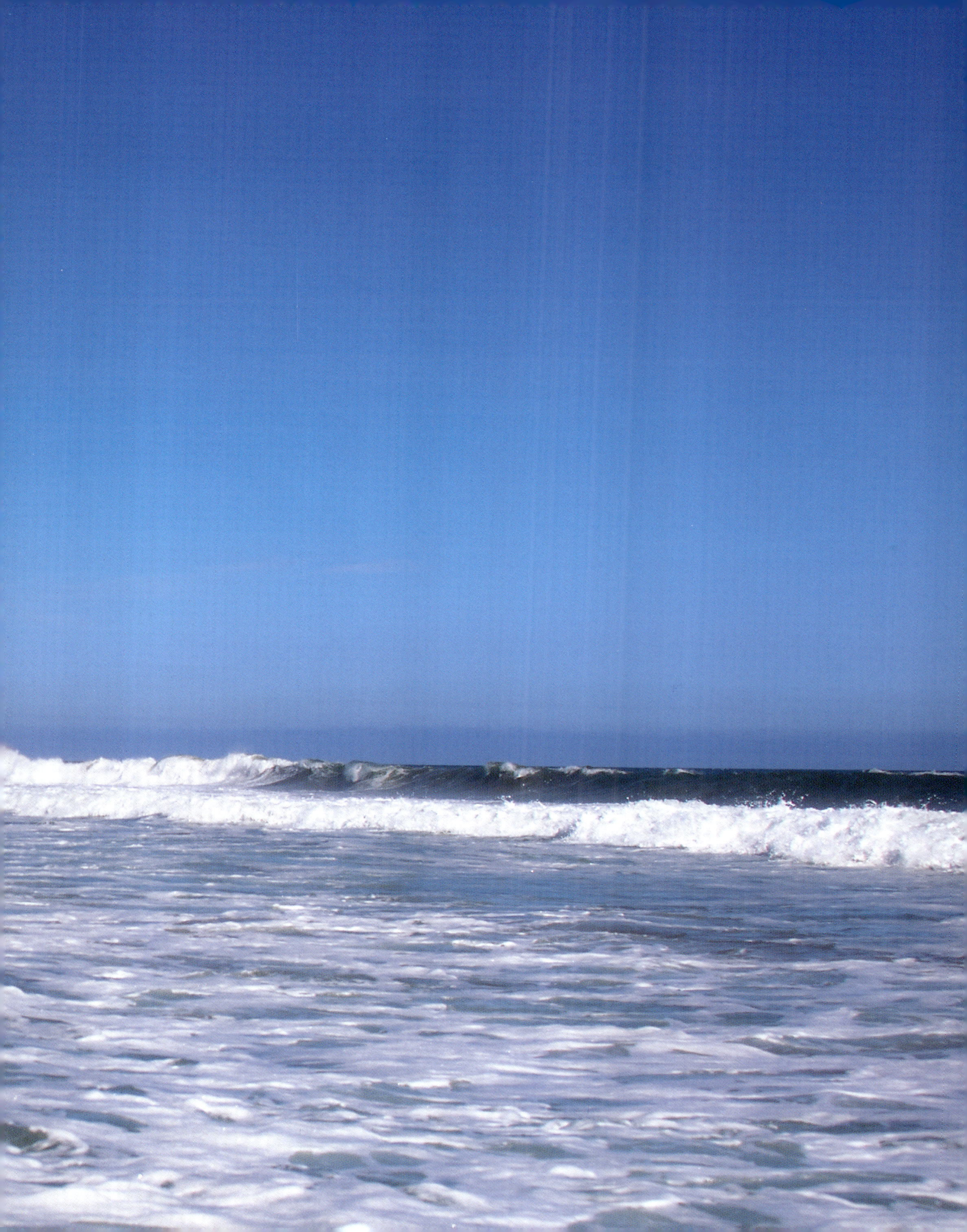

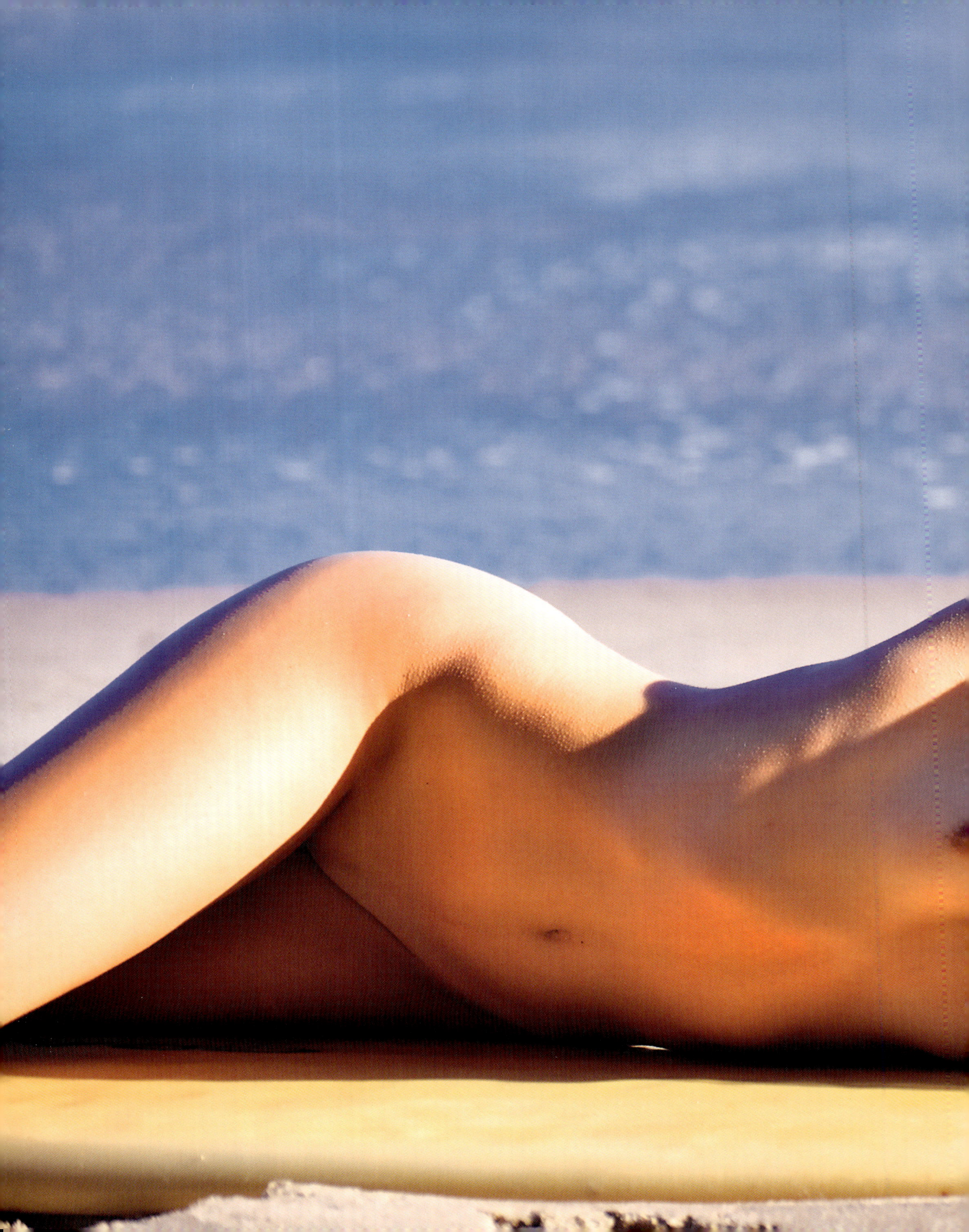

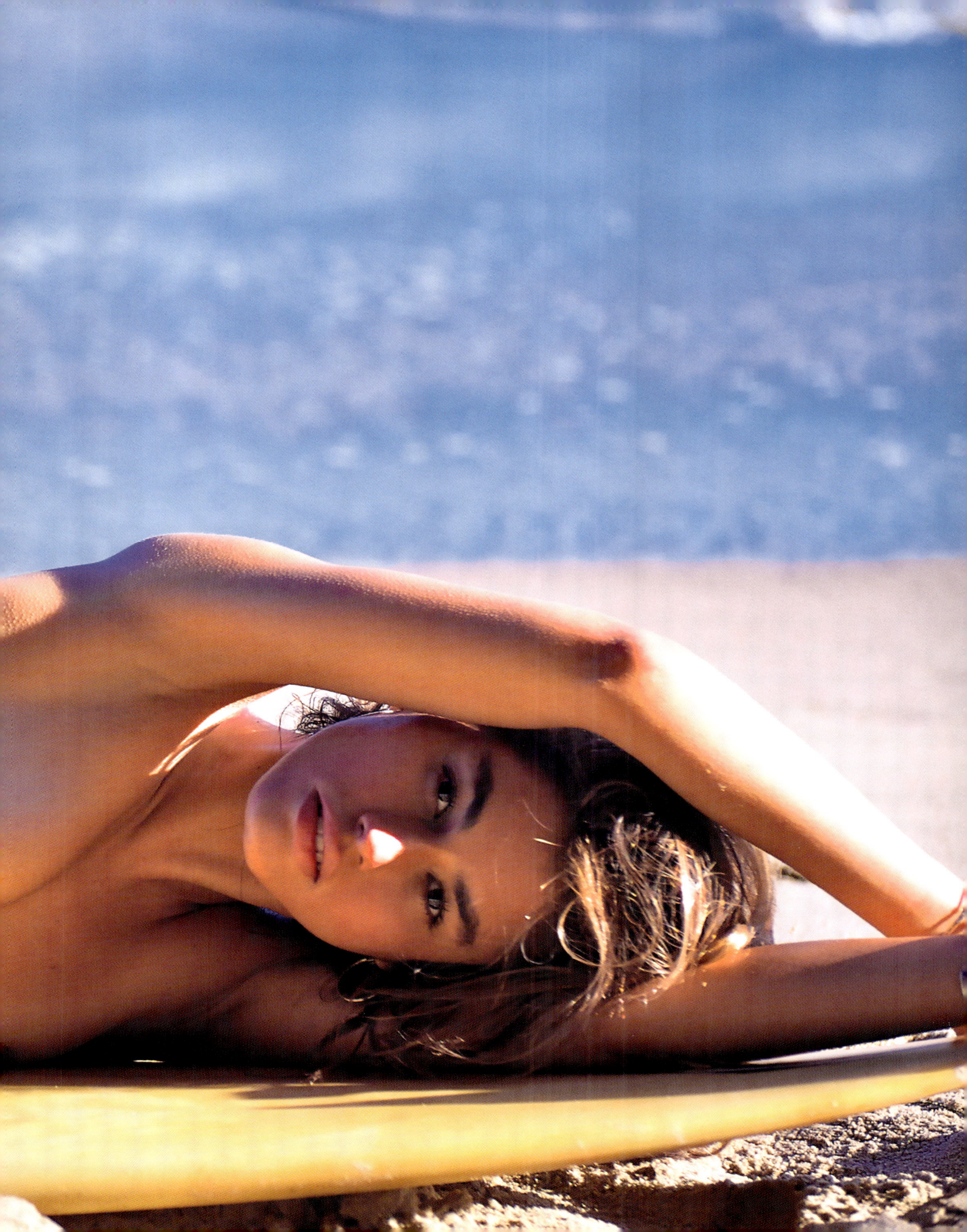

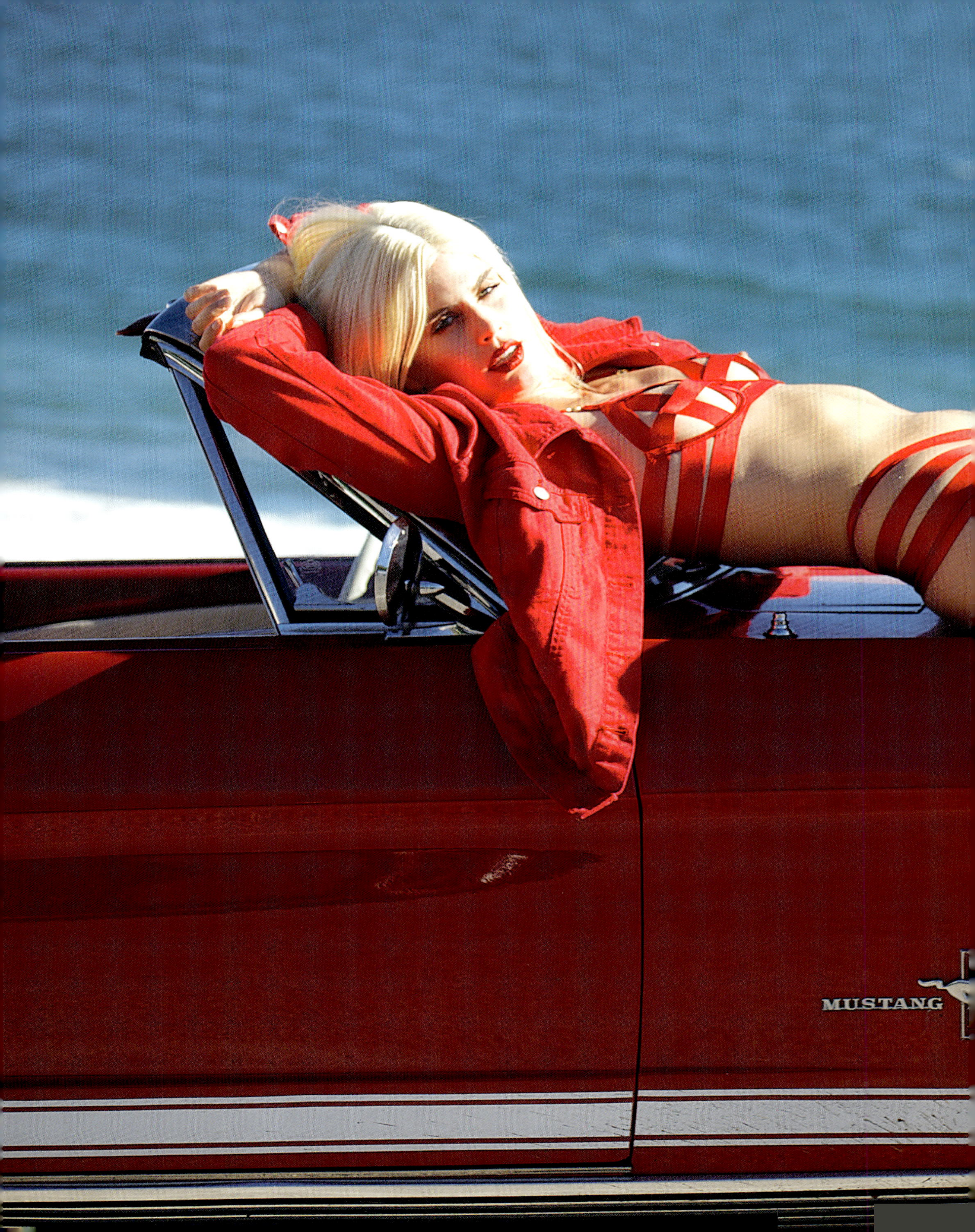
MUSTANG

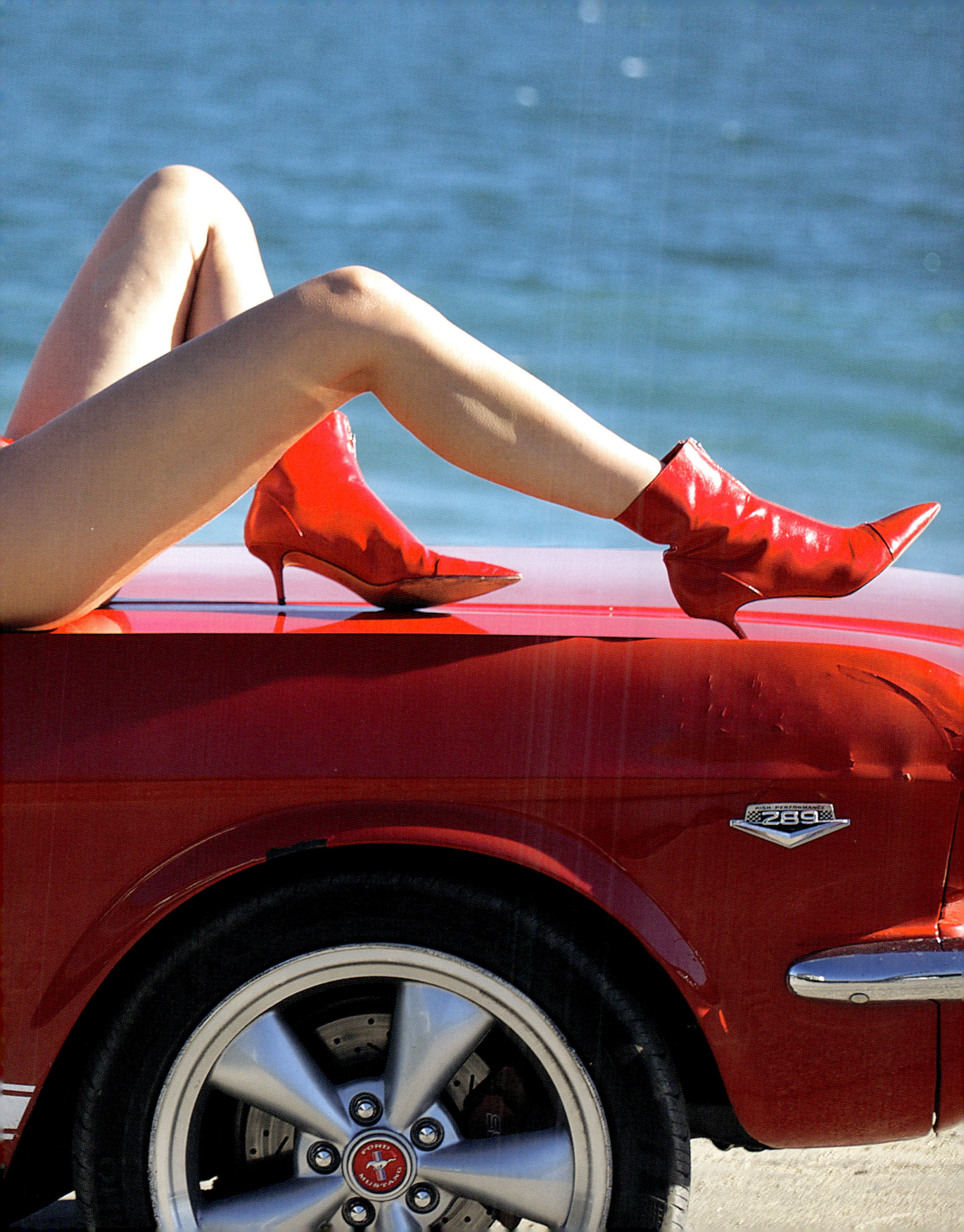

HIGH PERFORMANCE
289
FORD
MUSTANG

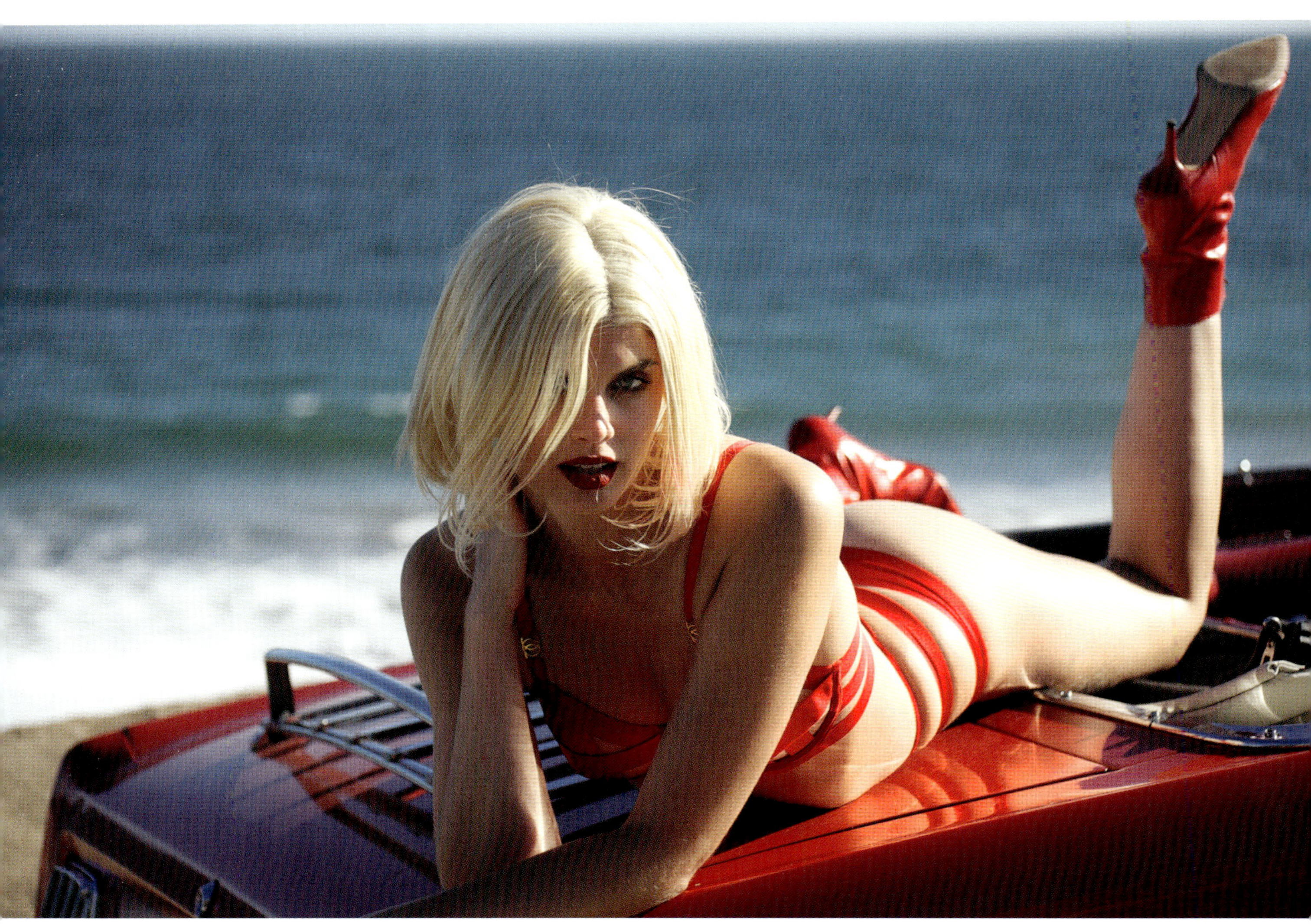

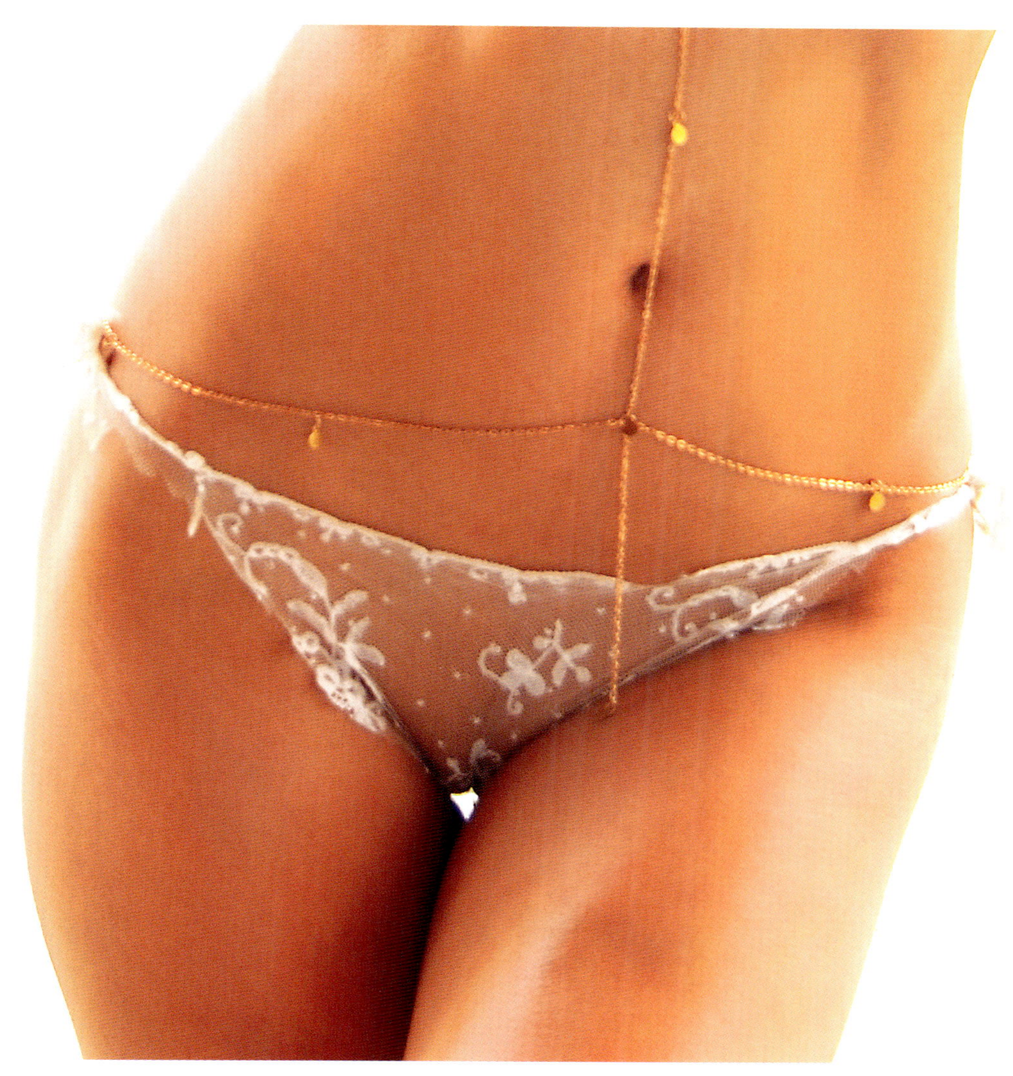

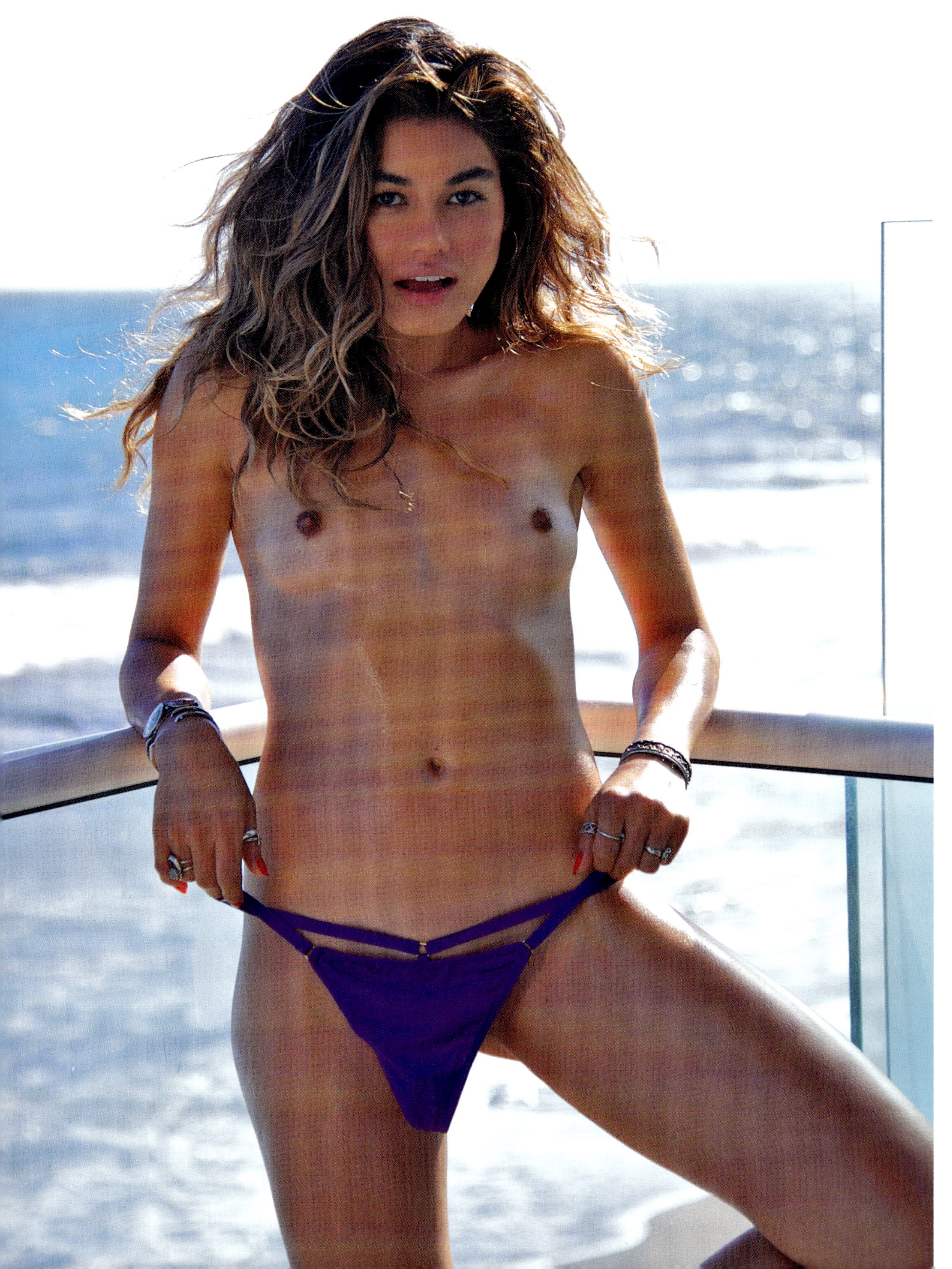

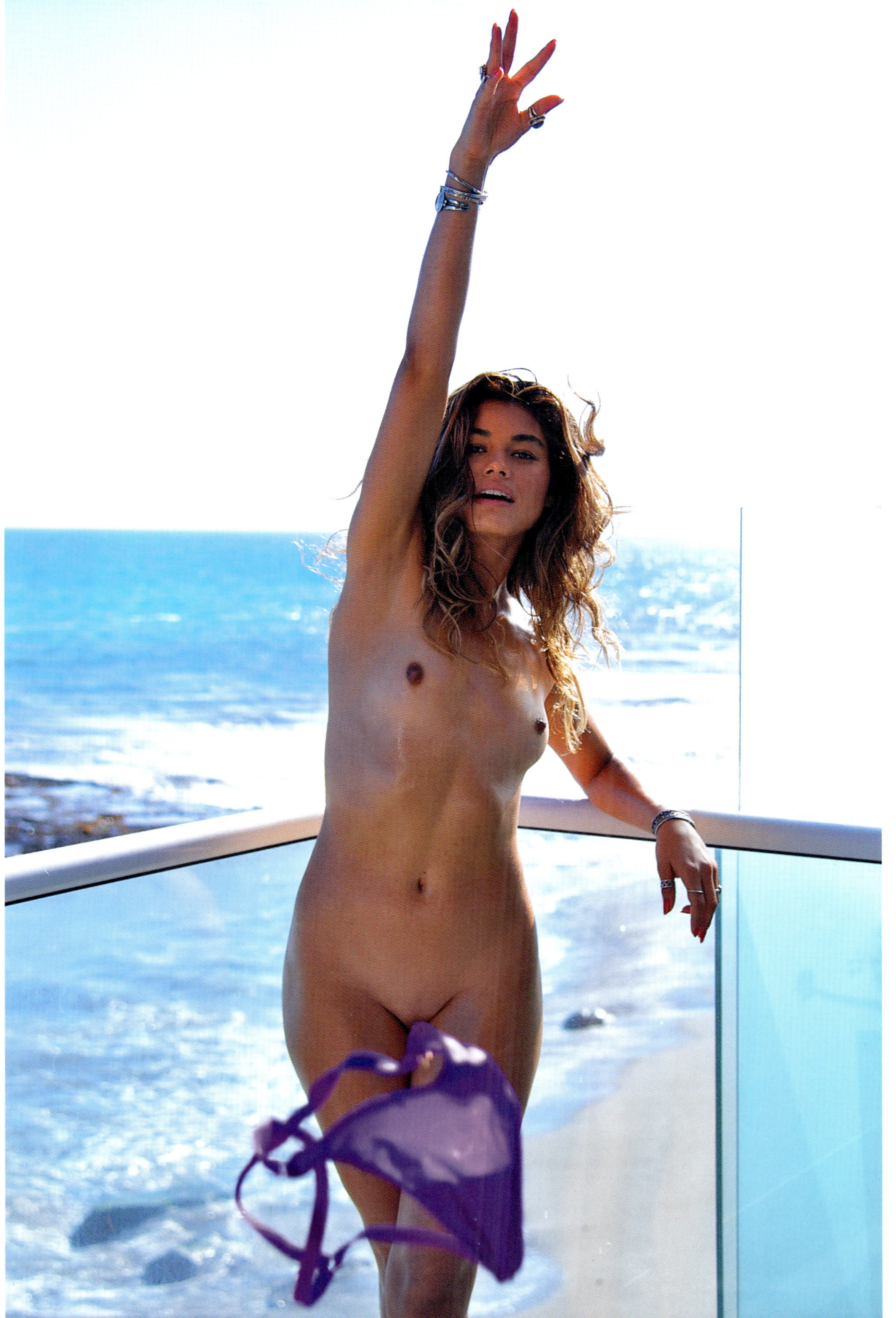

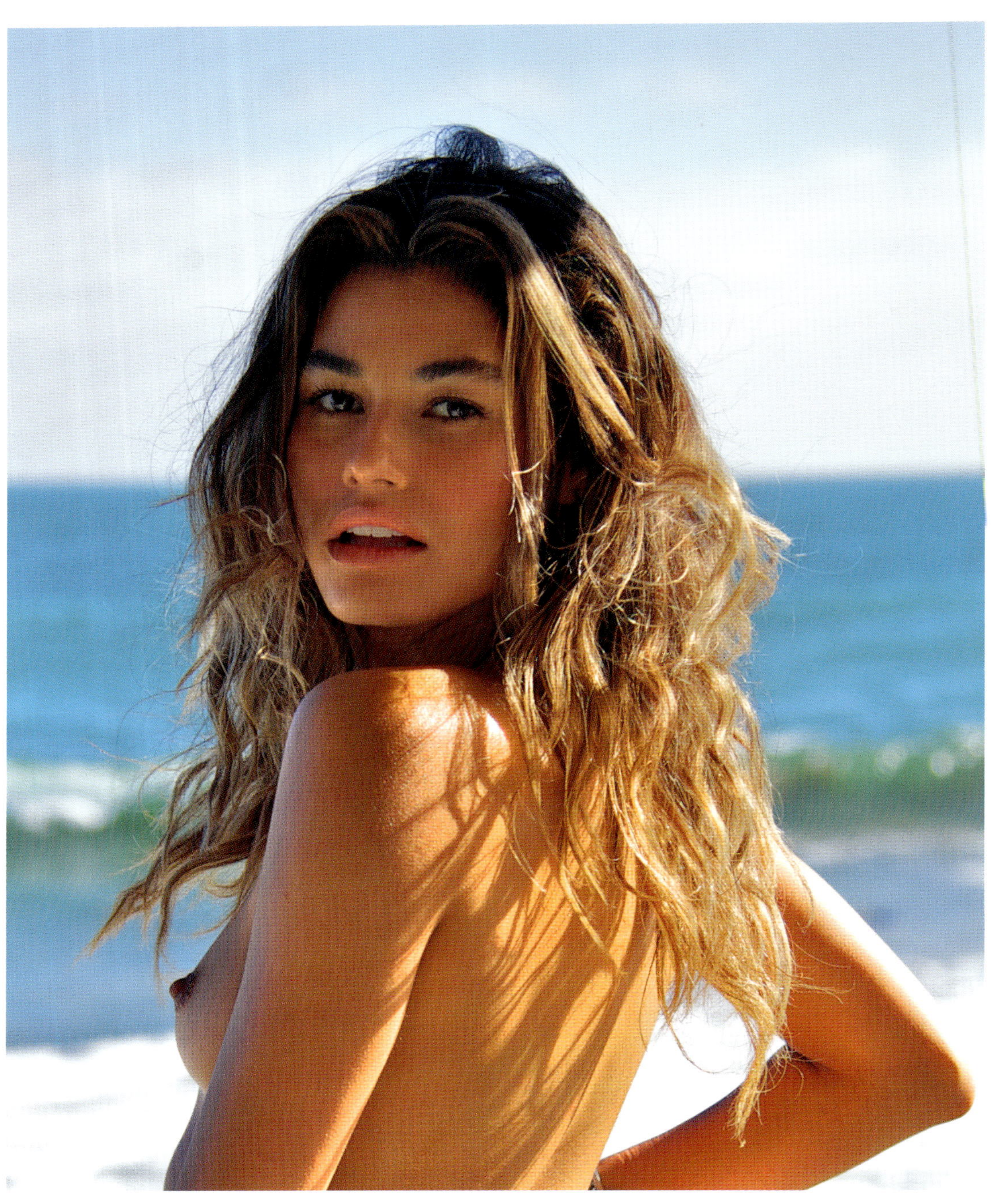

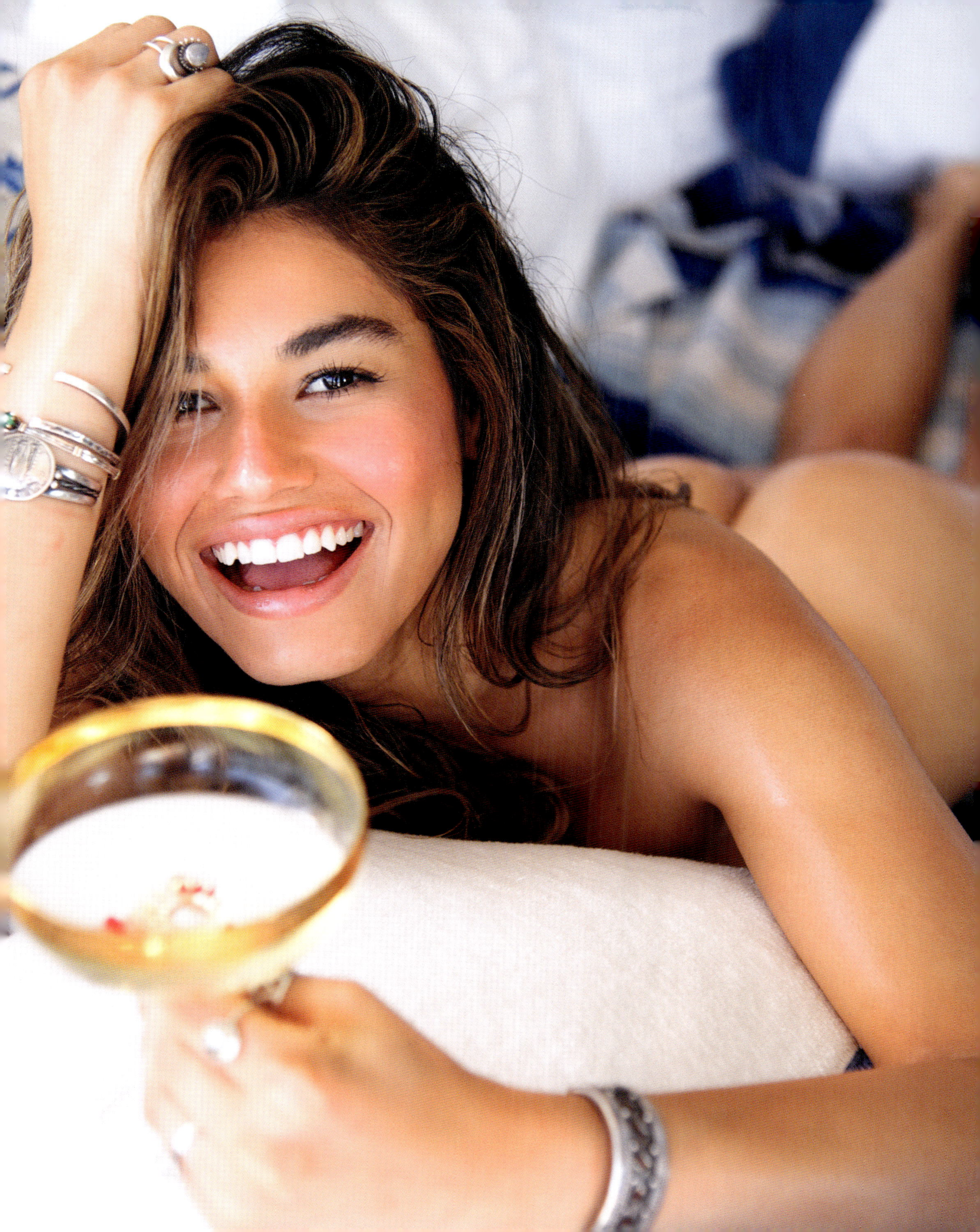

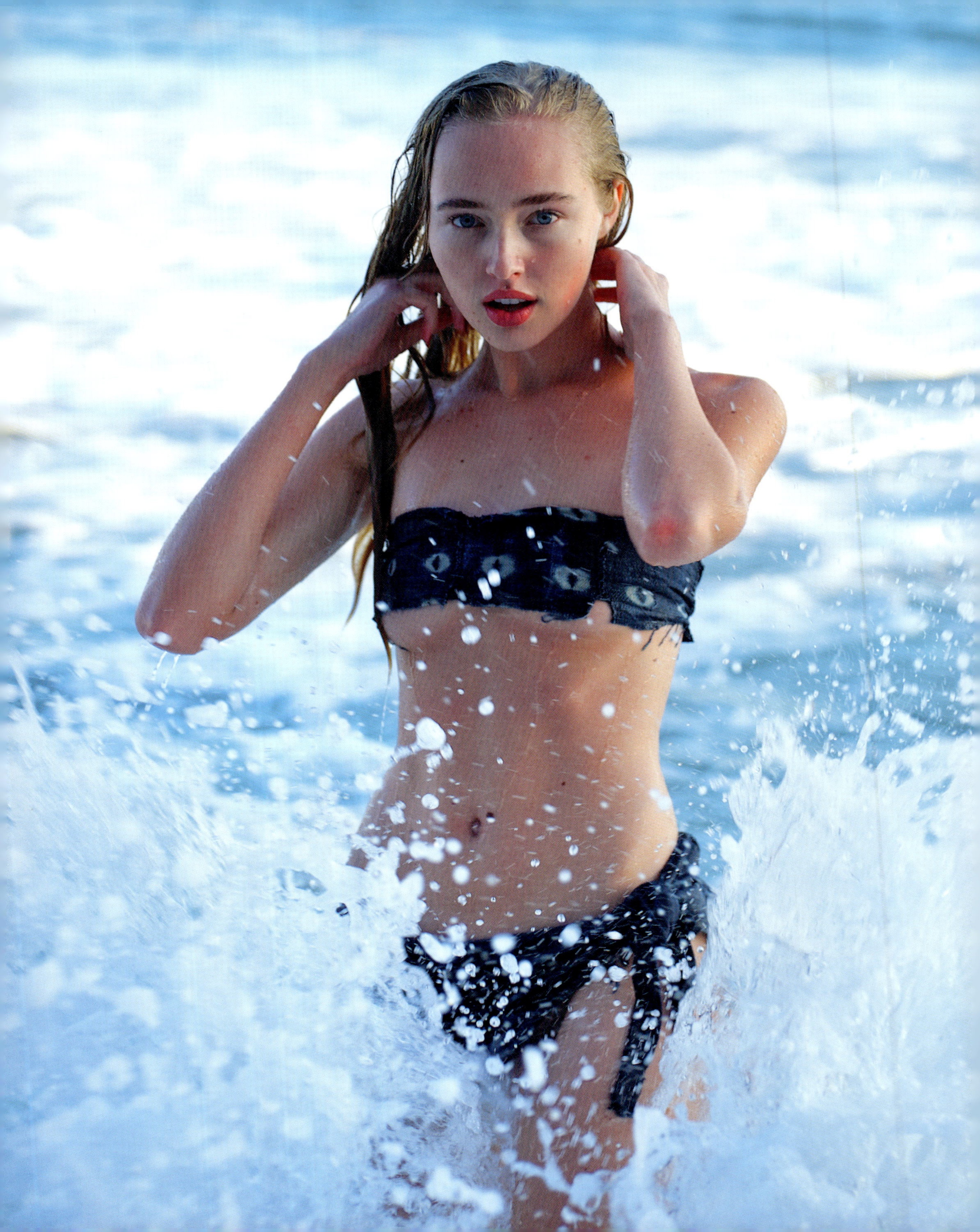

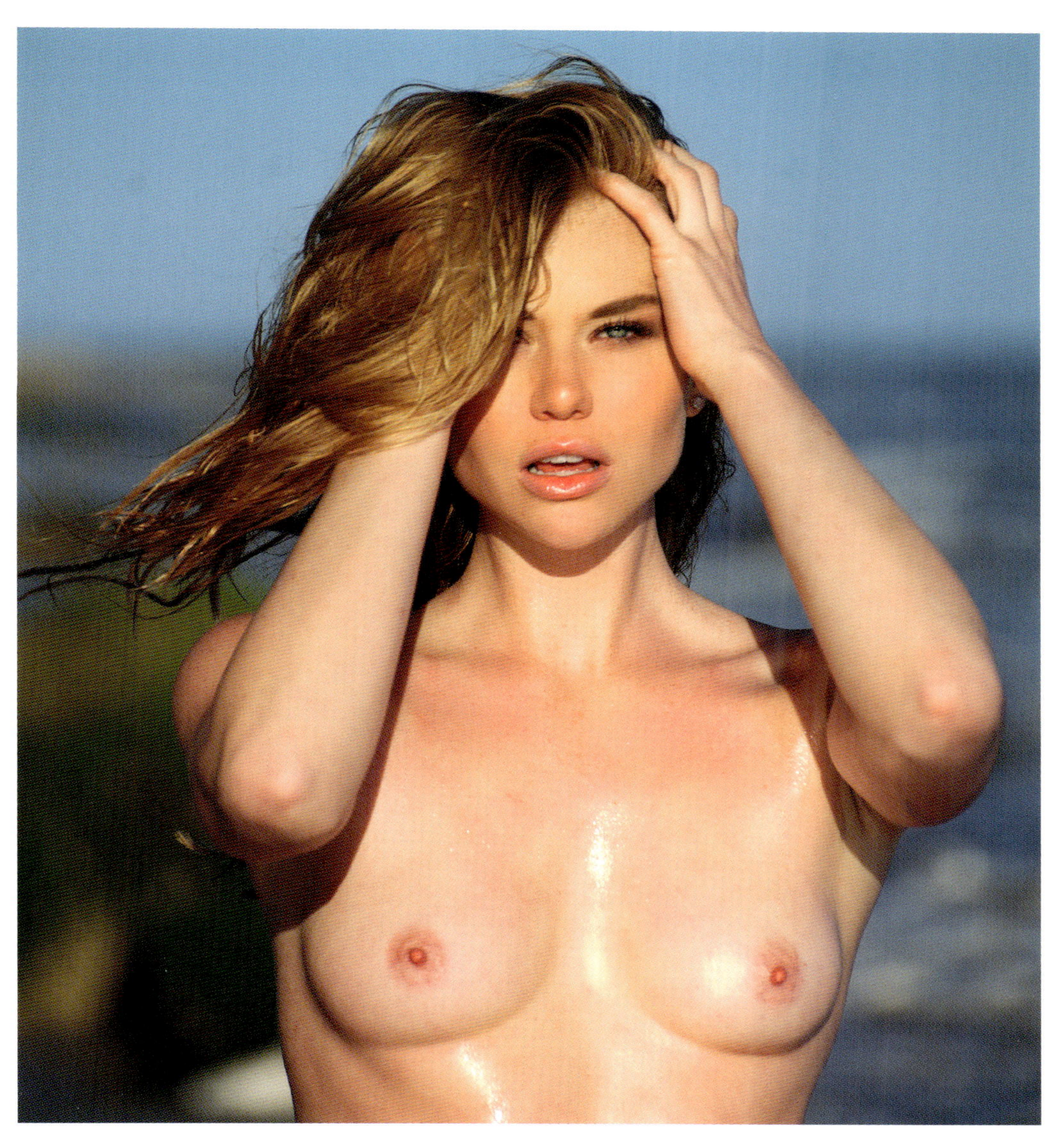

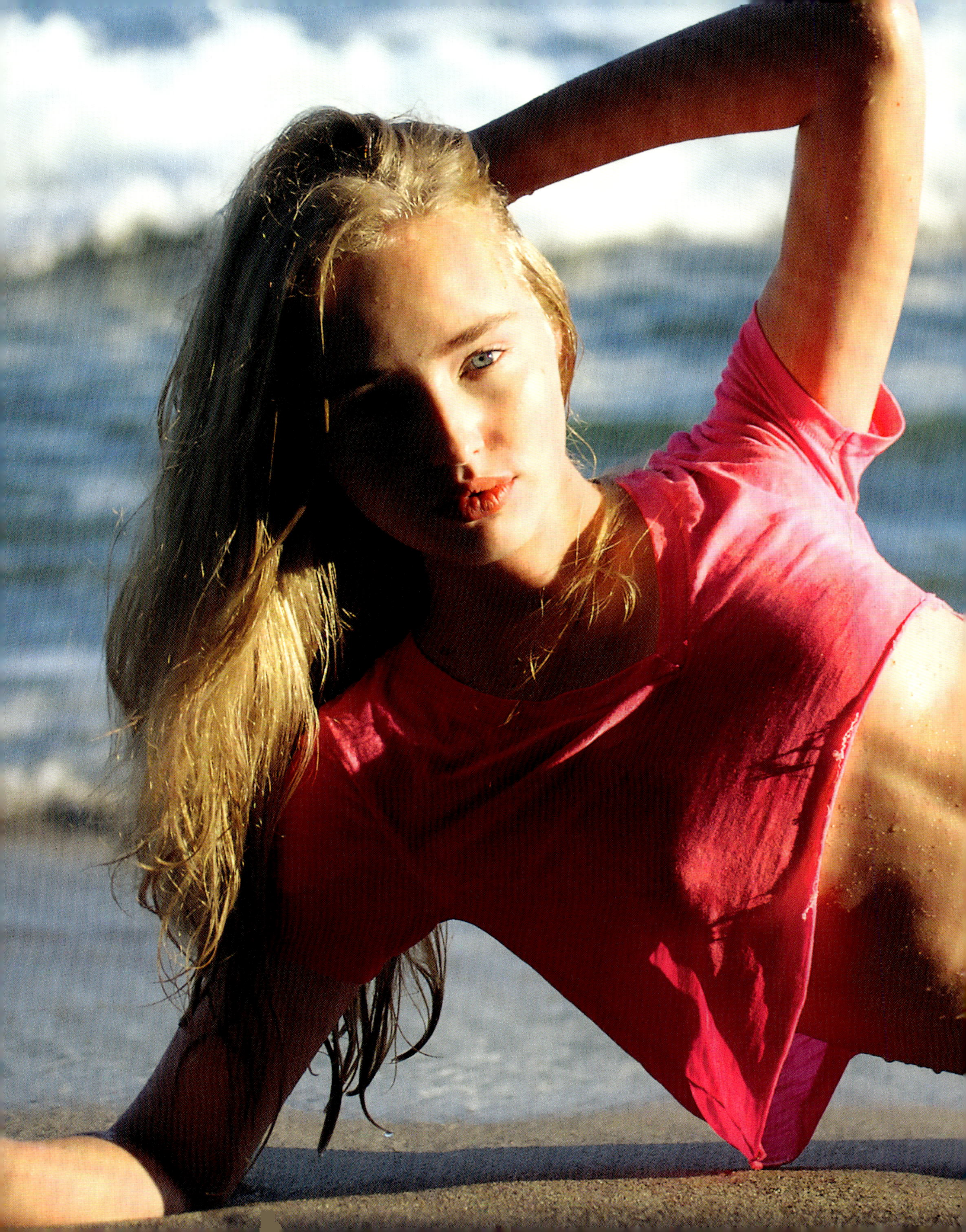

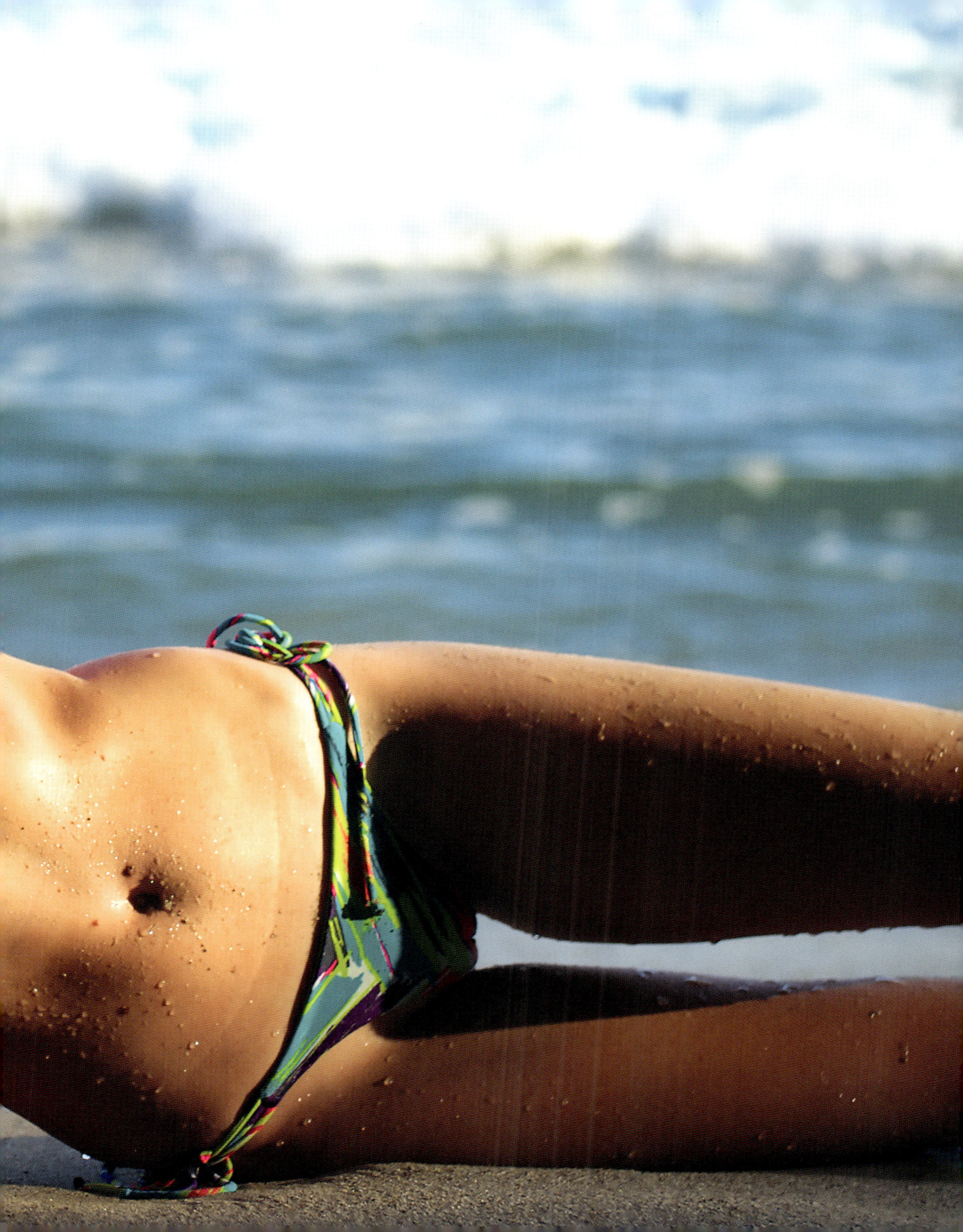

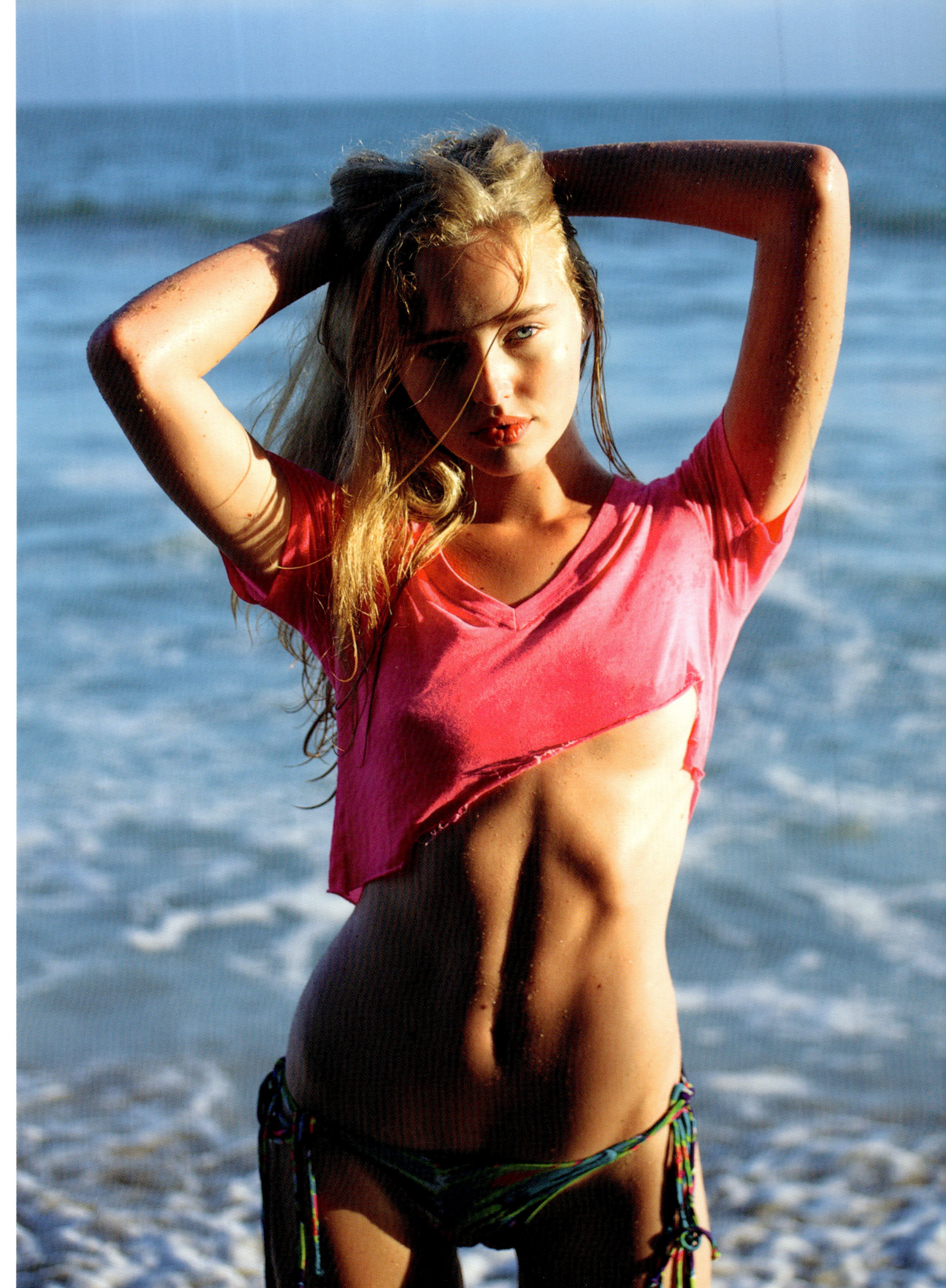

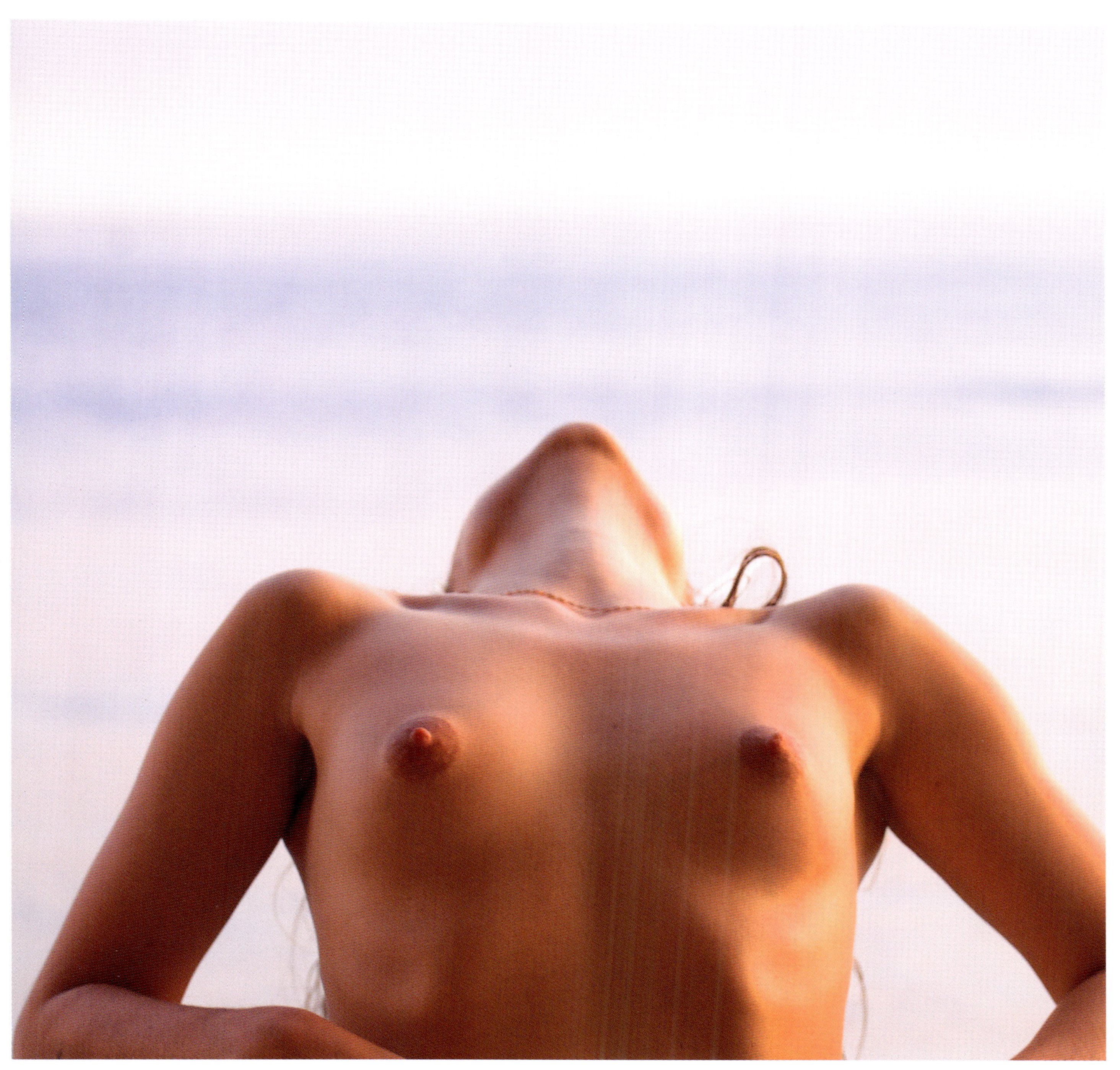

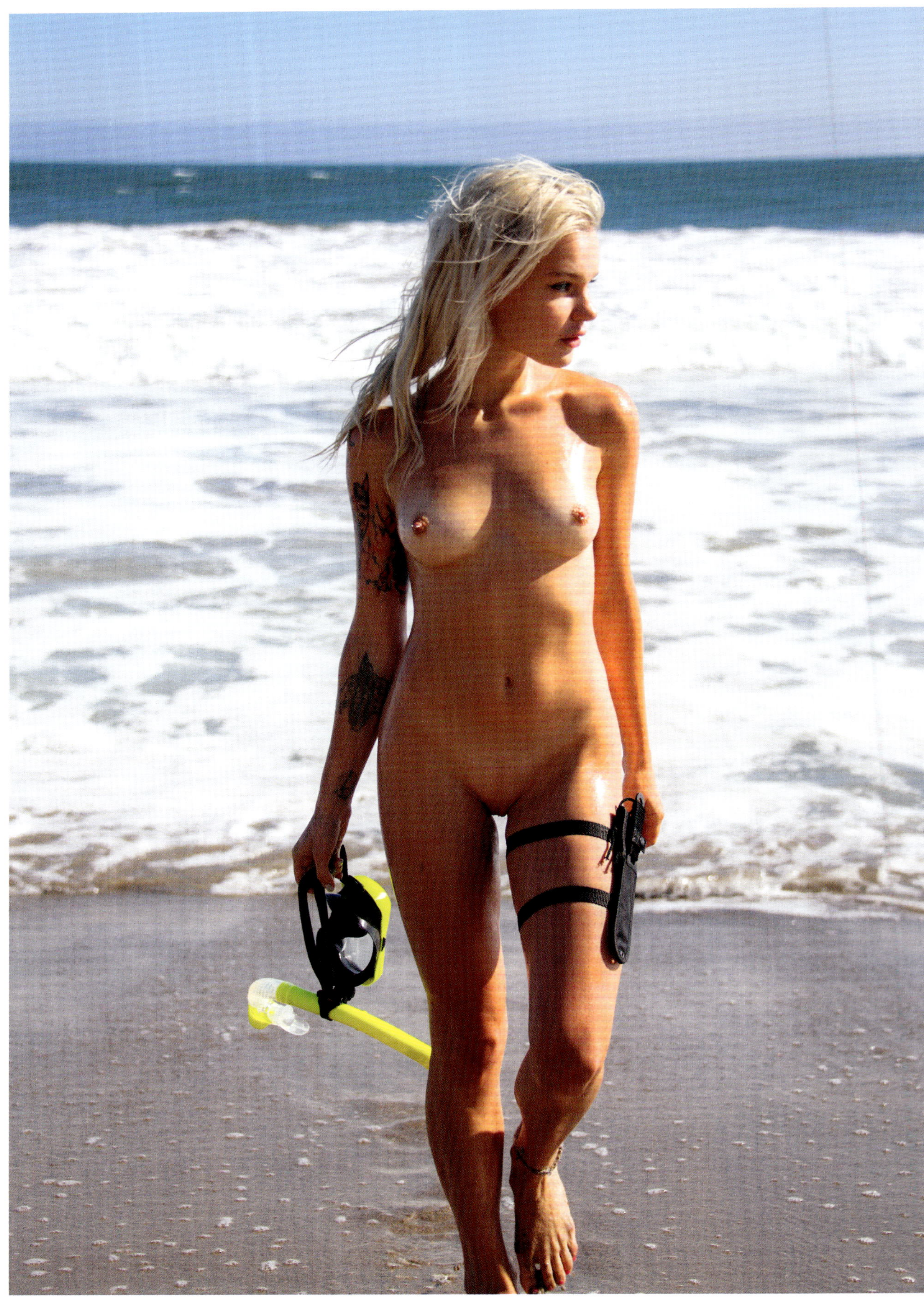

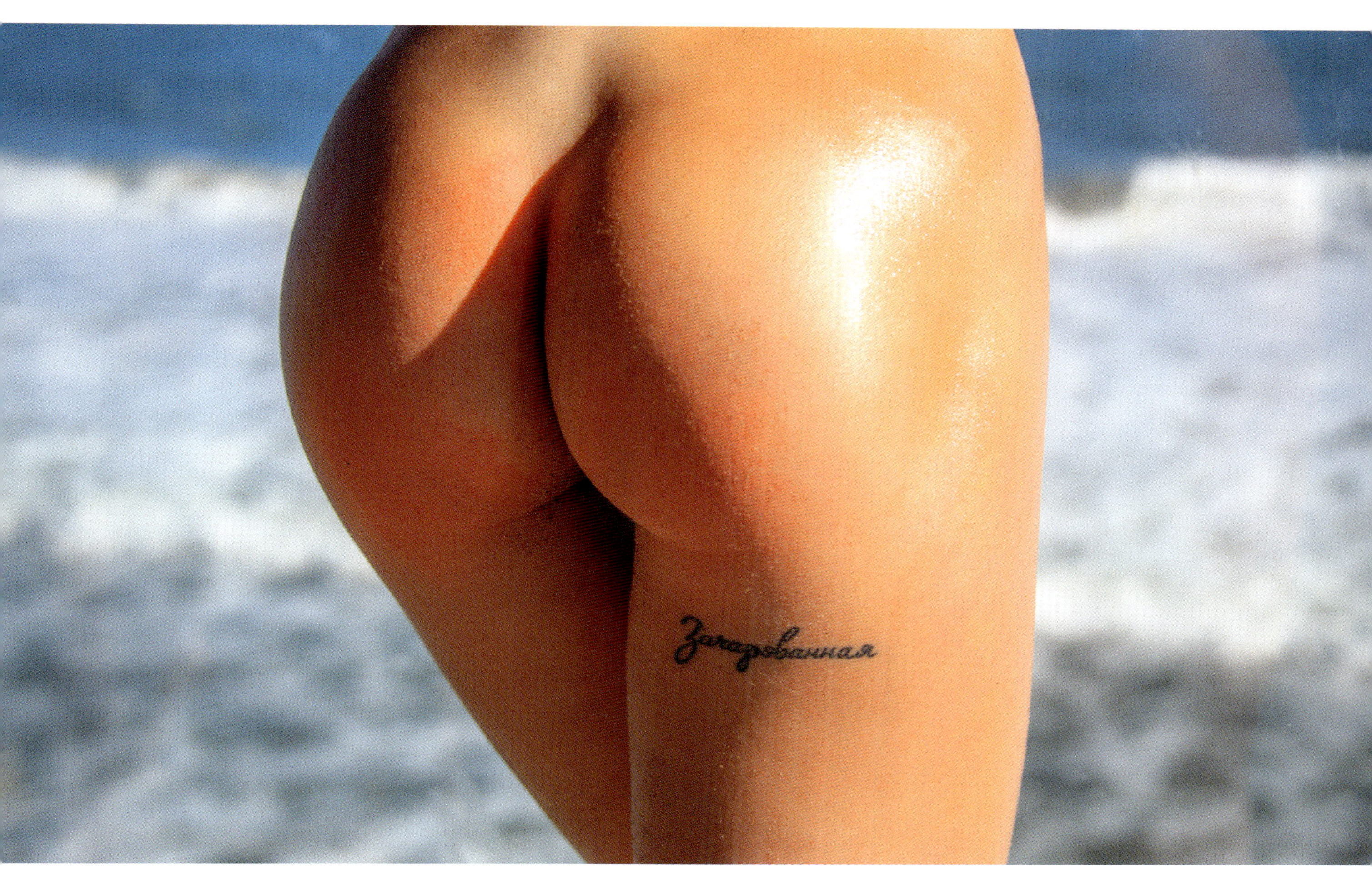
Зачарованная

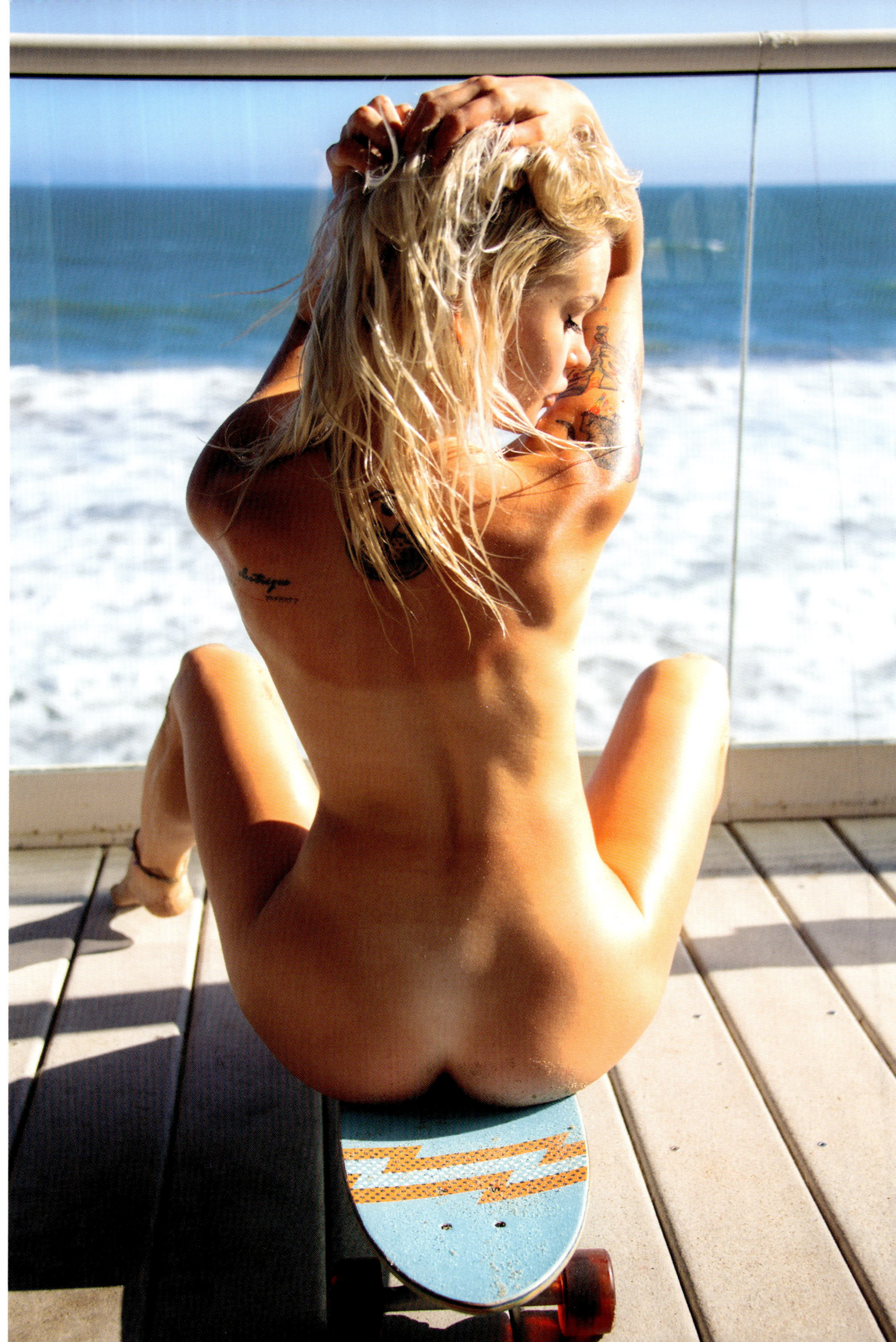

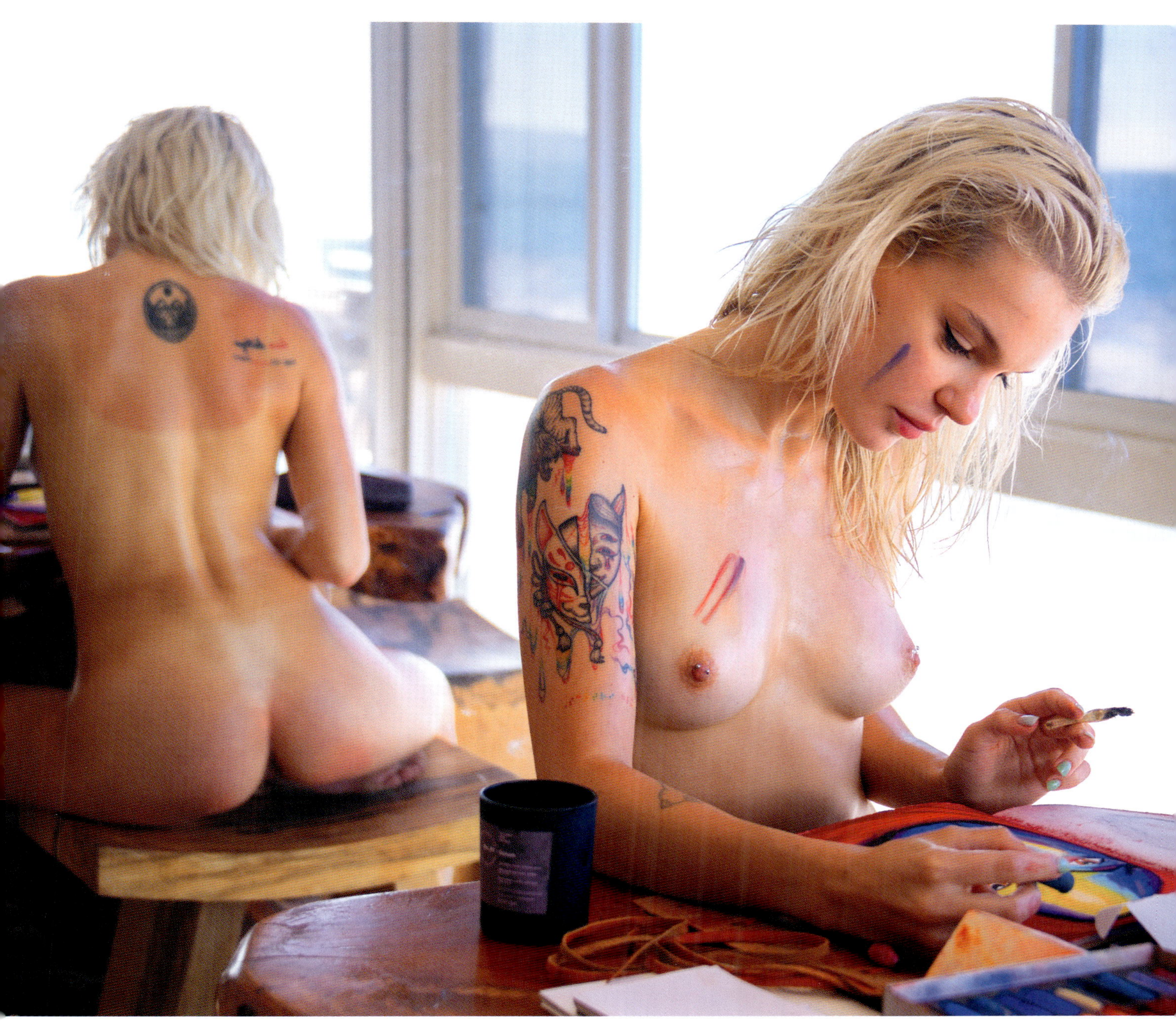

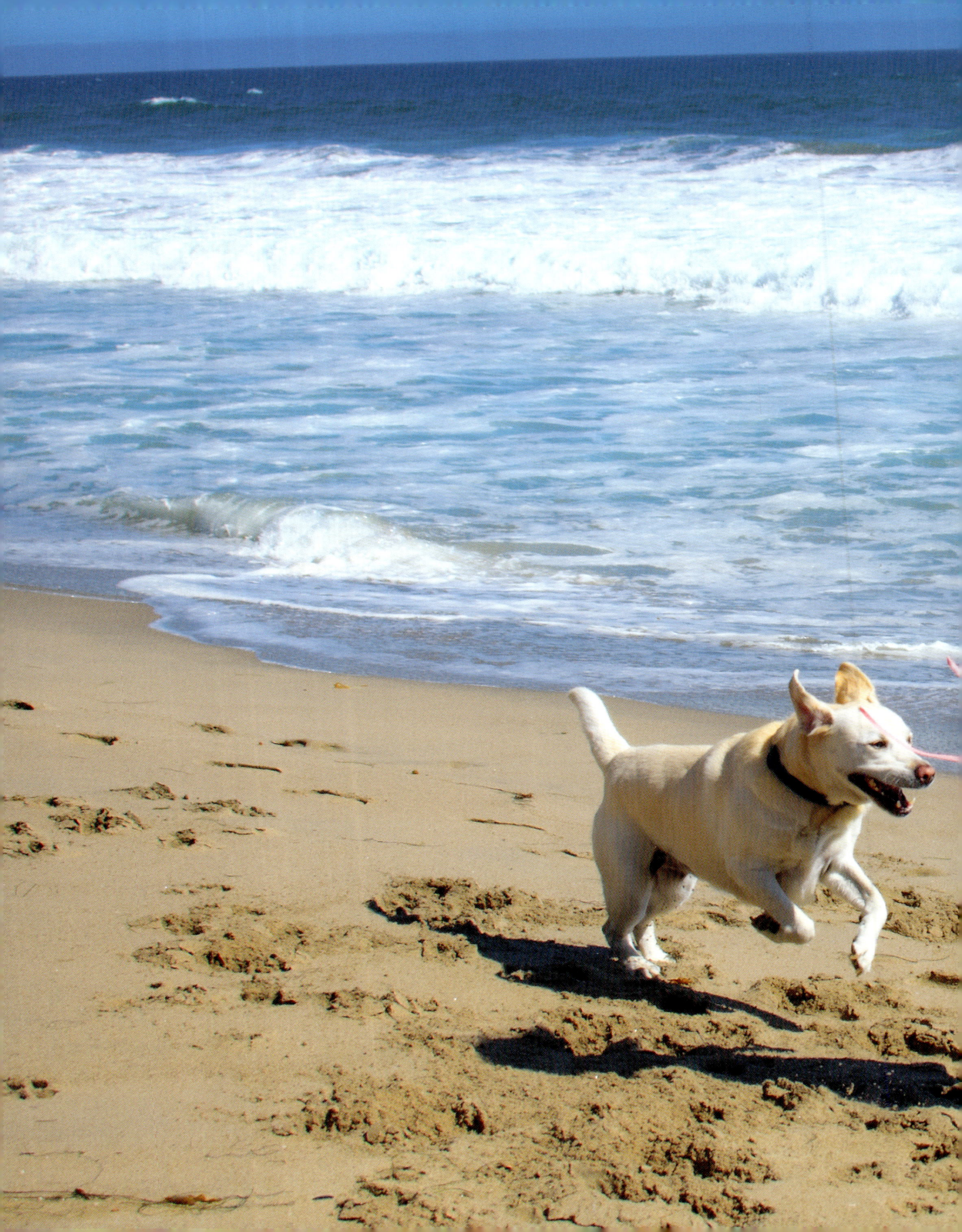

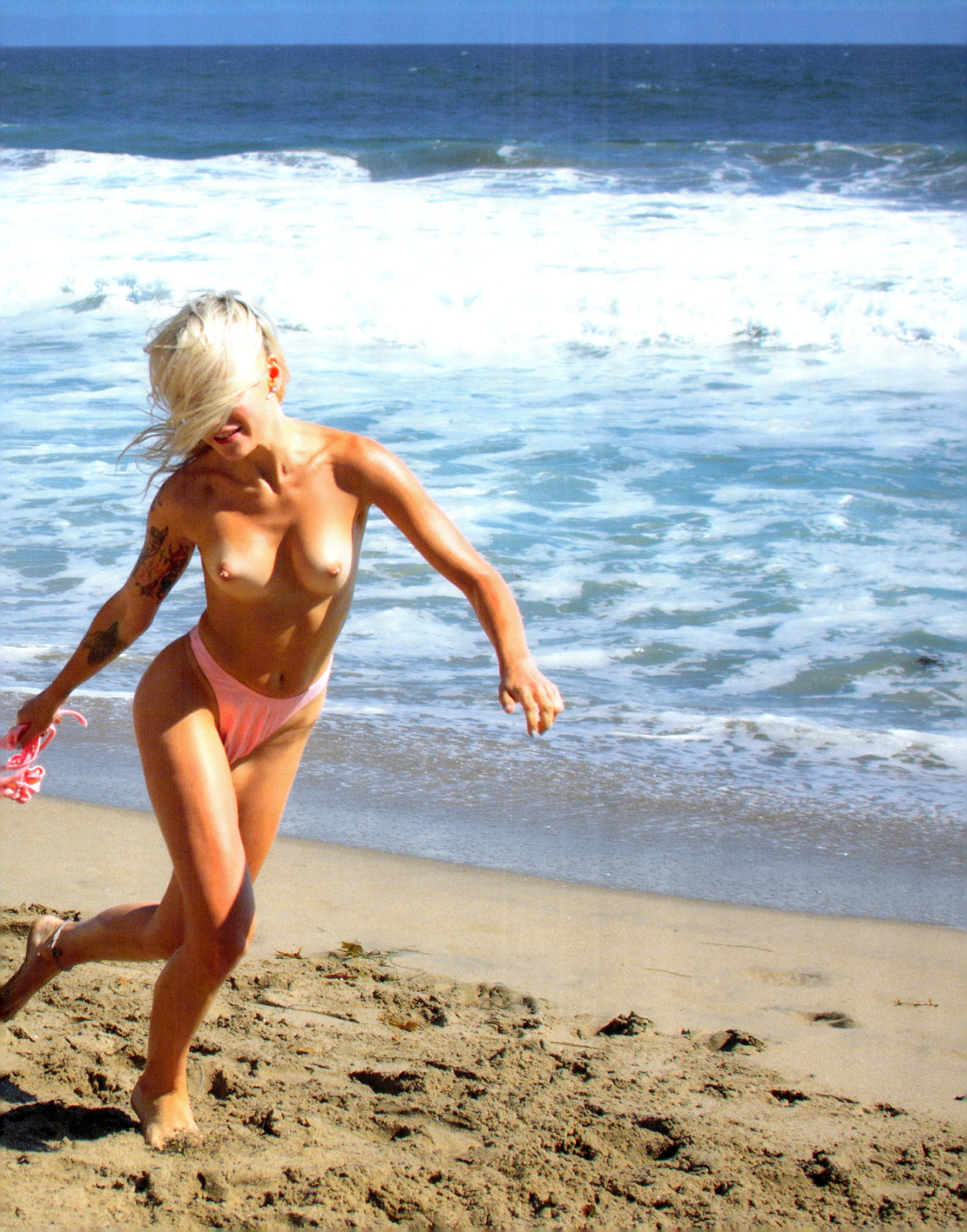

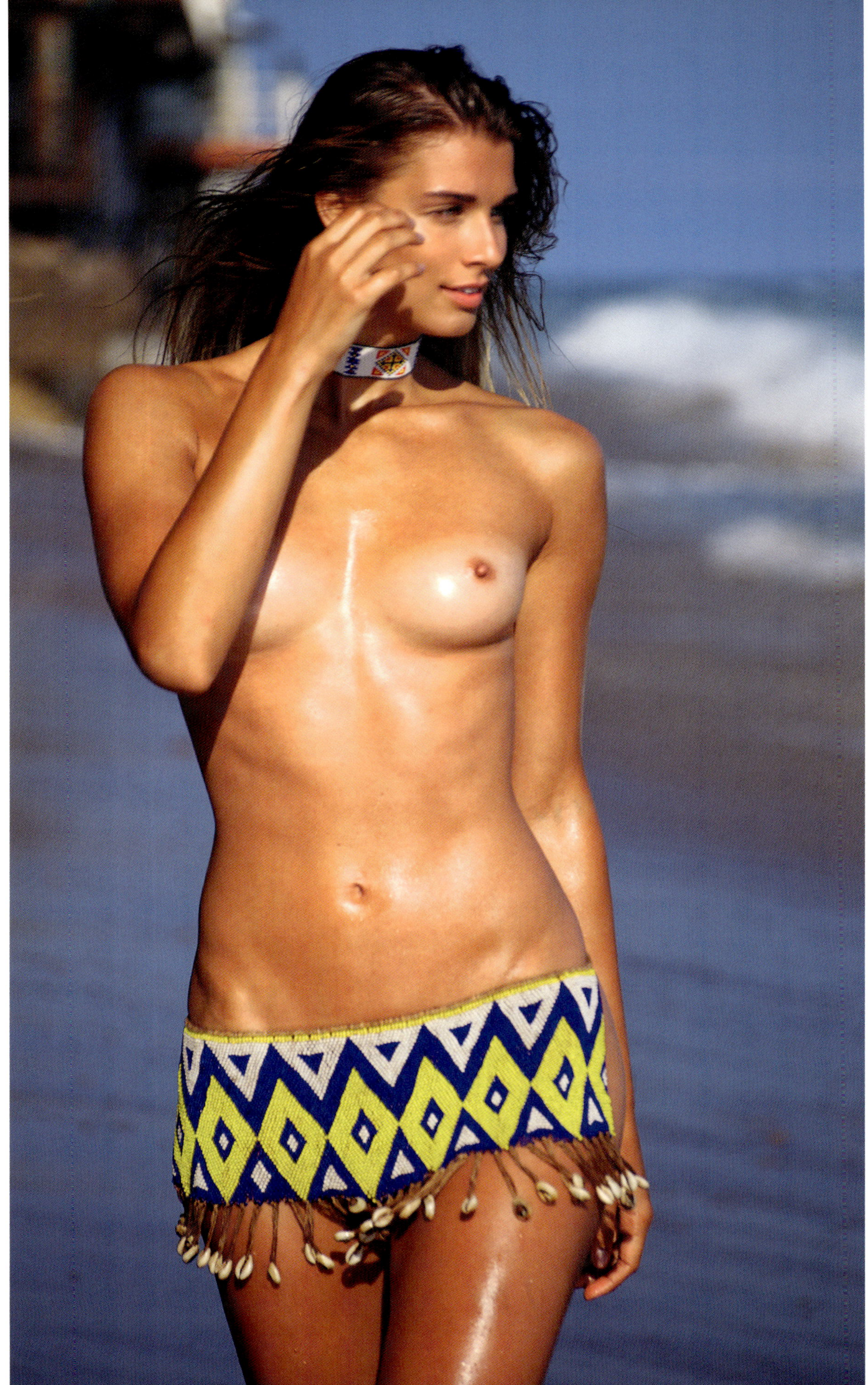

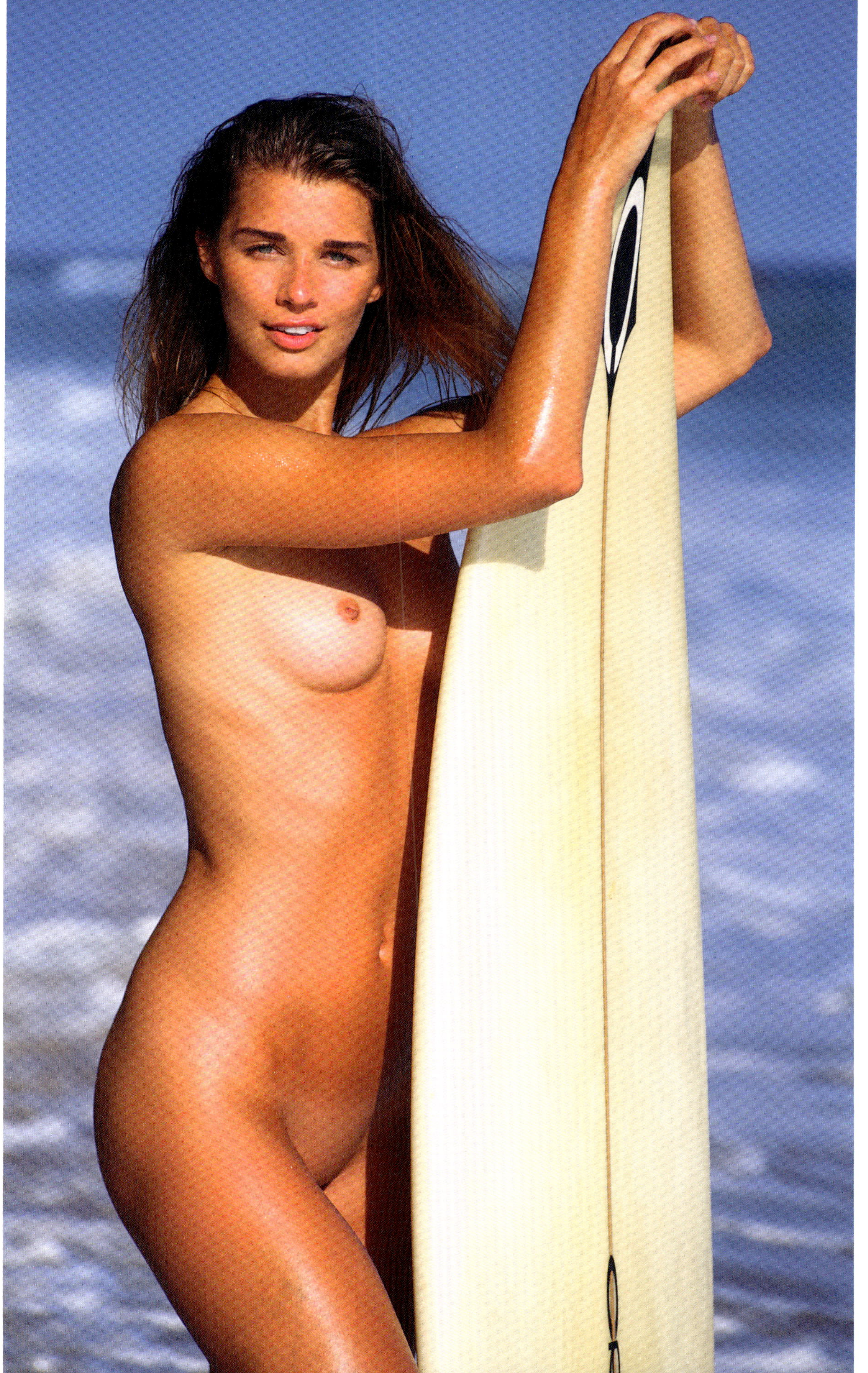

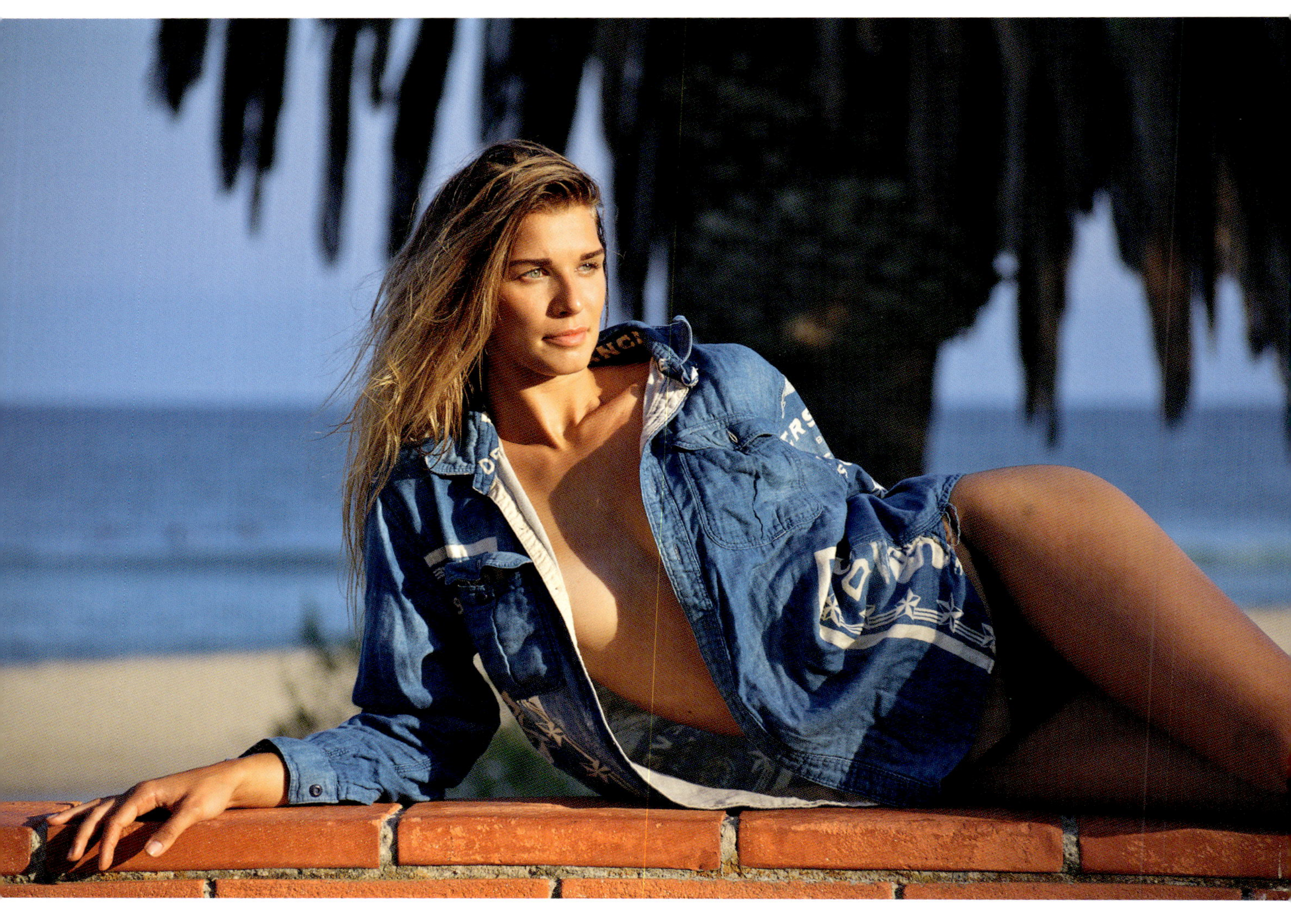

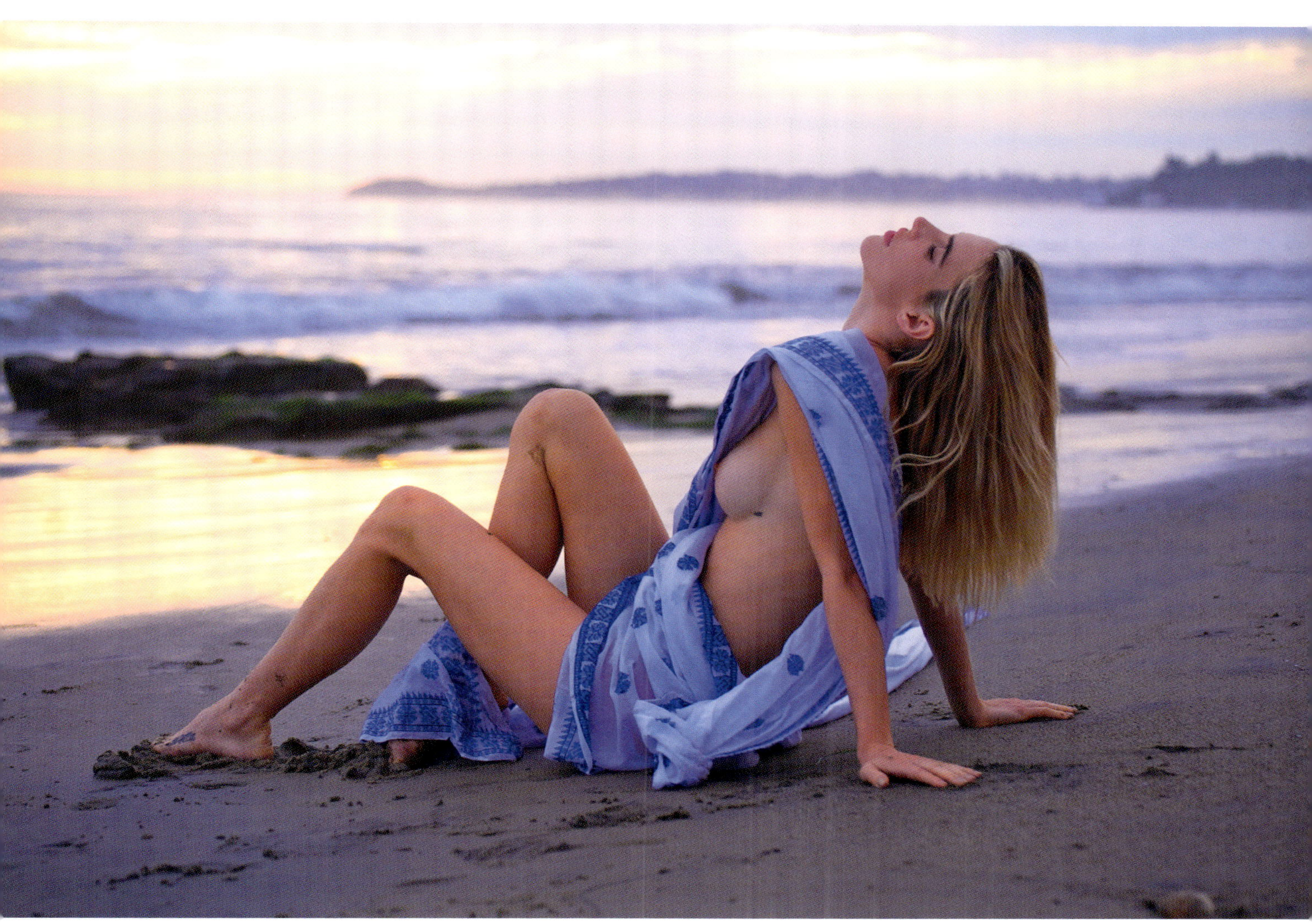

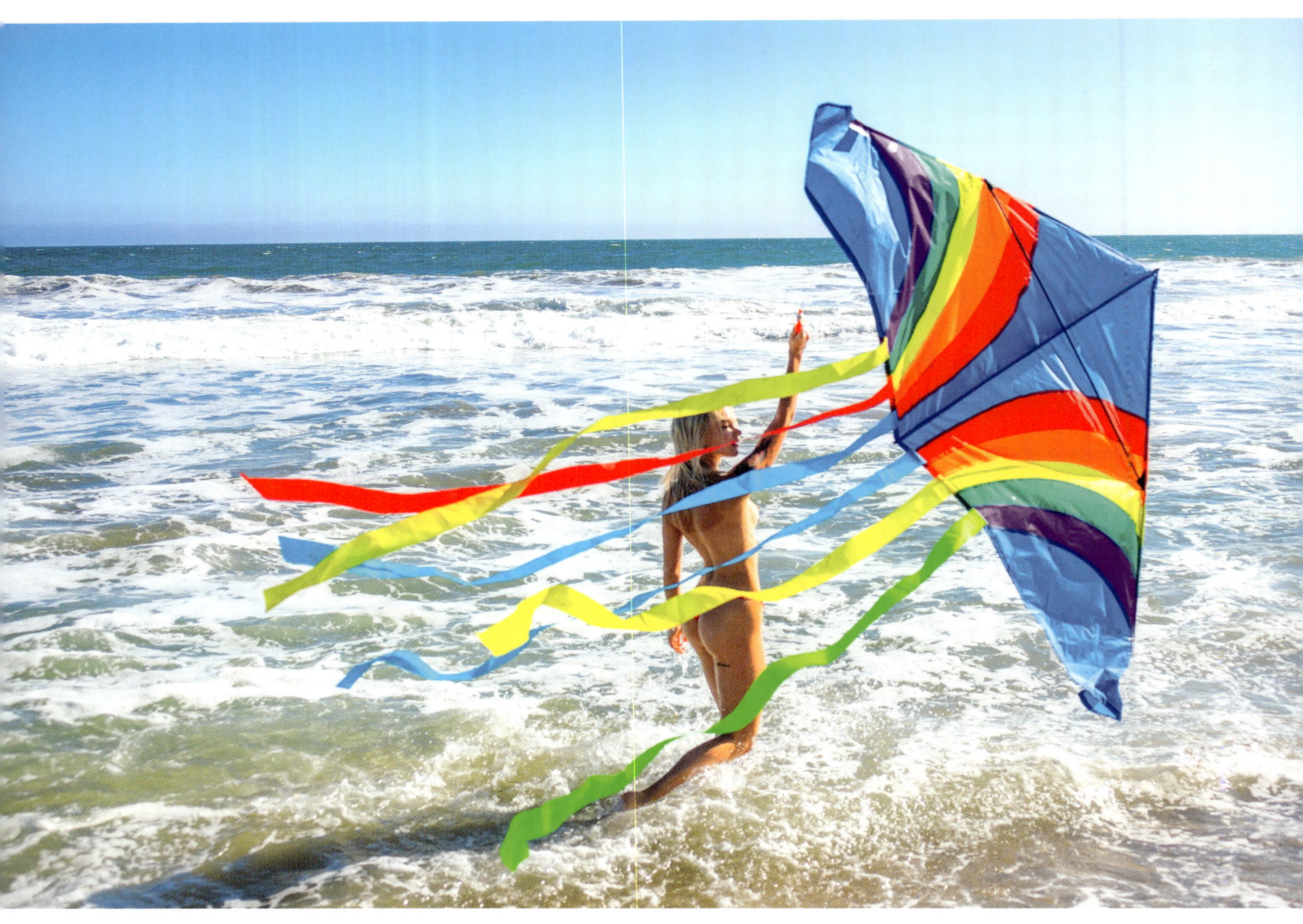

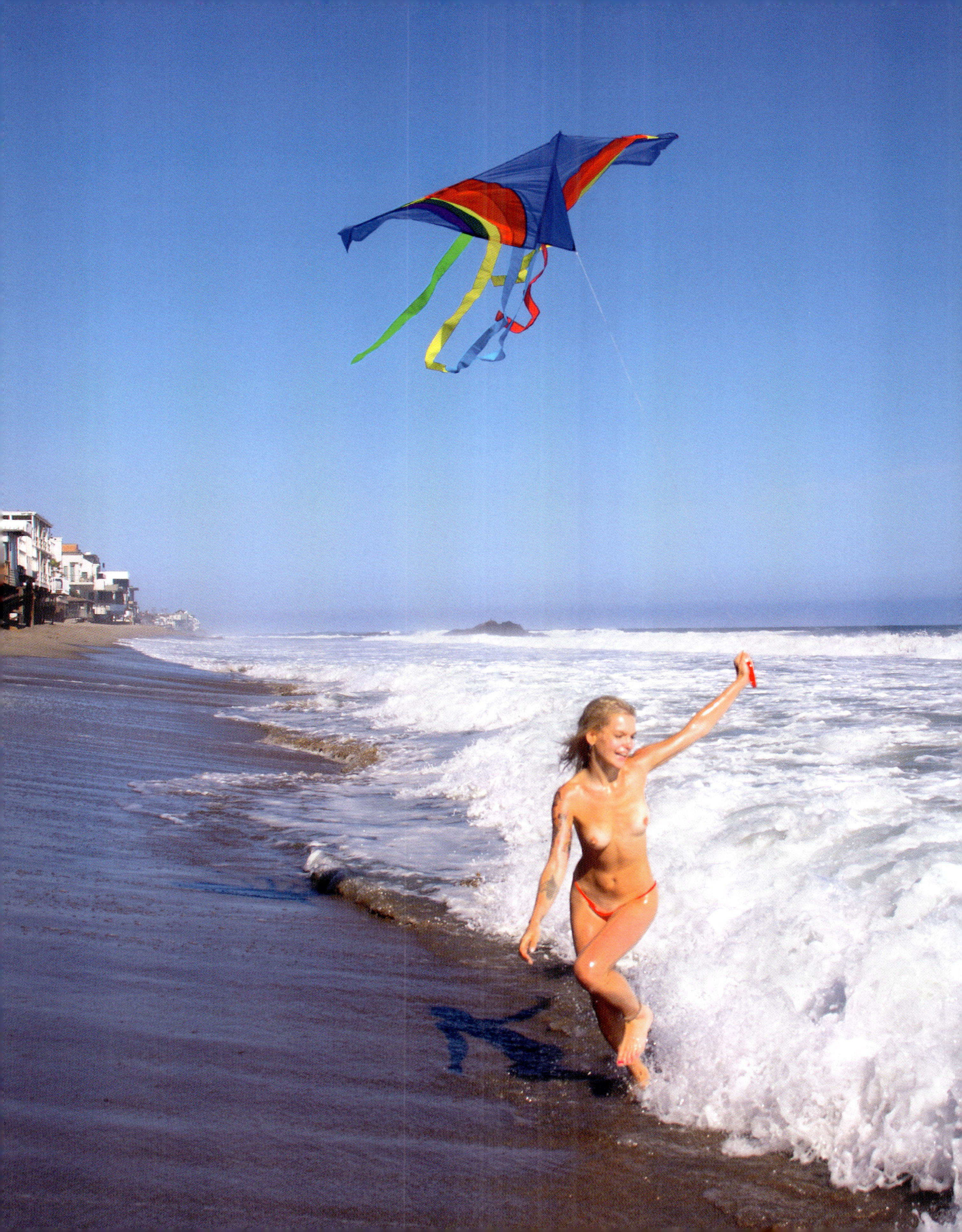

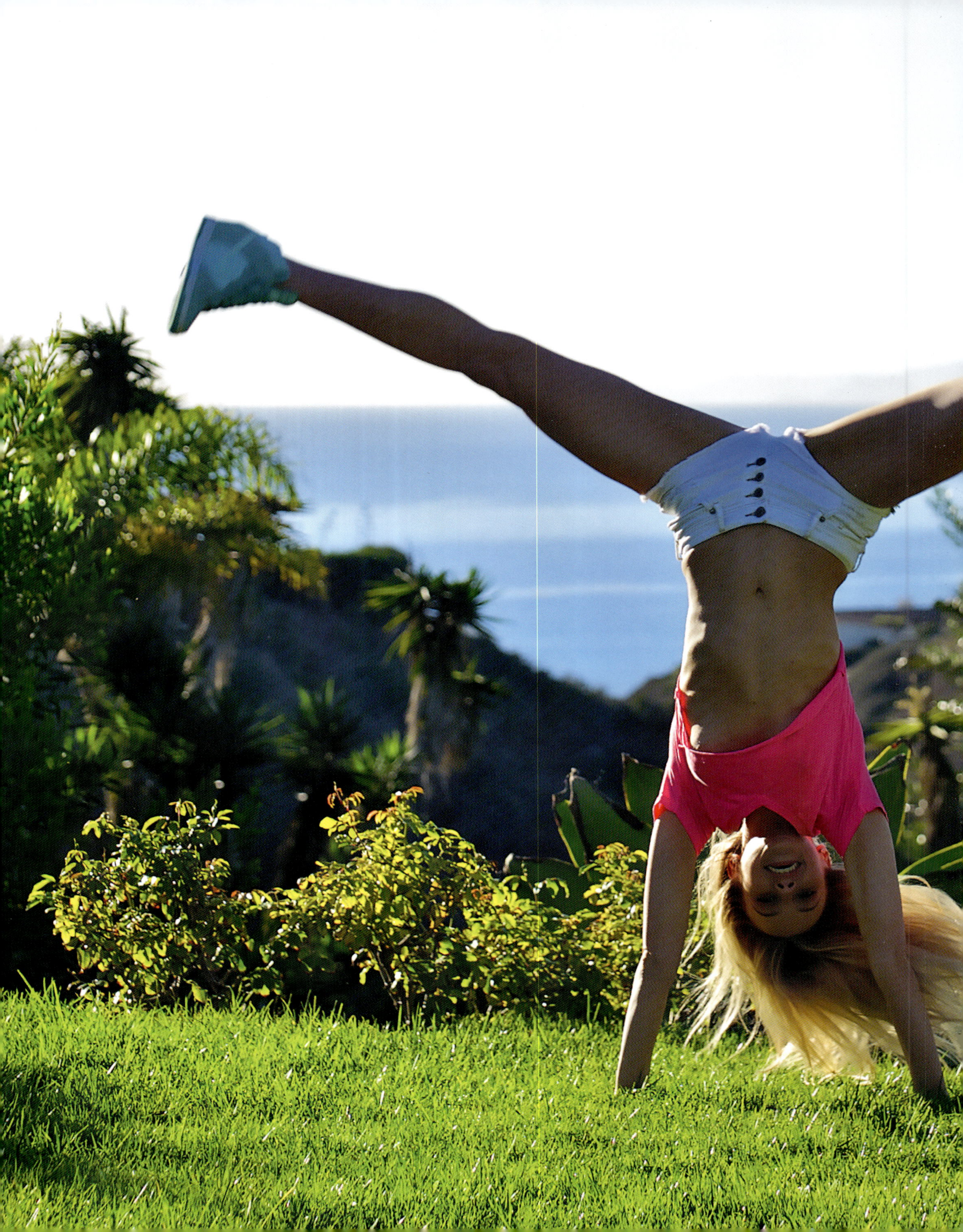

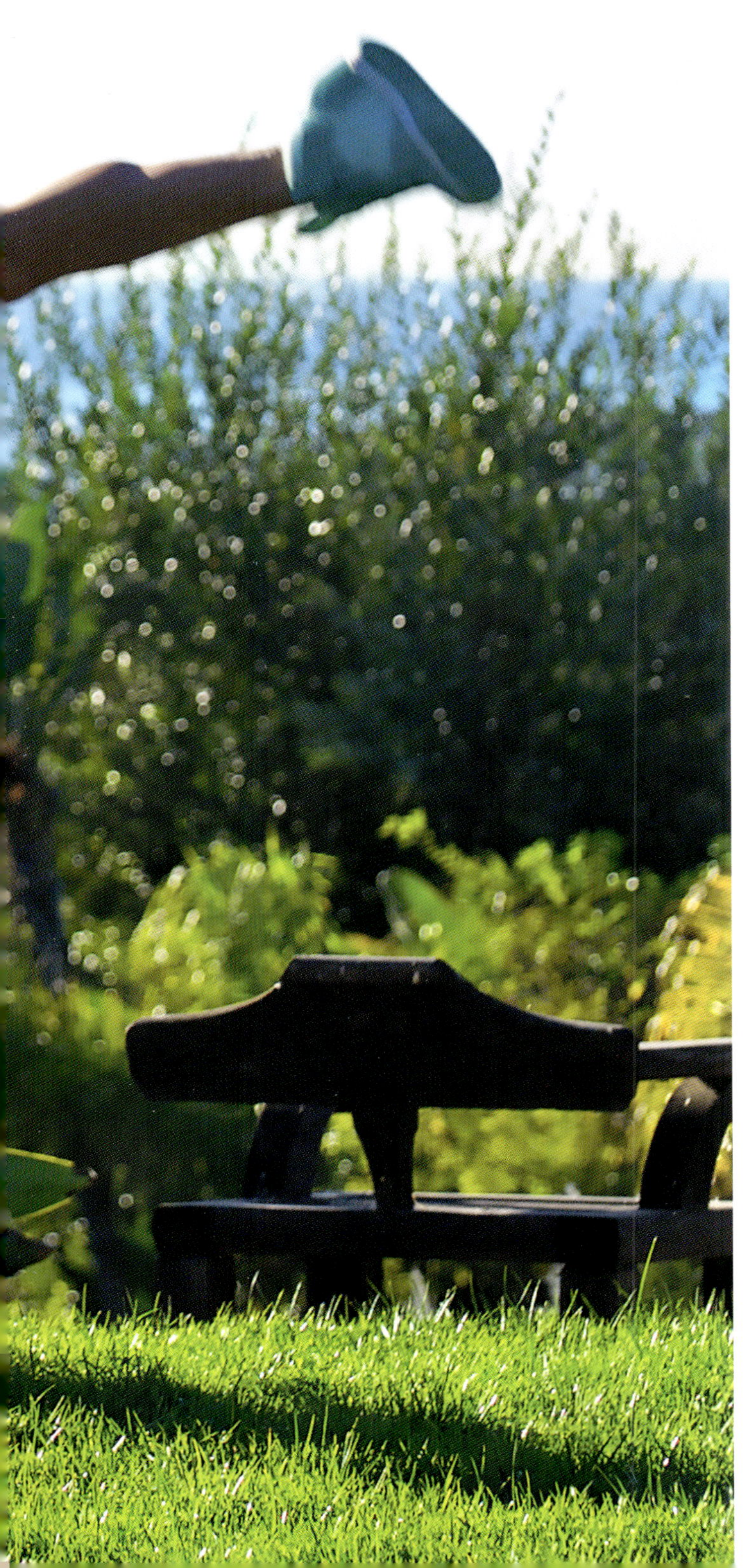

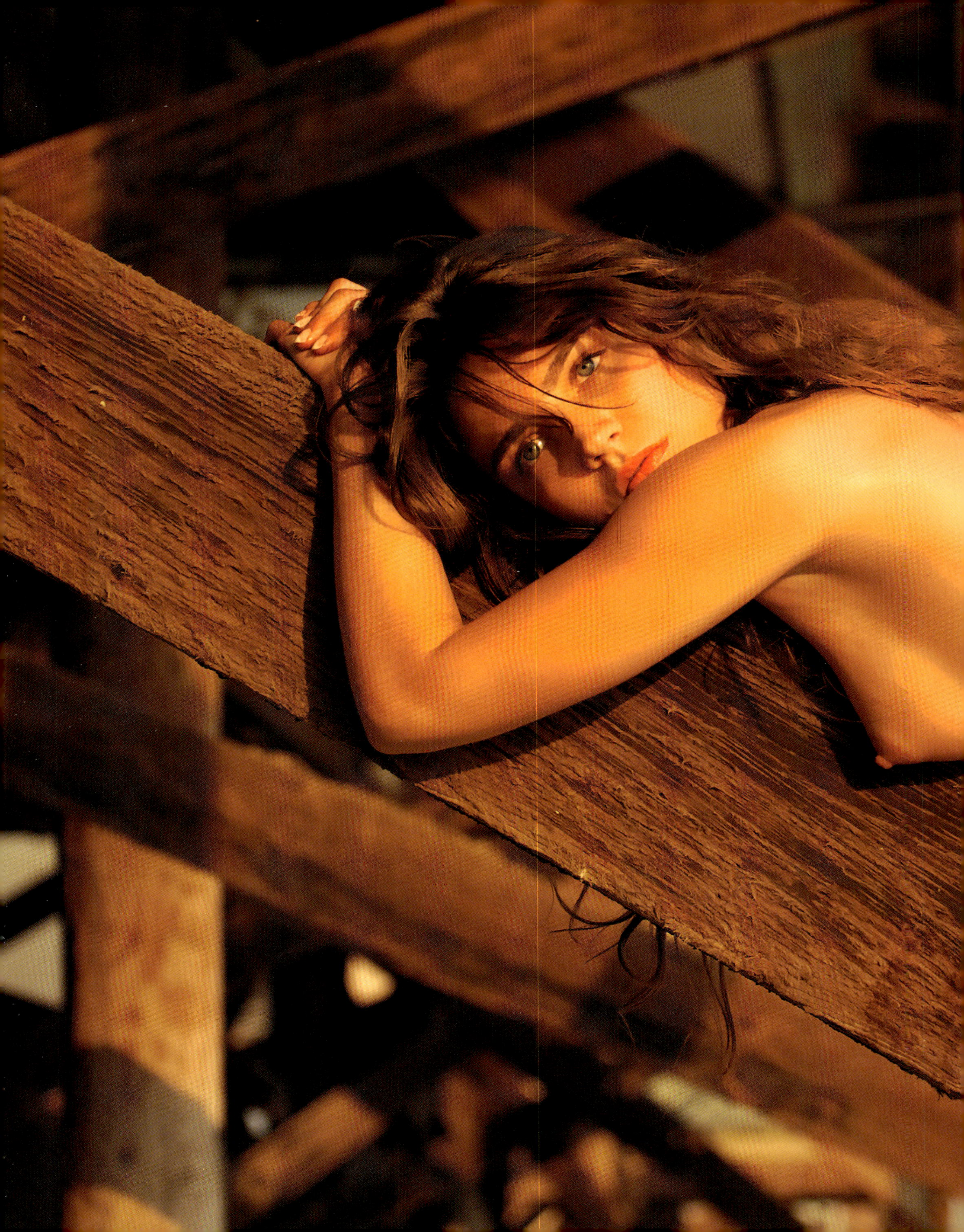

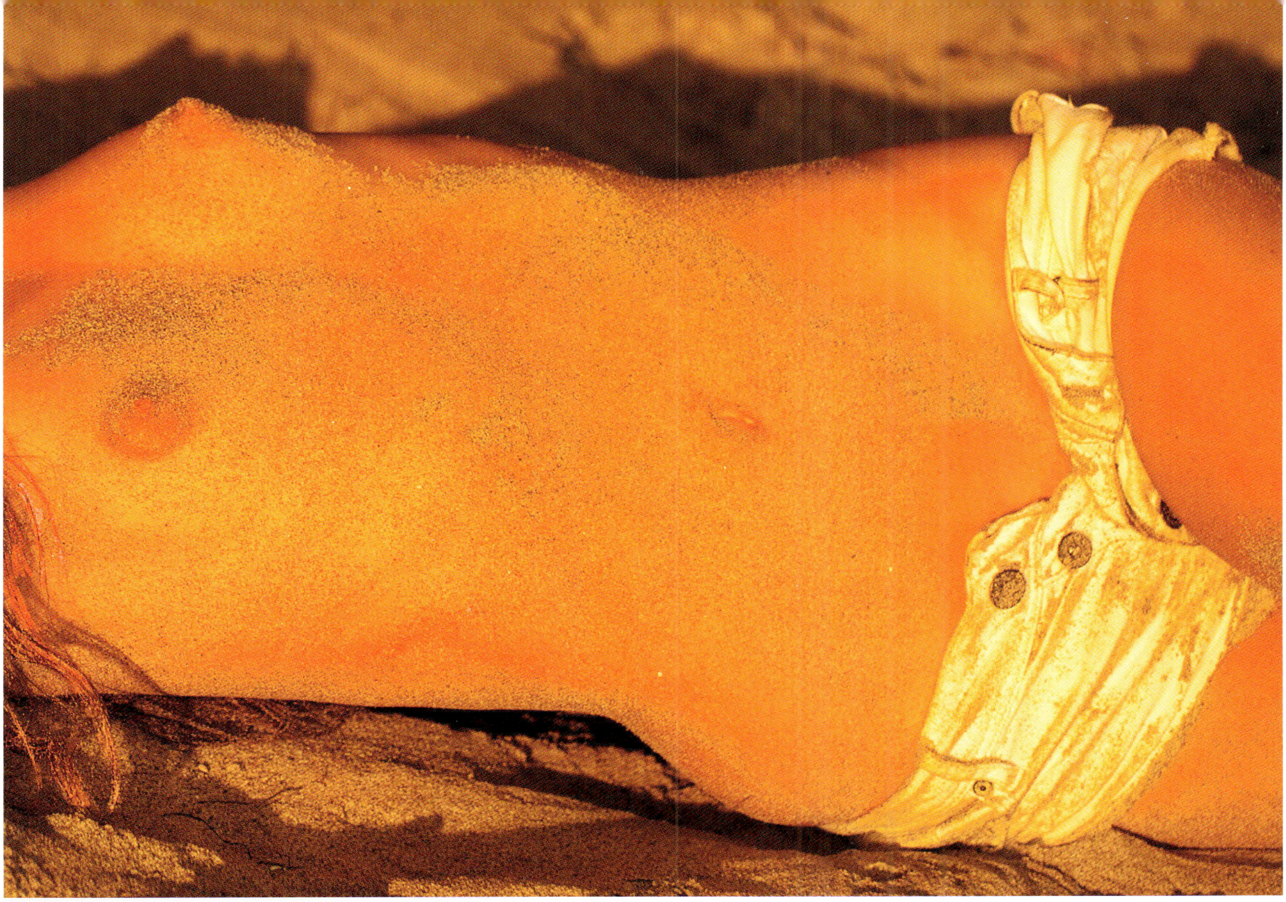

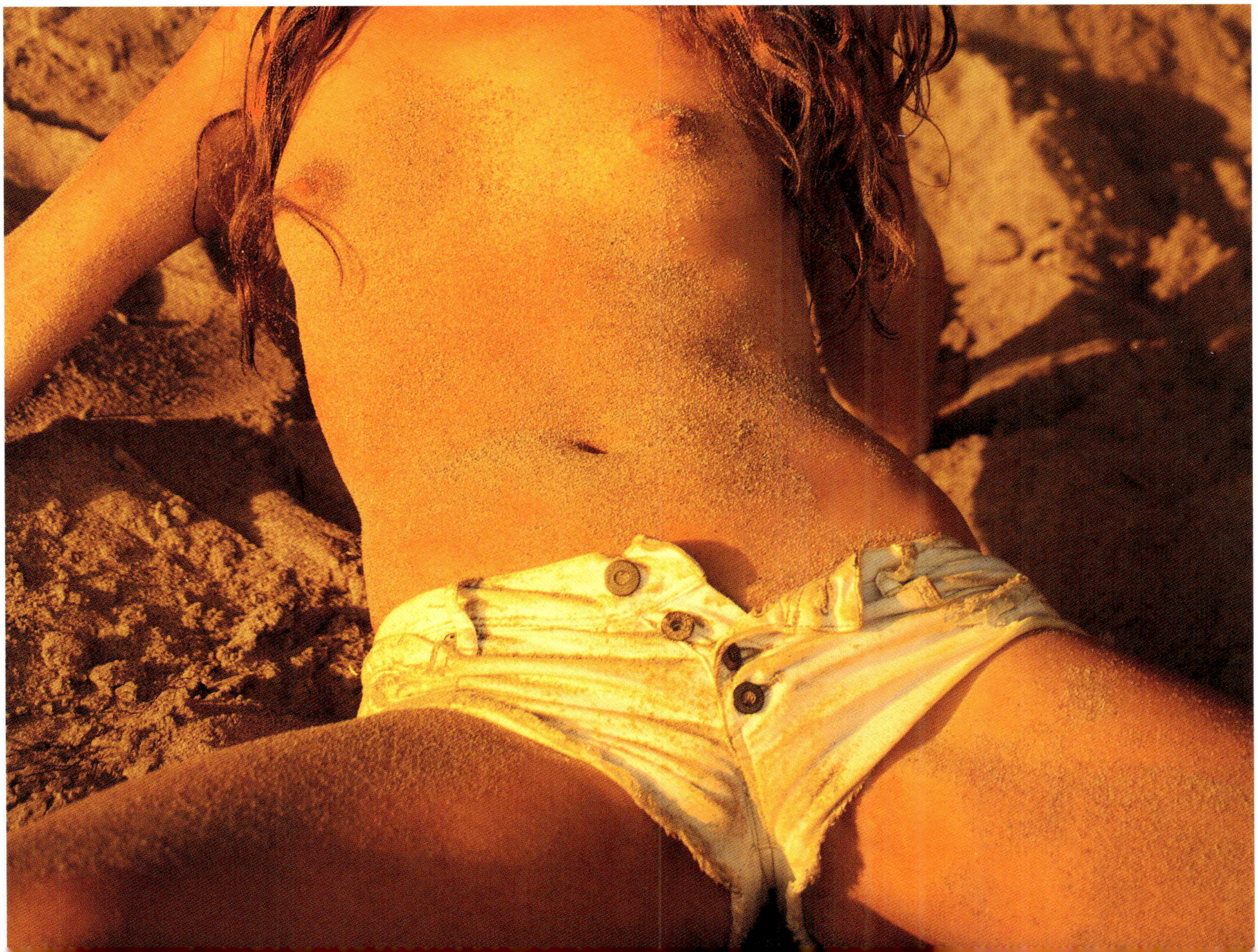

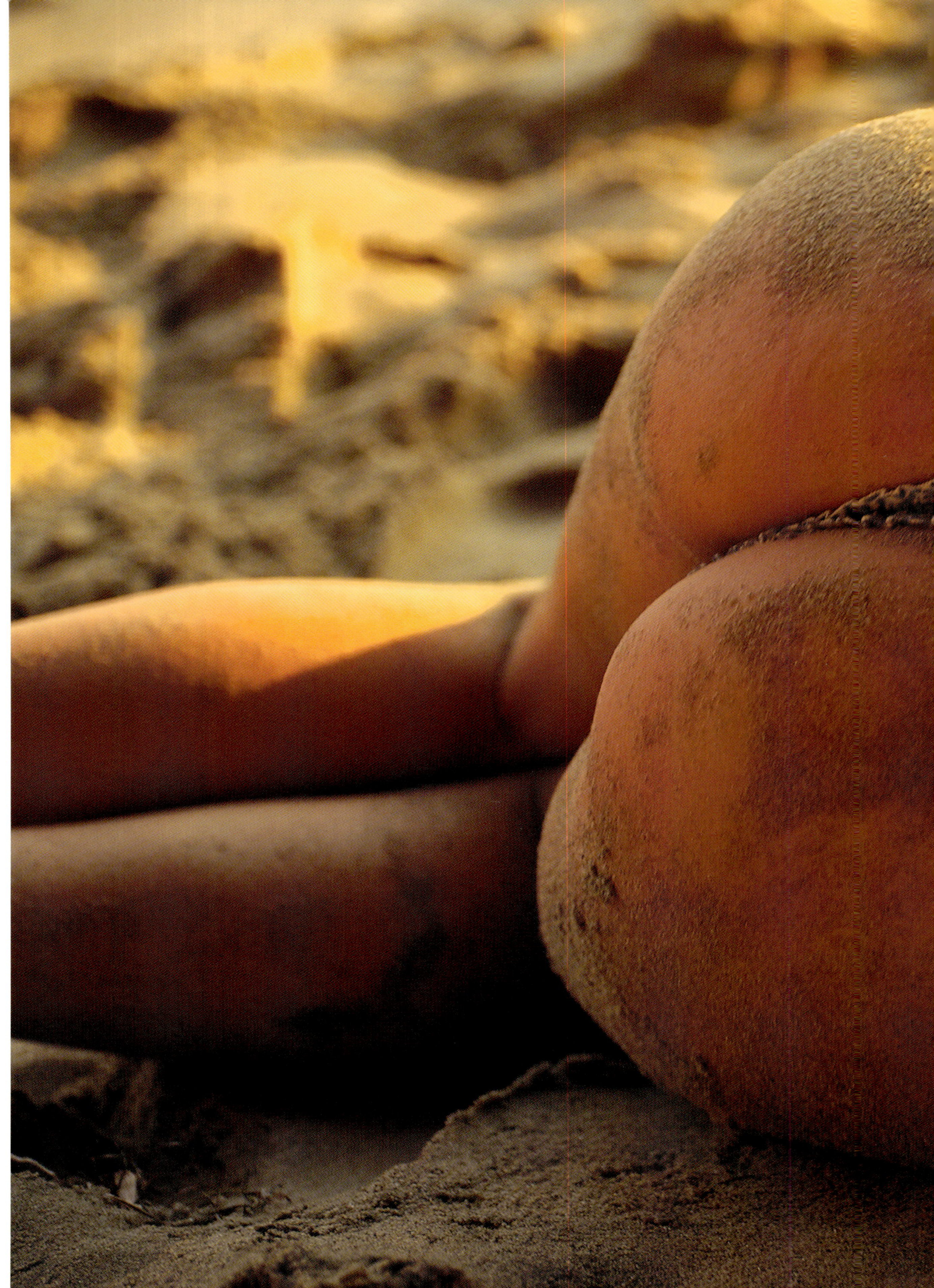

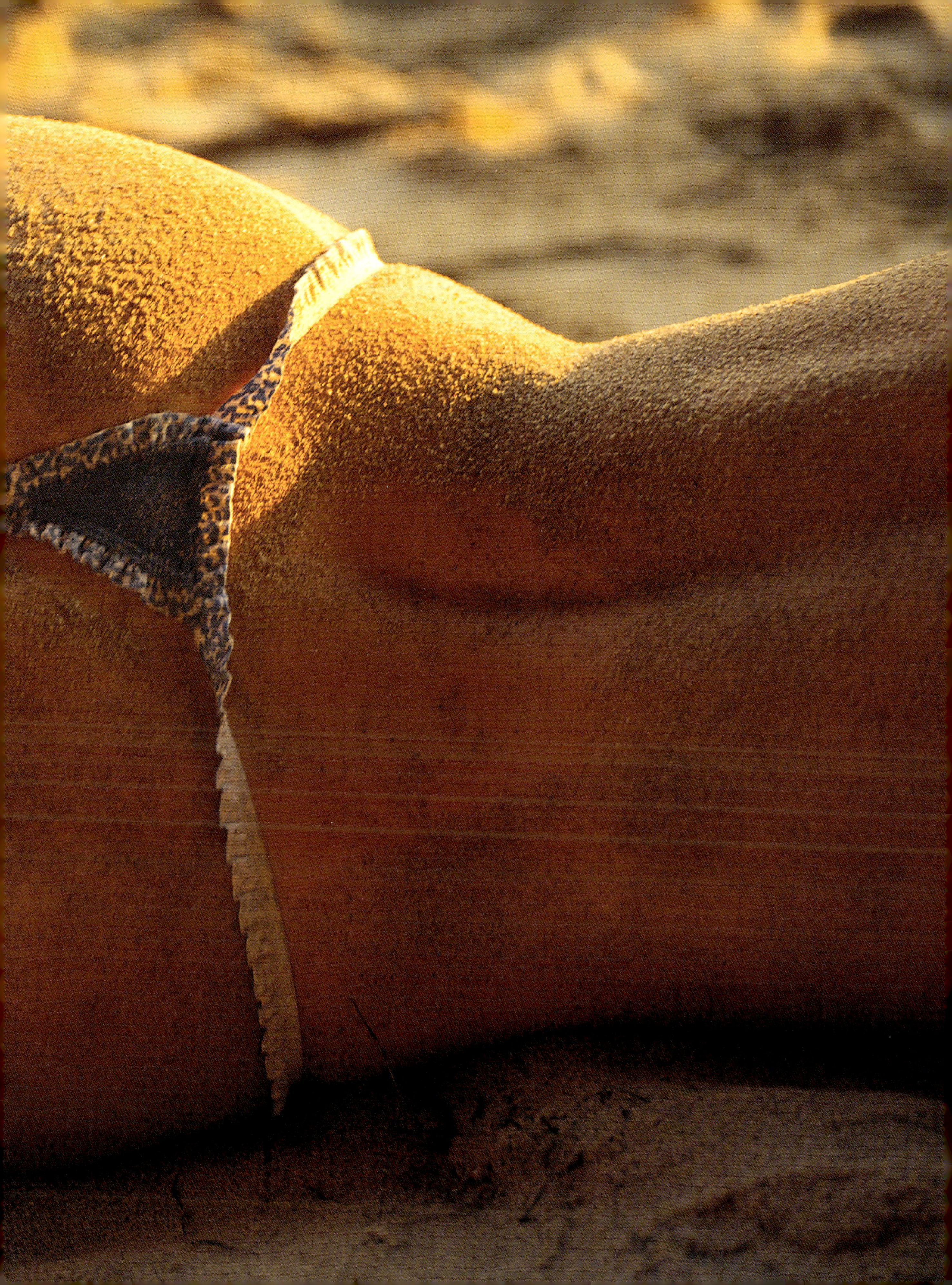

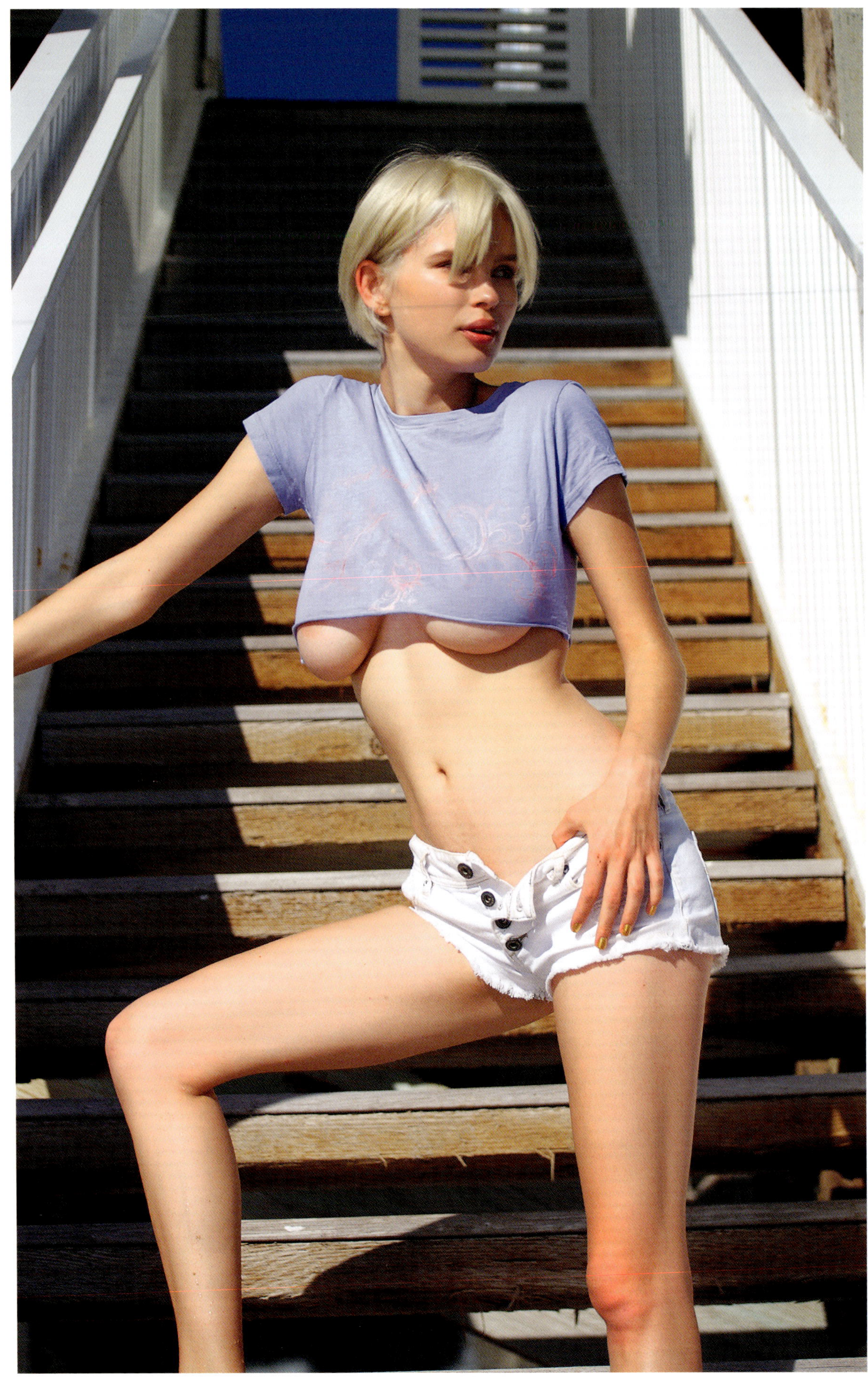

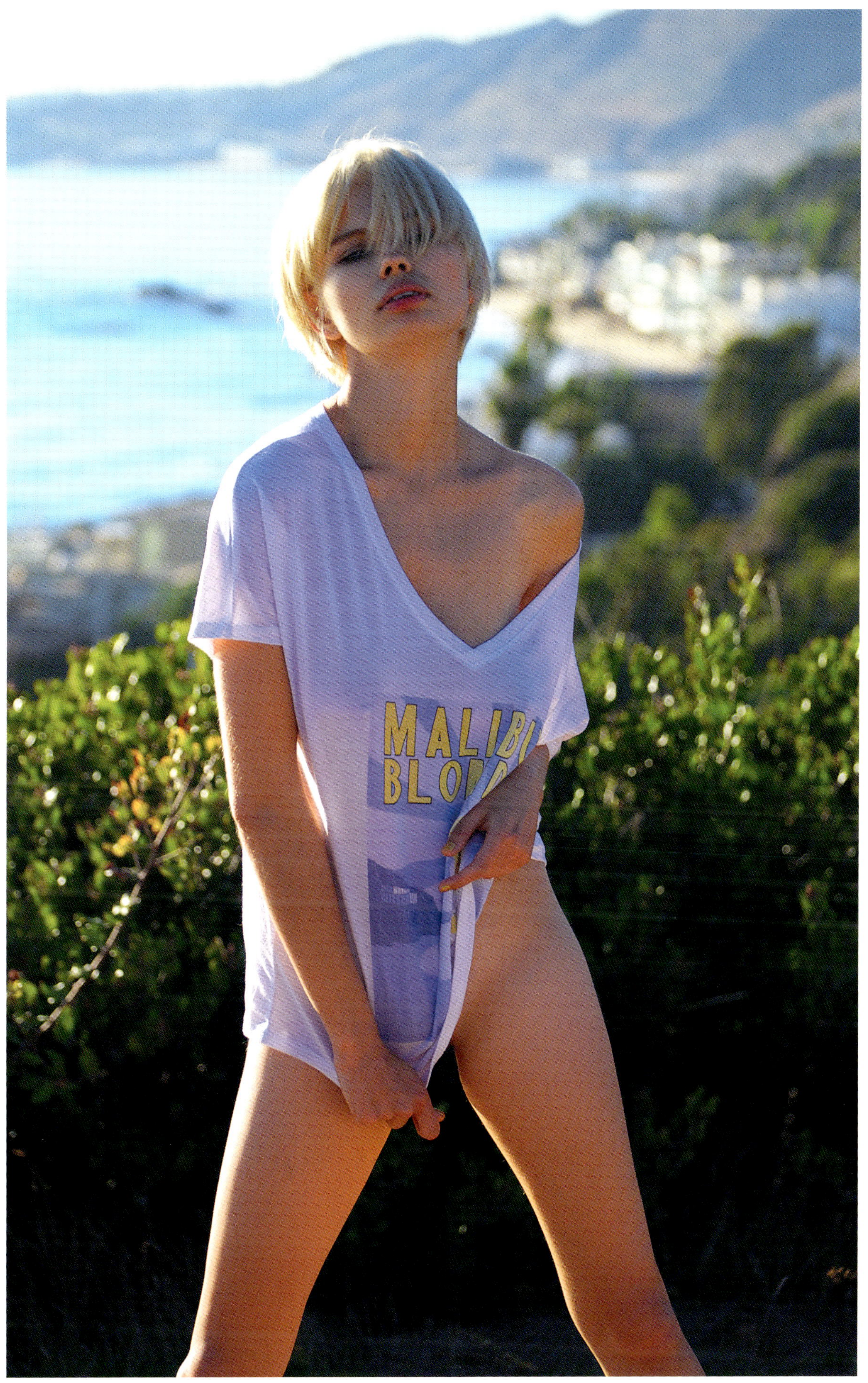
MALIBU
BLONDE

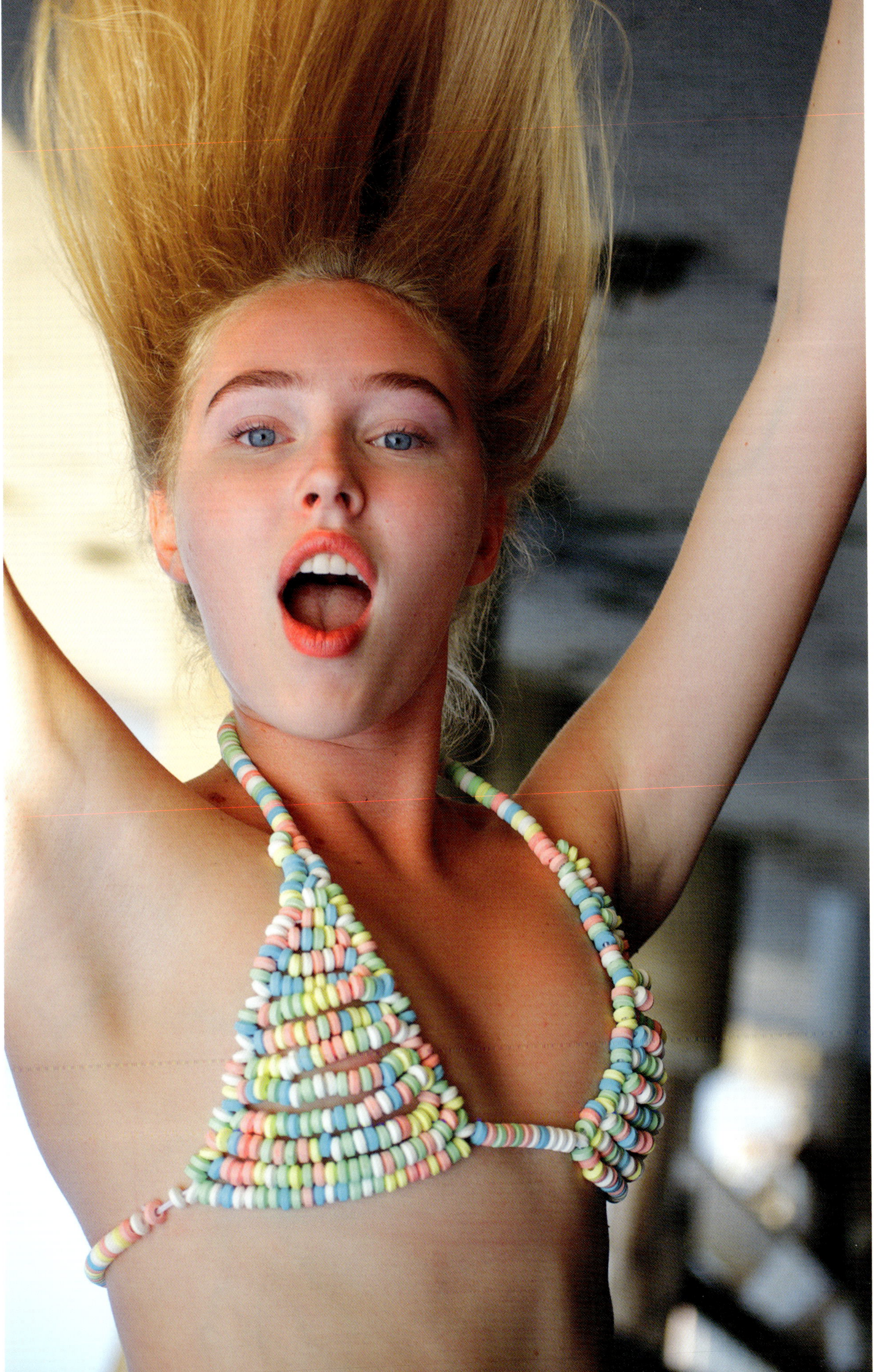

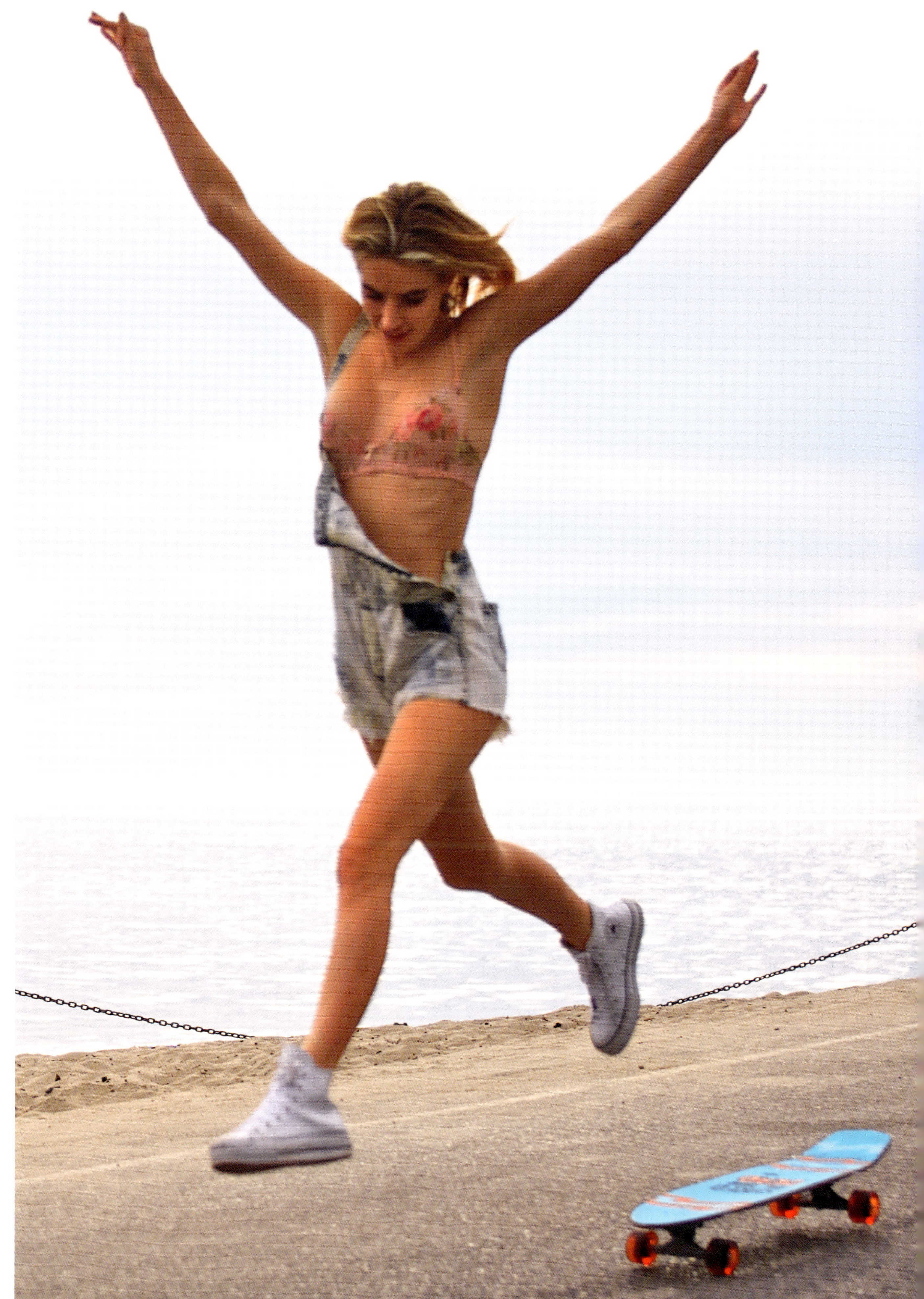

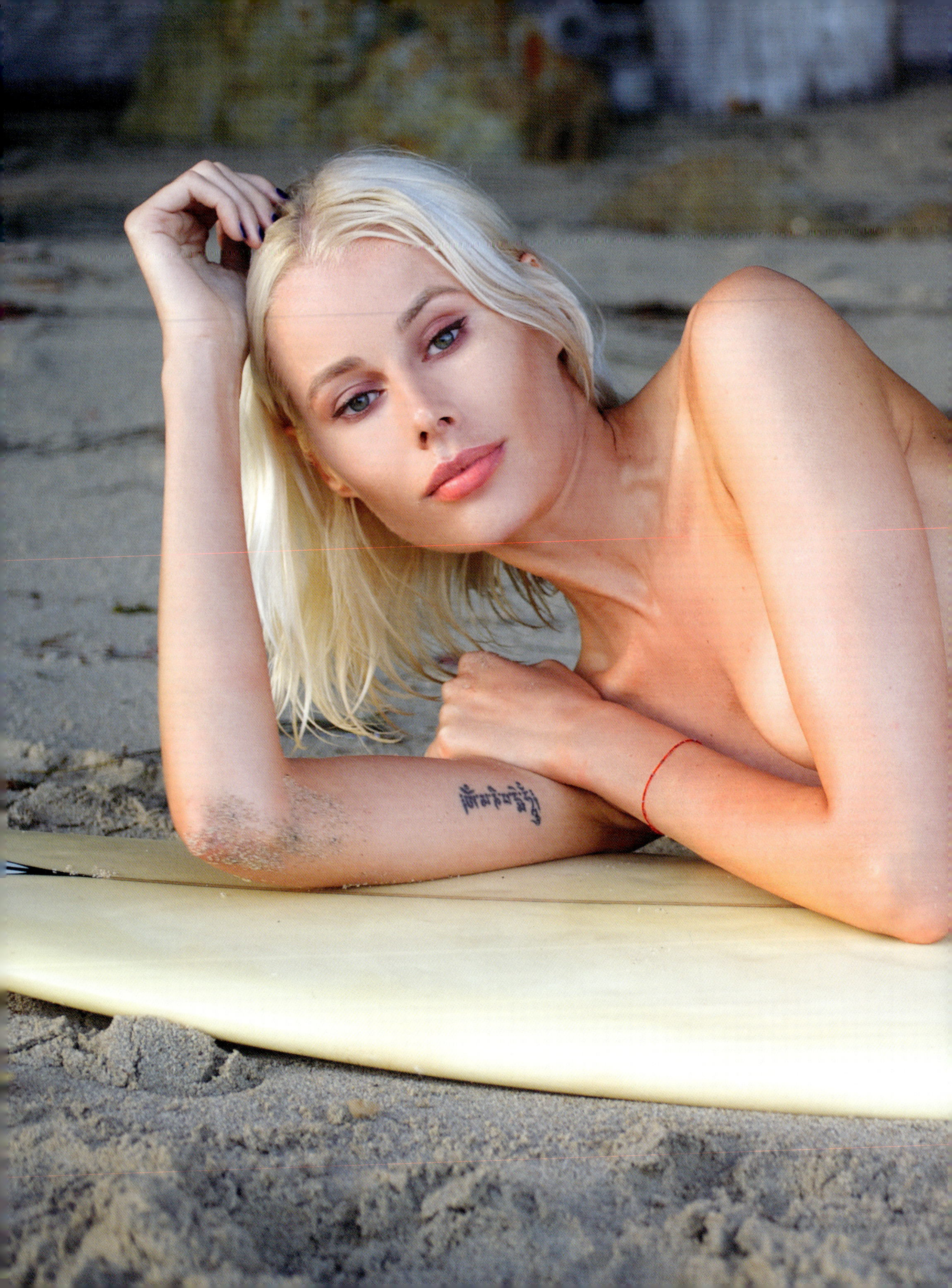

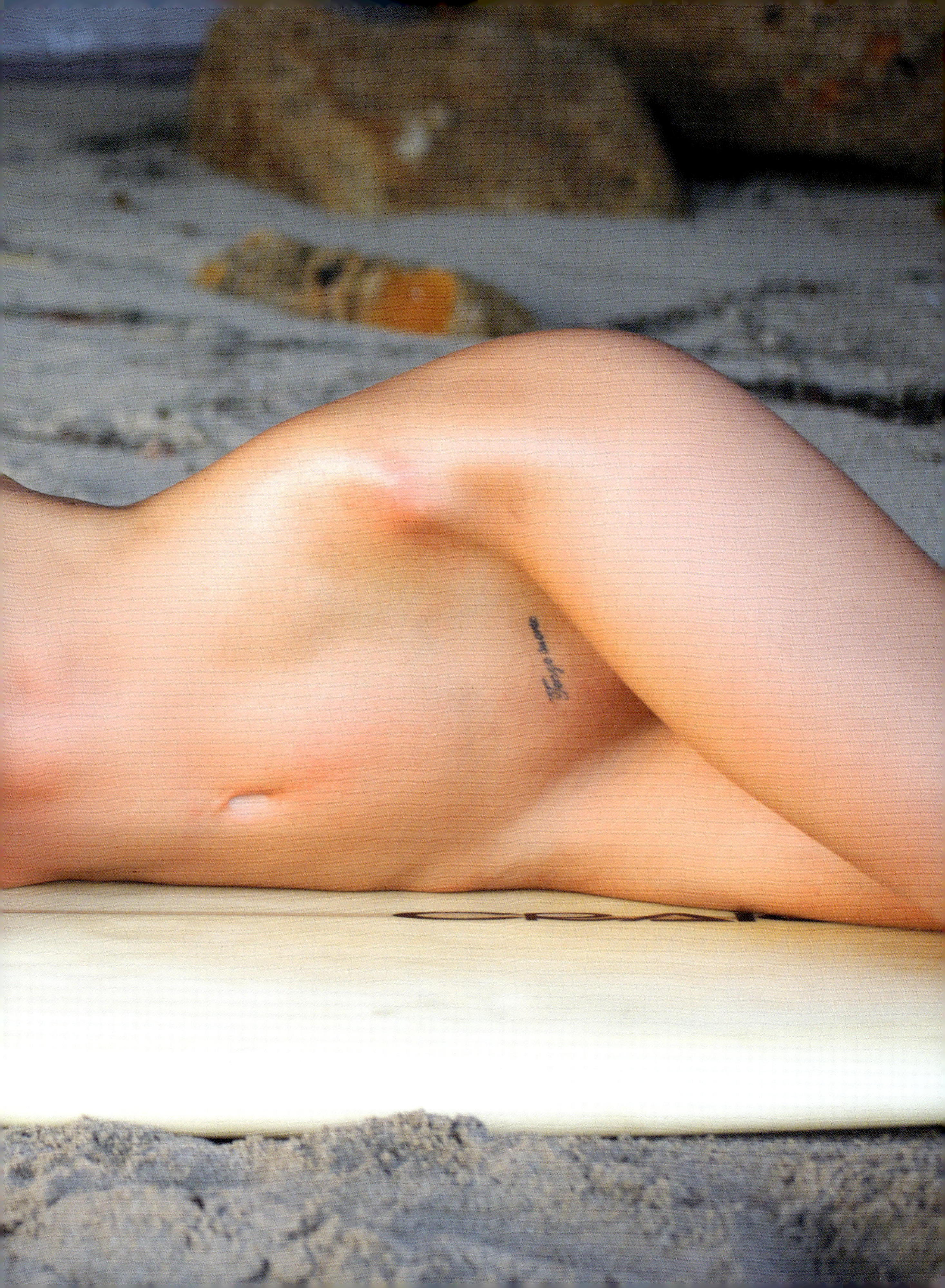

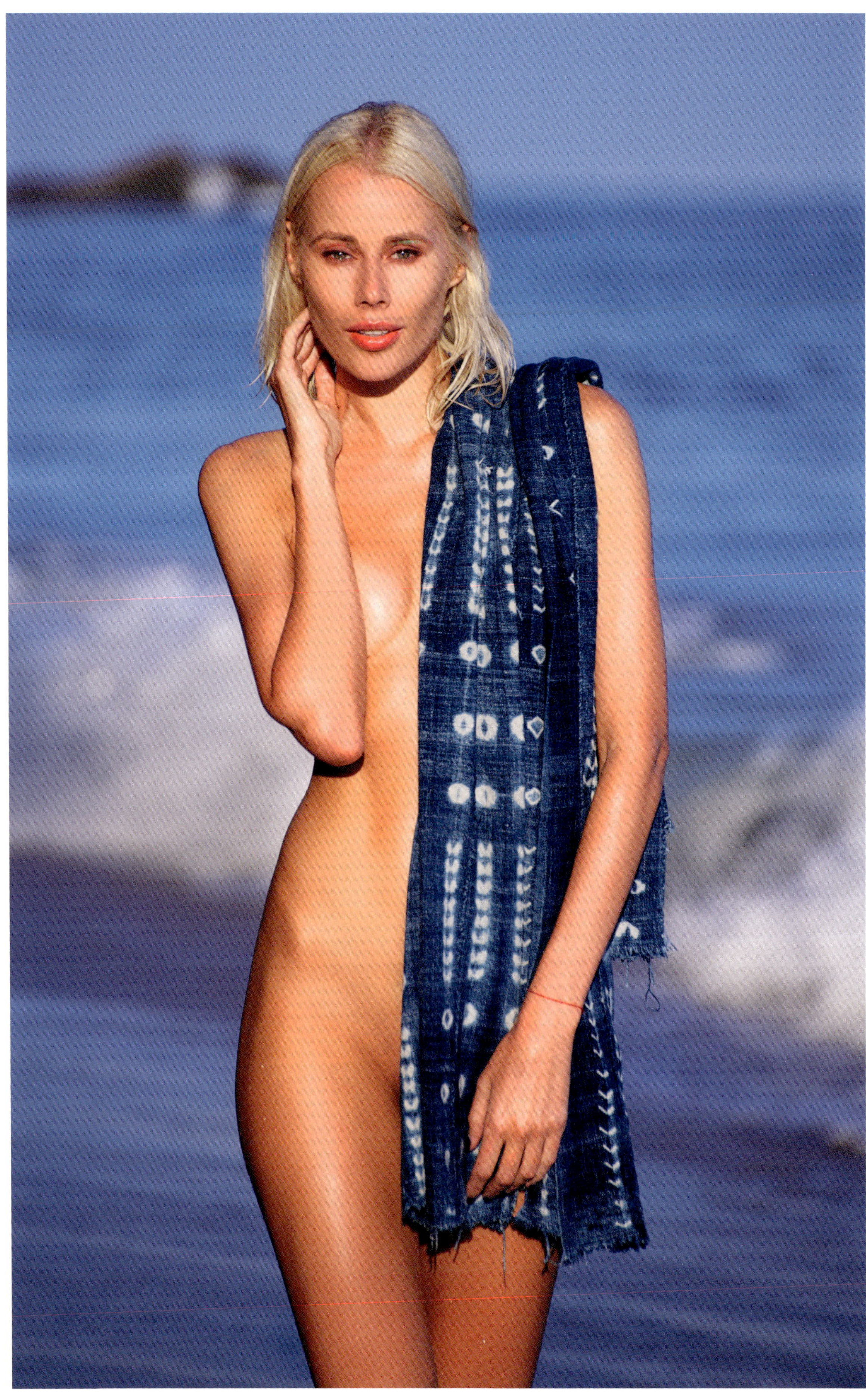

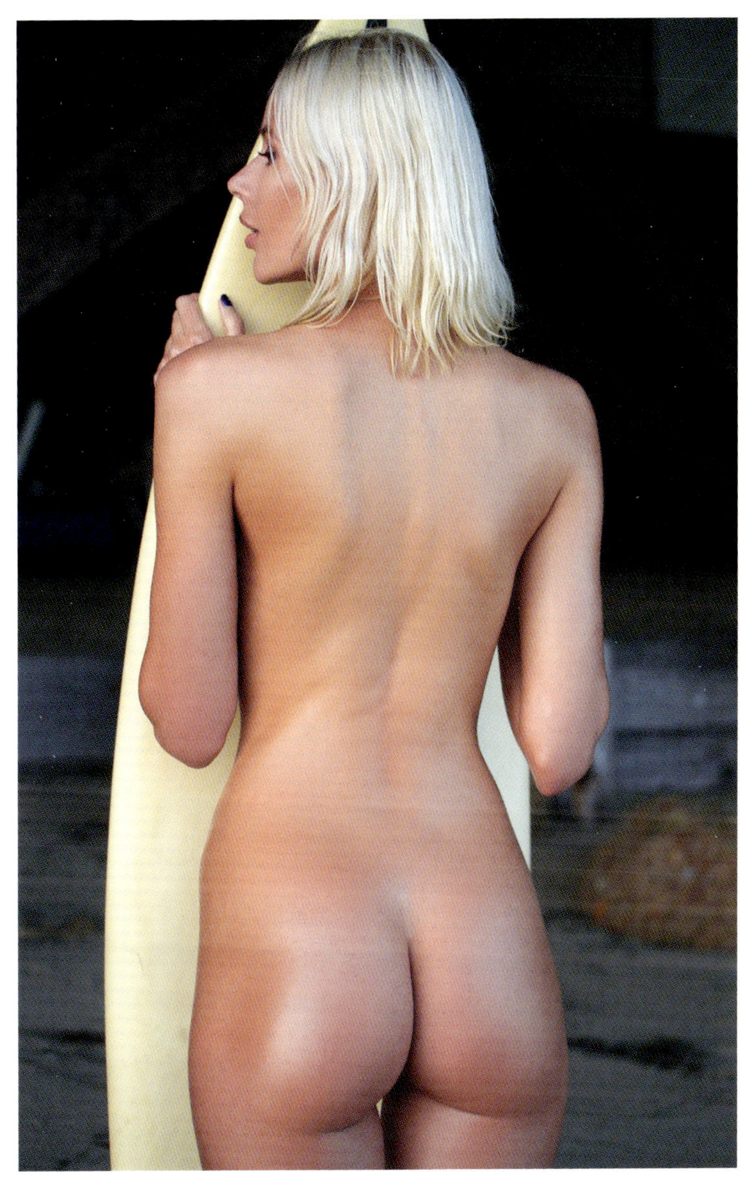

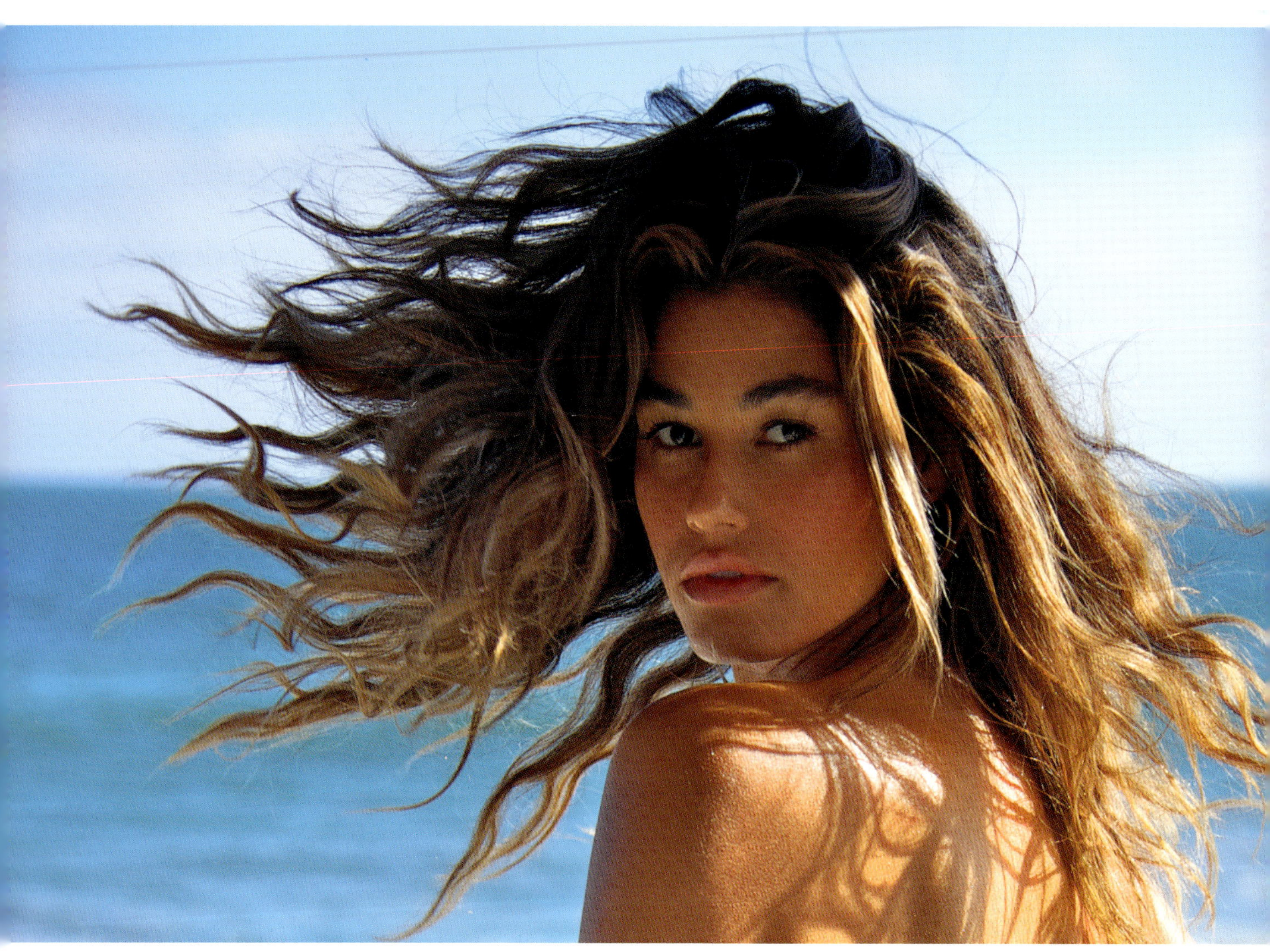

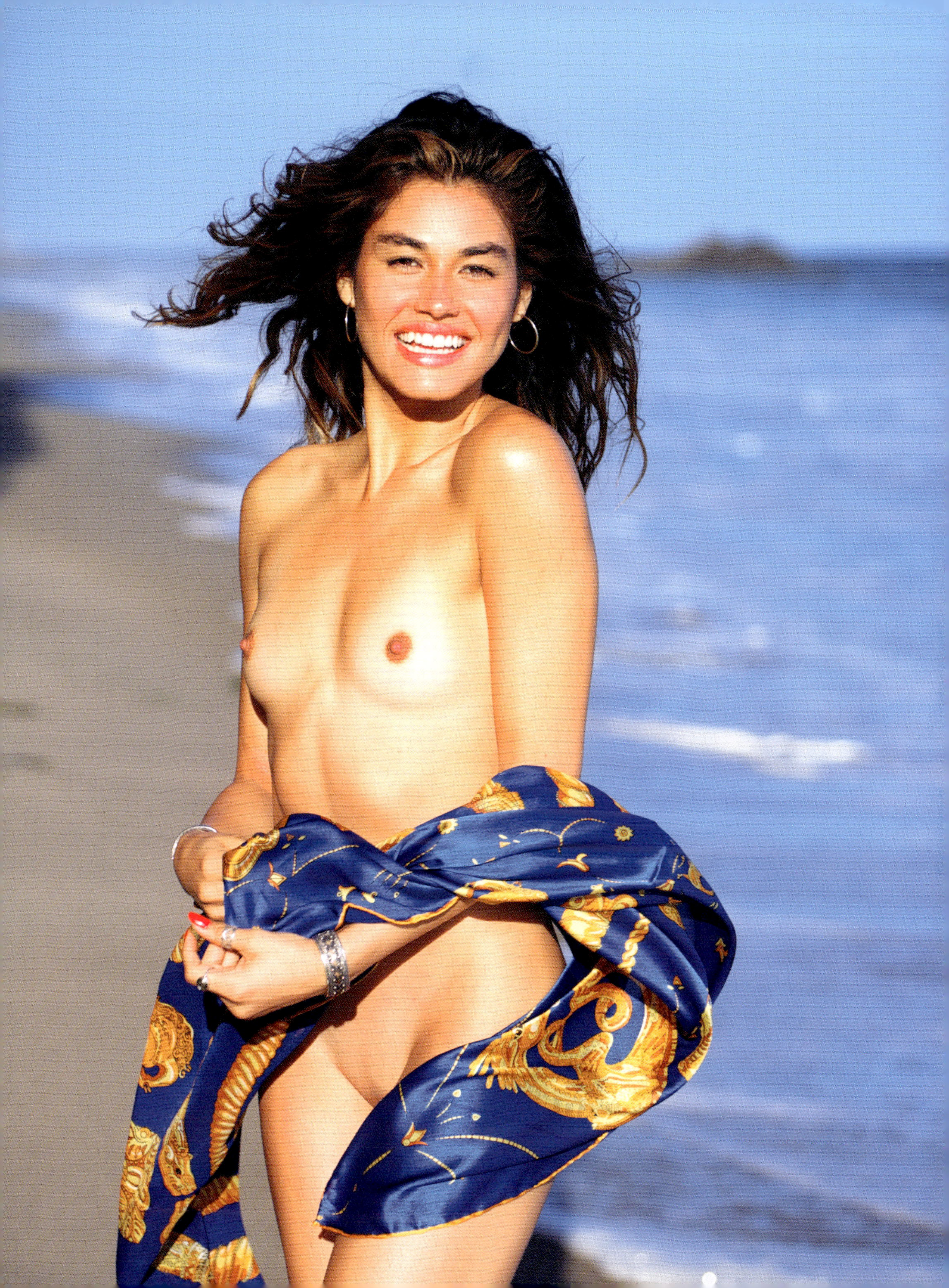

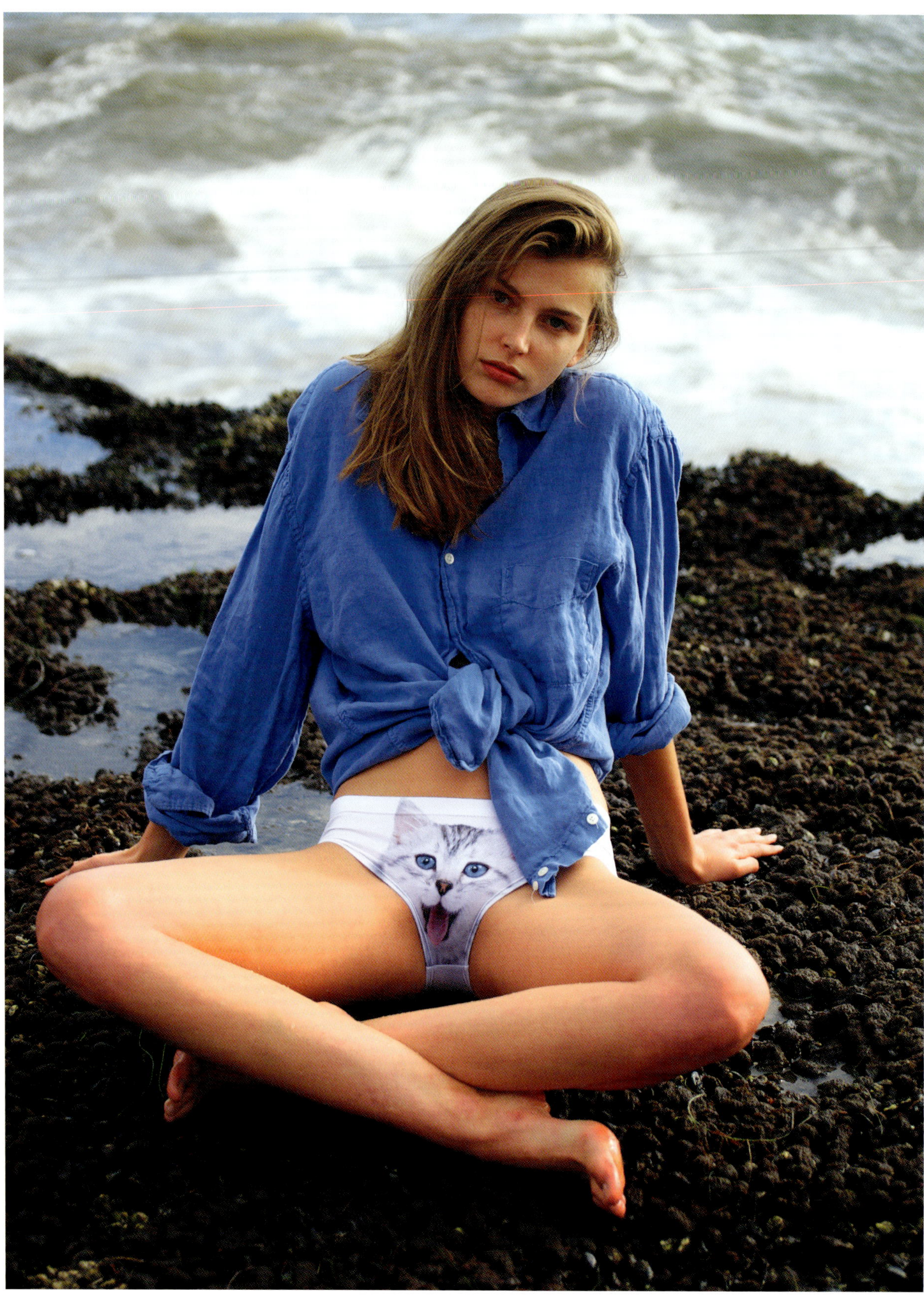

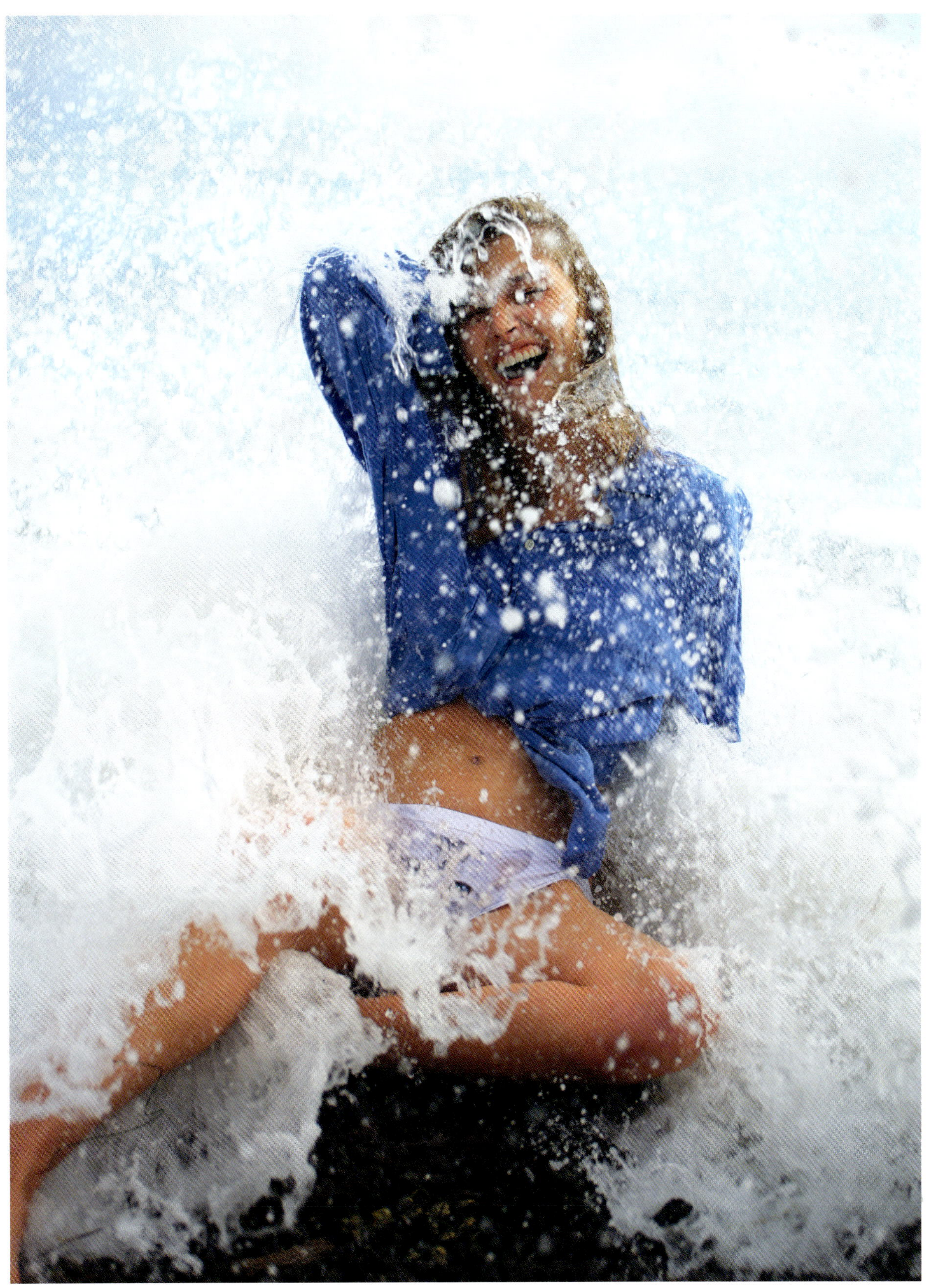

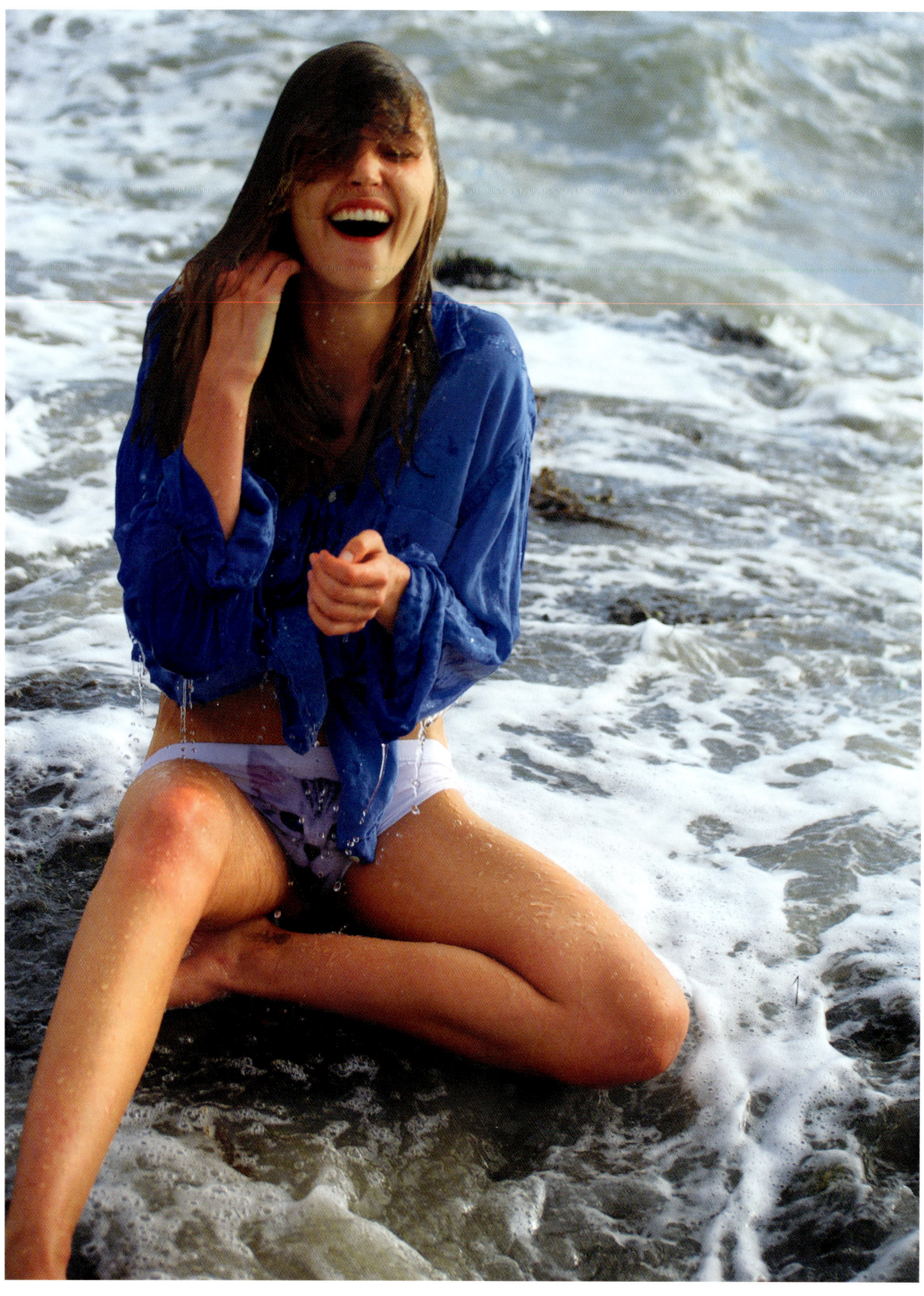

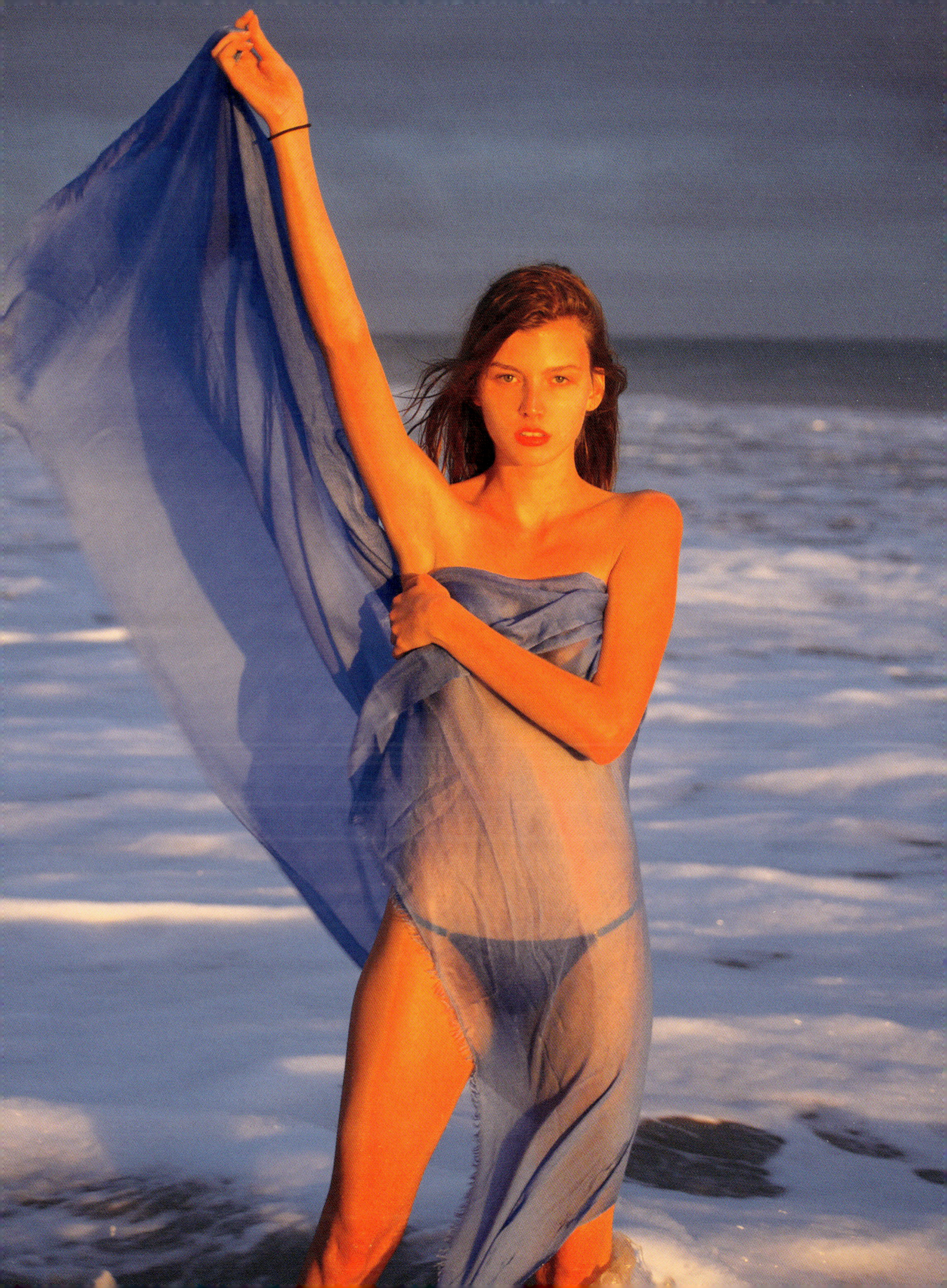

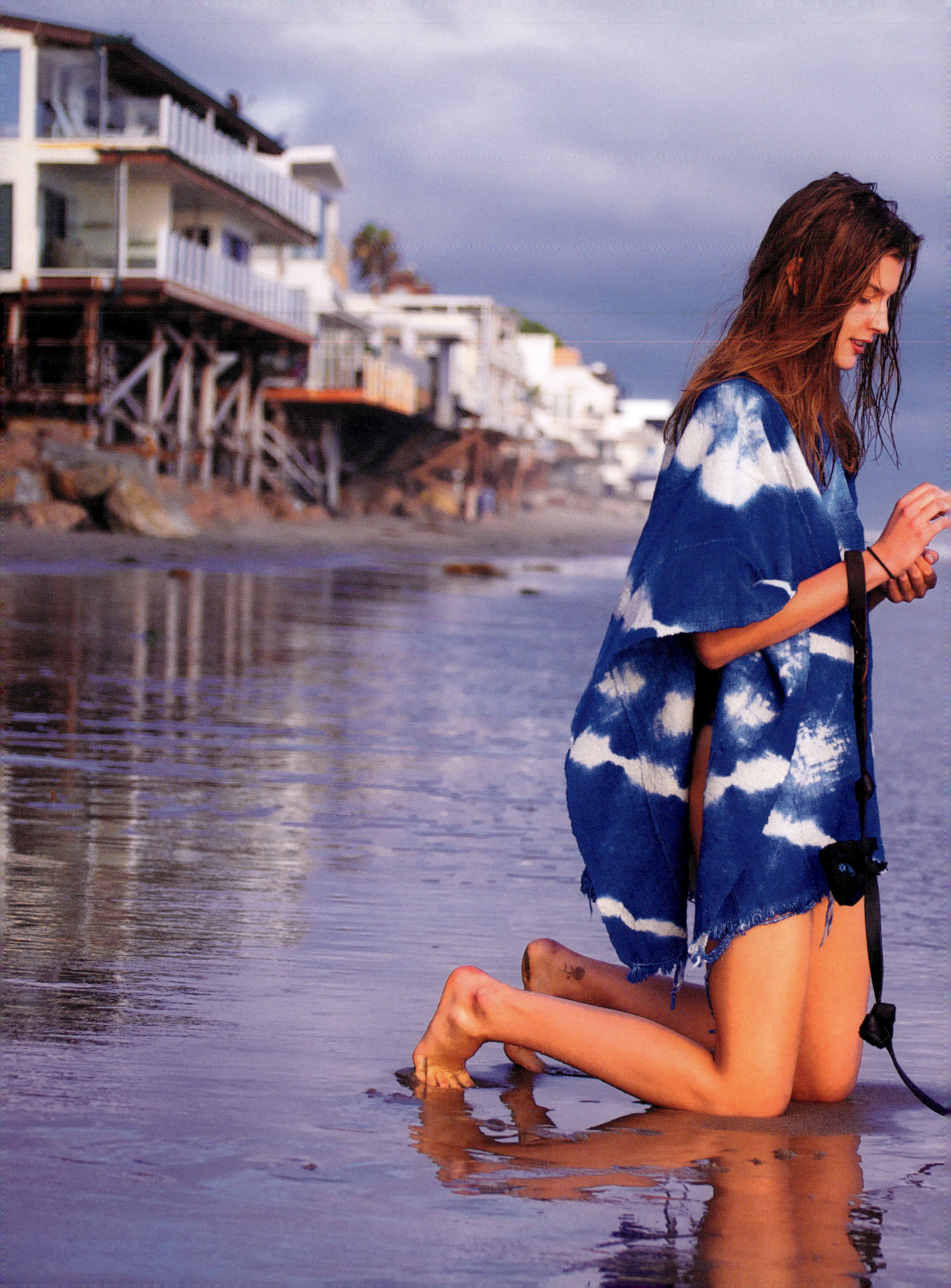

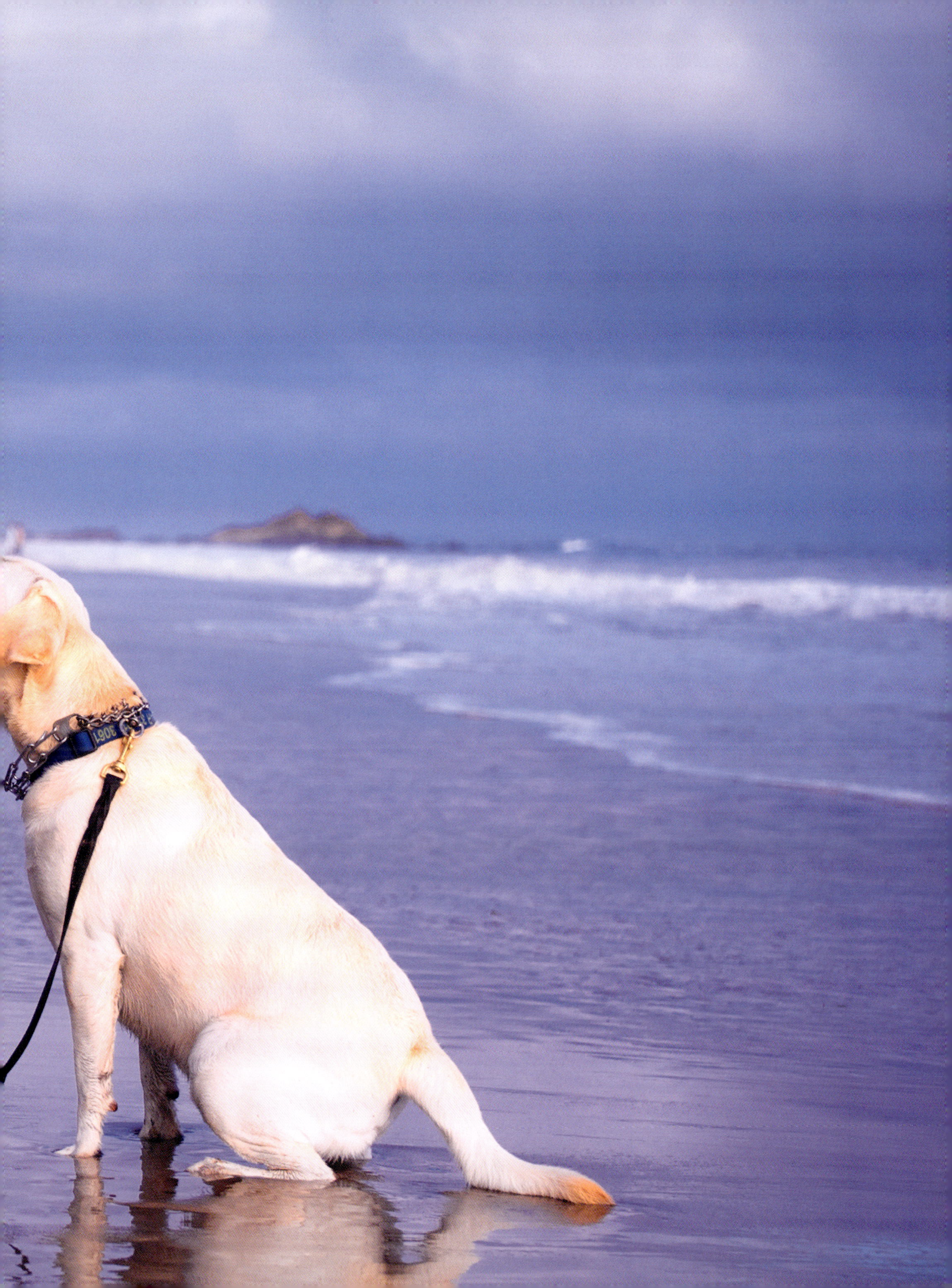

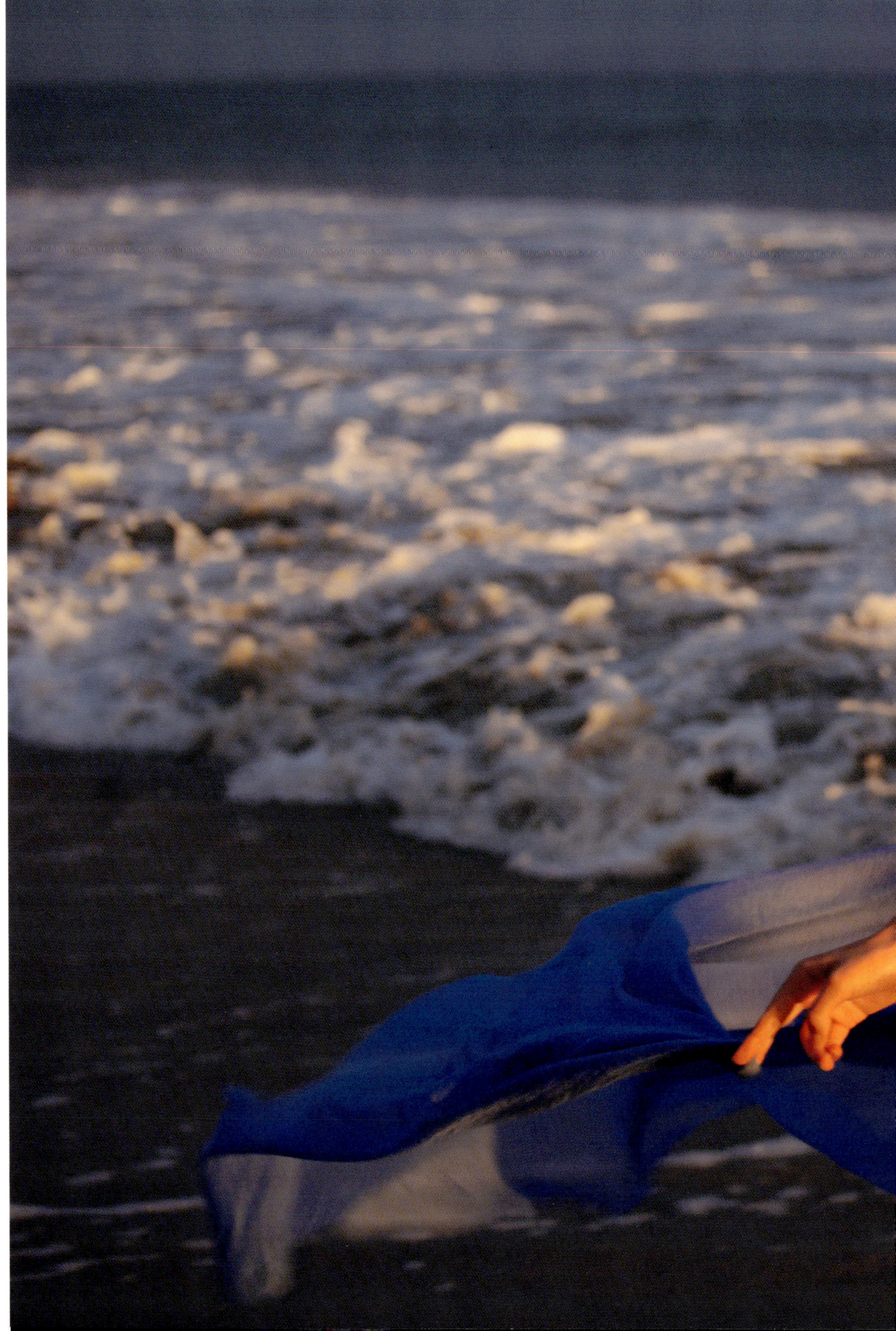

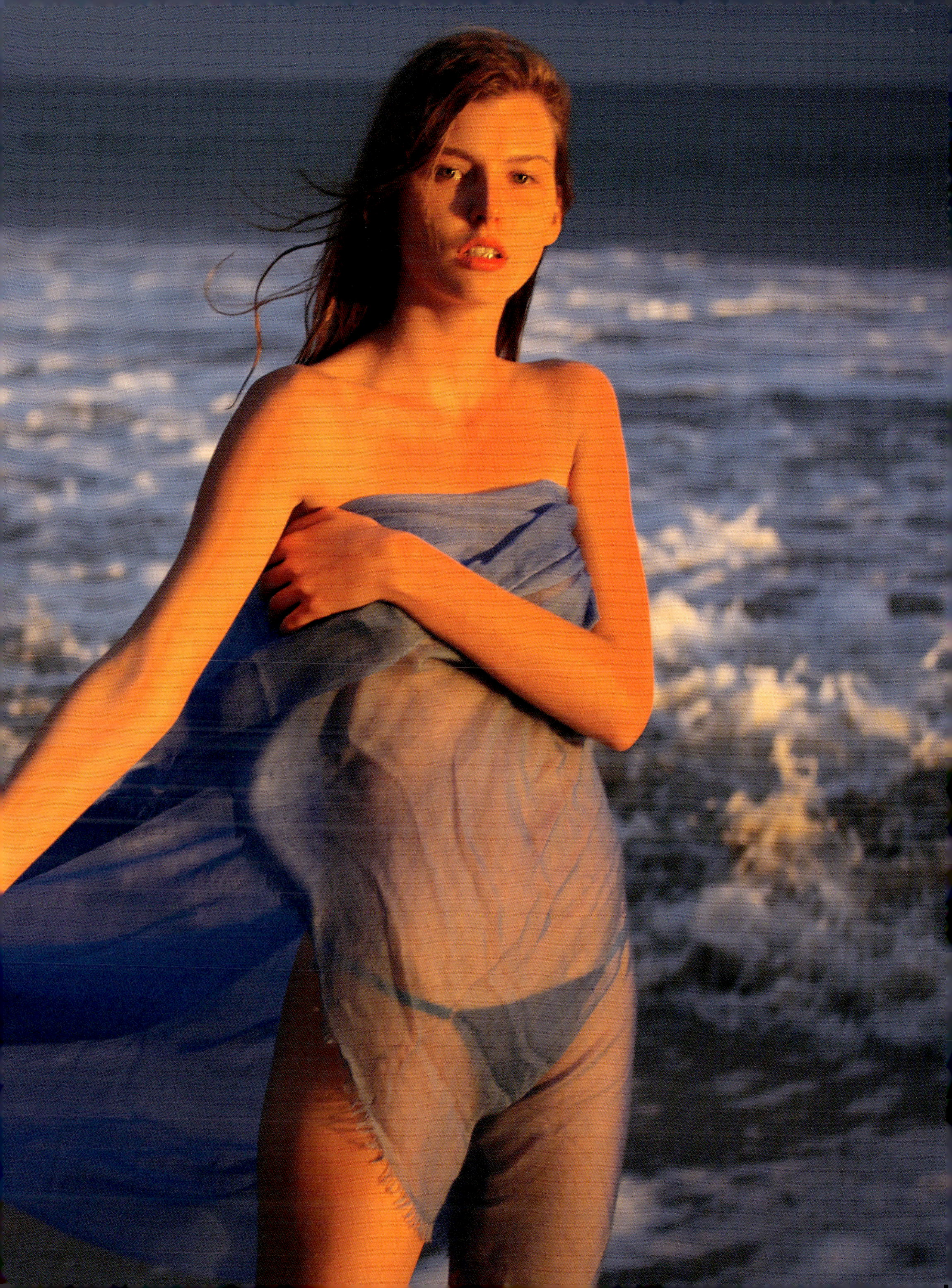

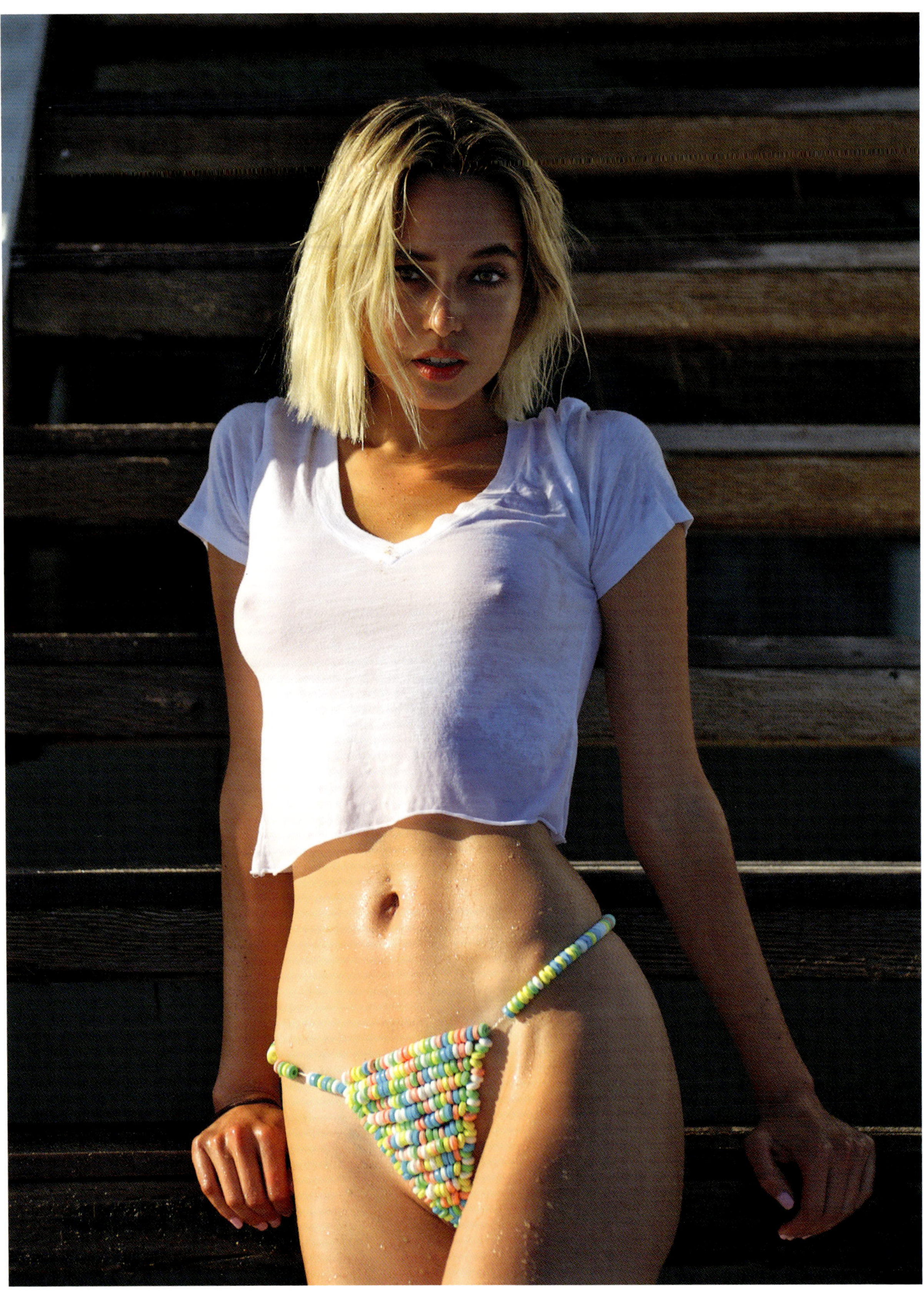

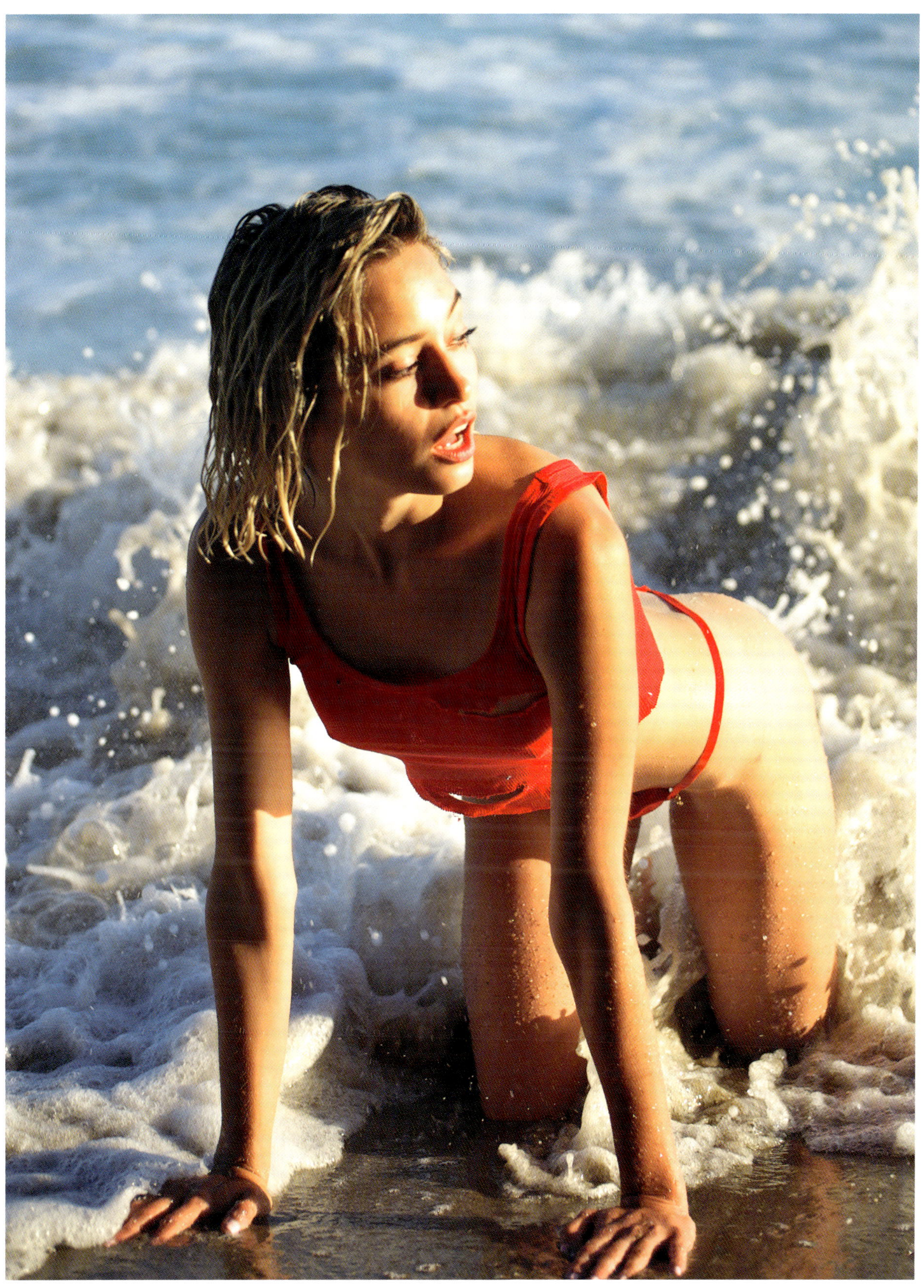

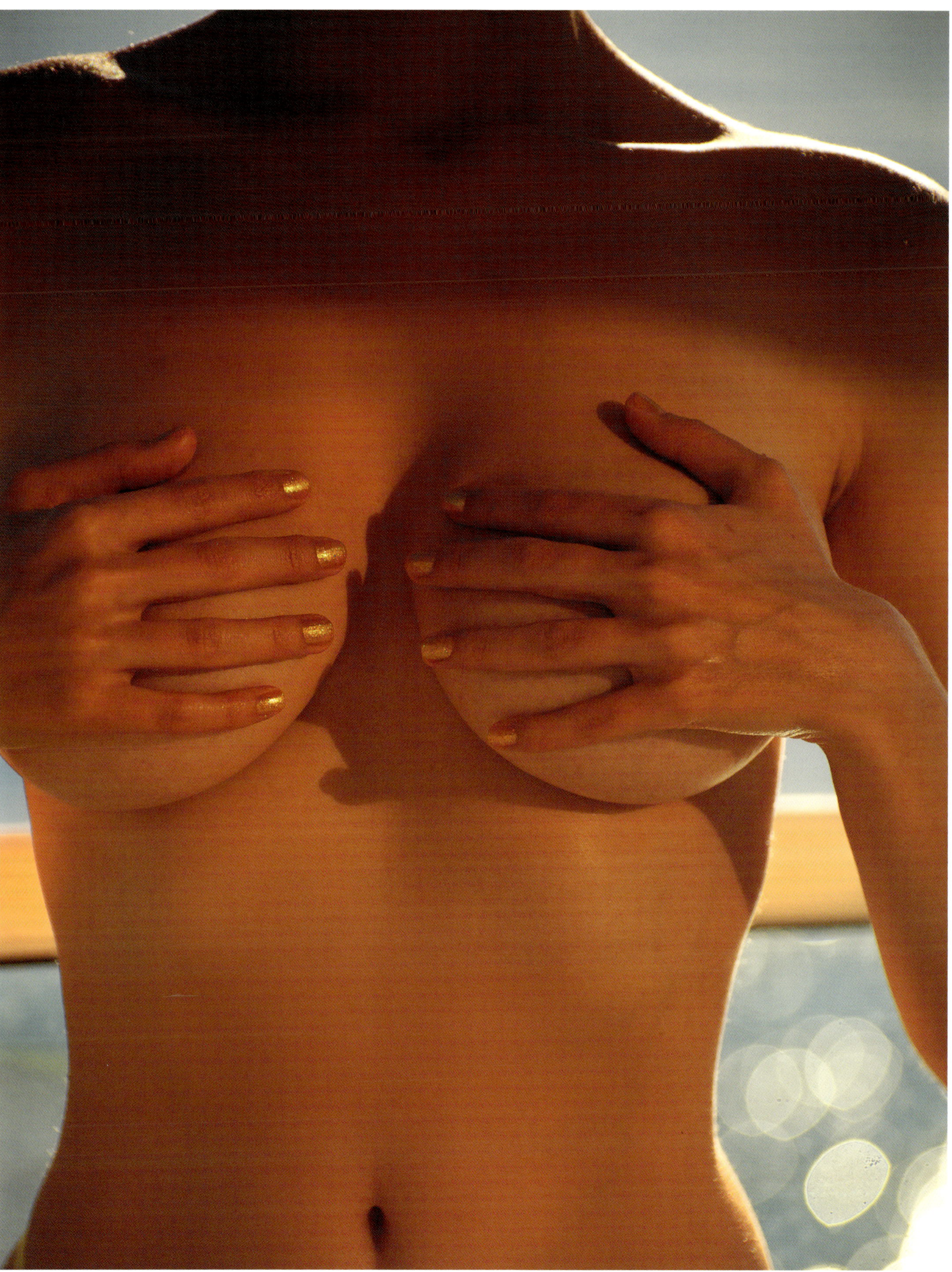

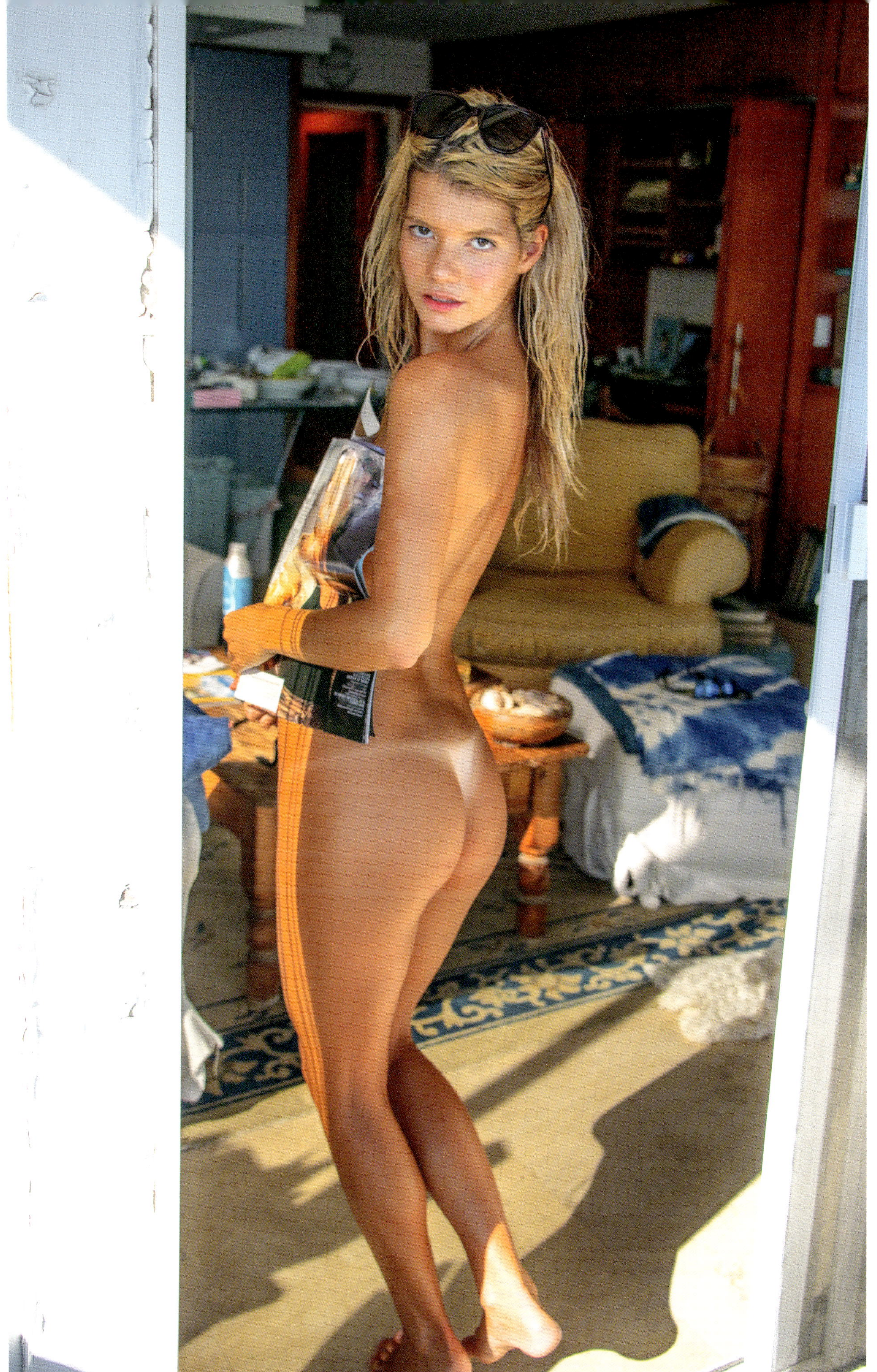

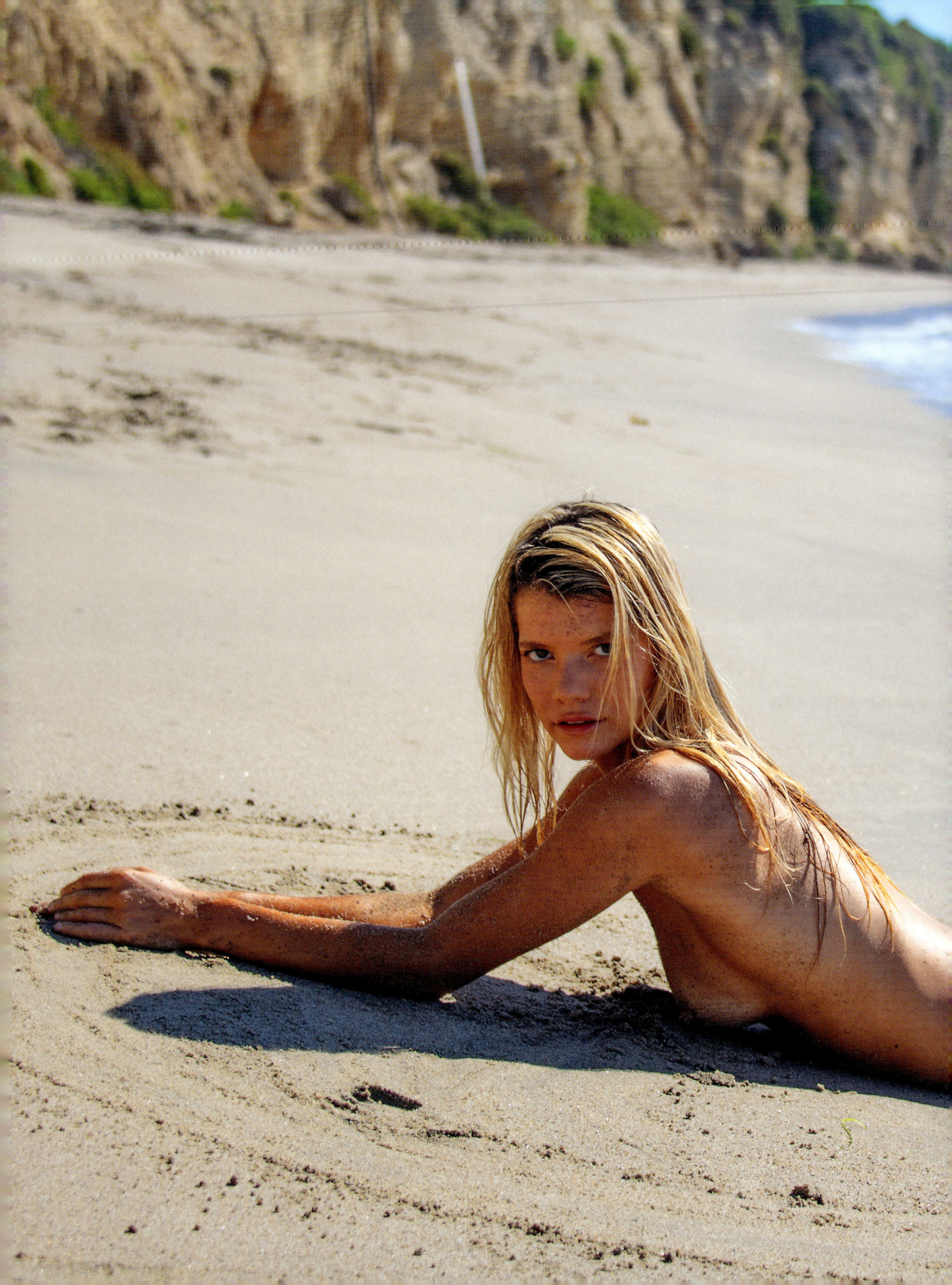

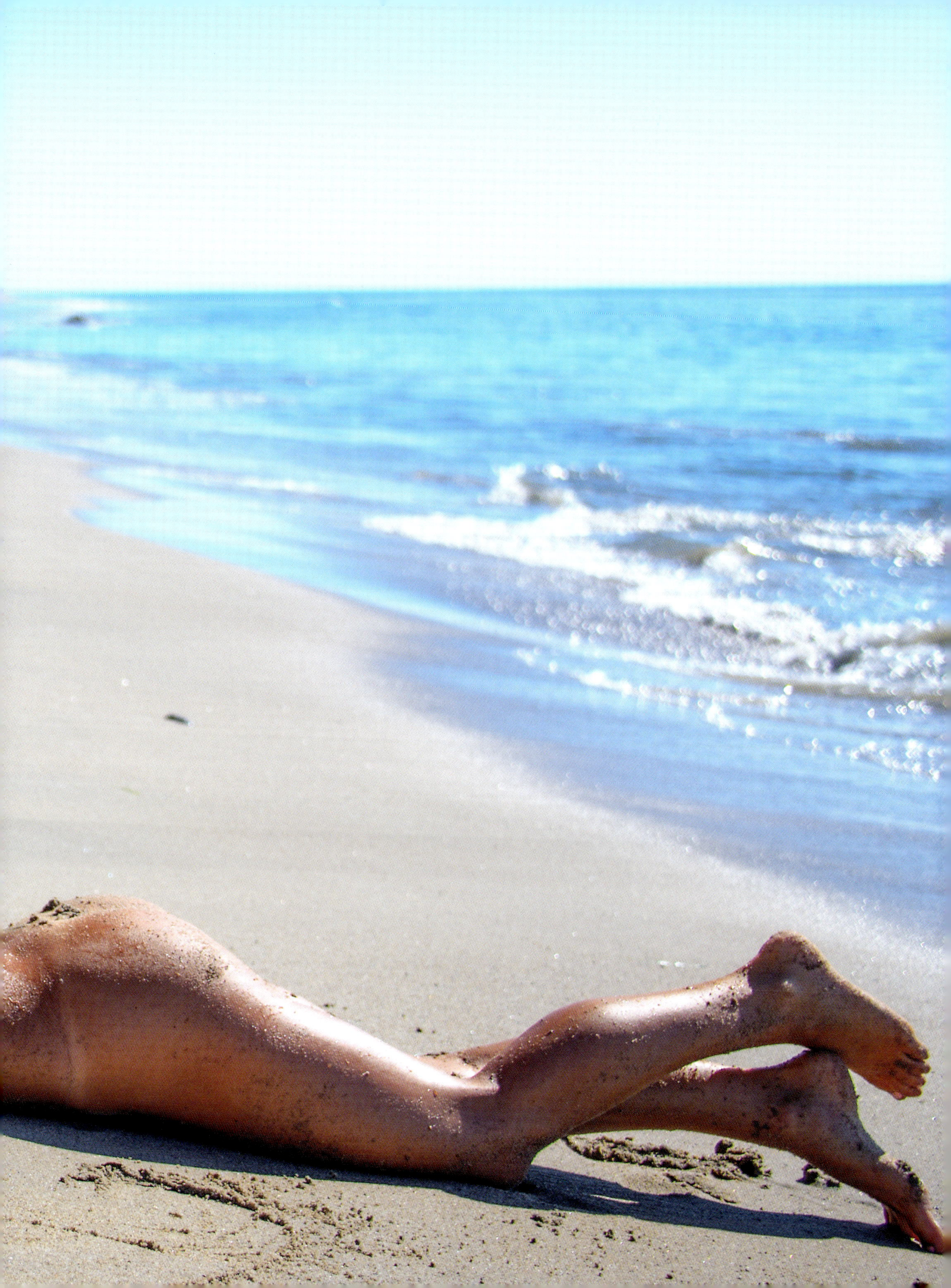

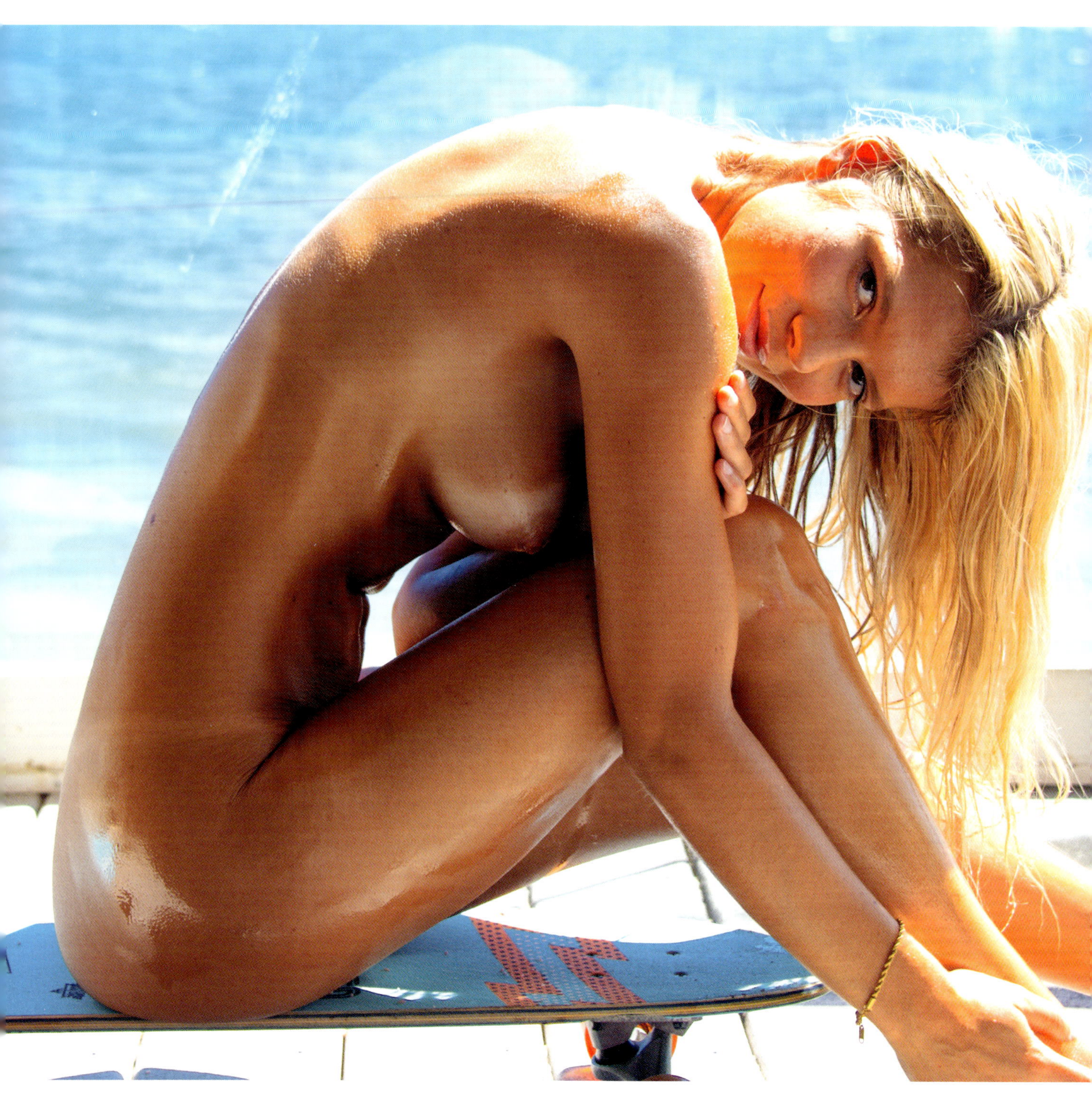

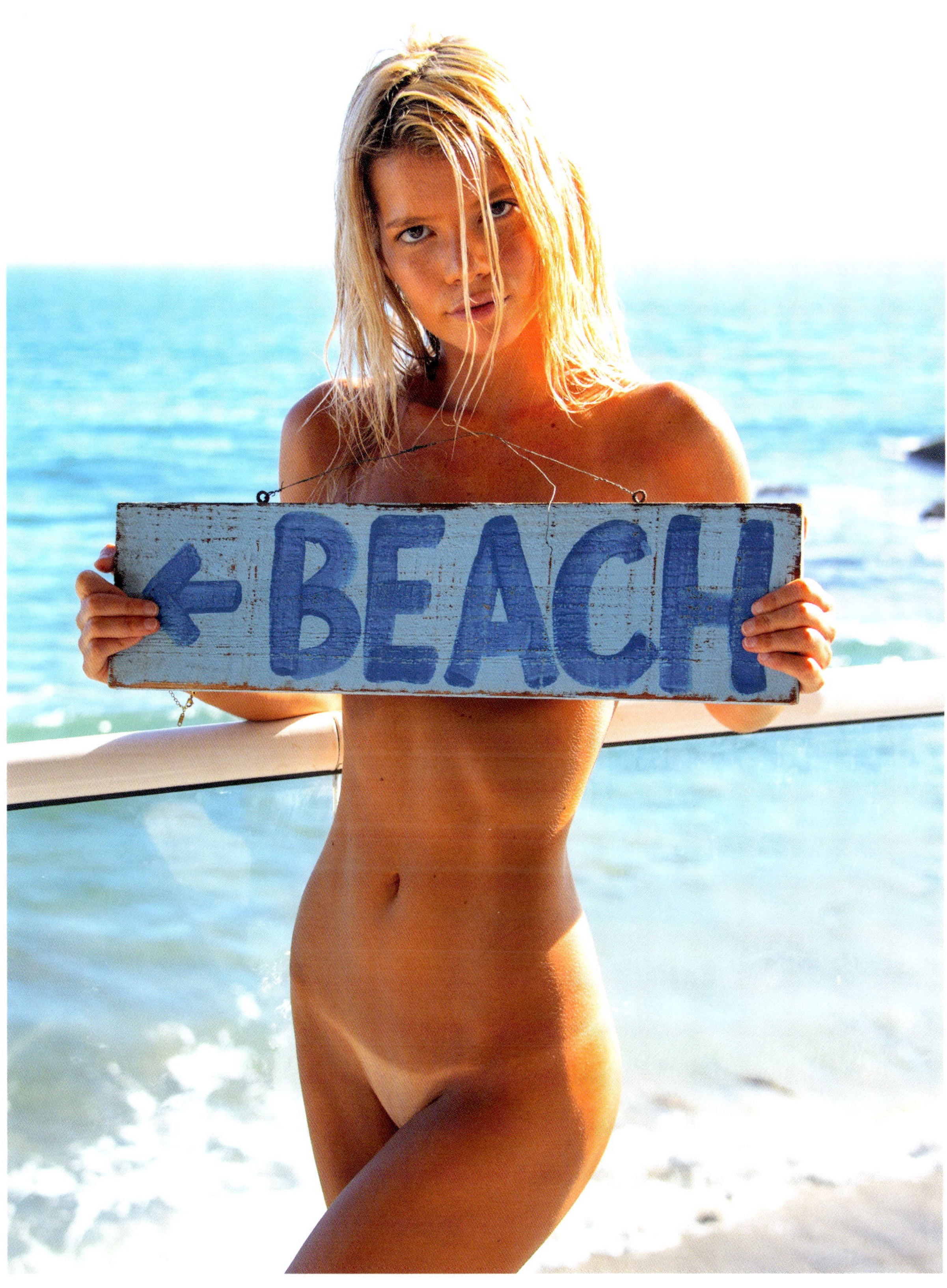
← BEACH!

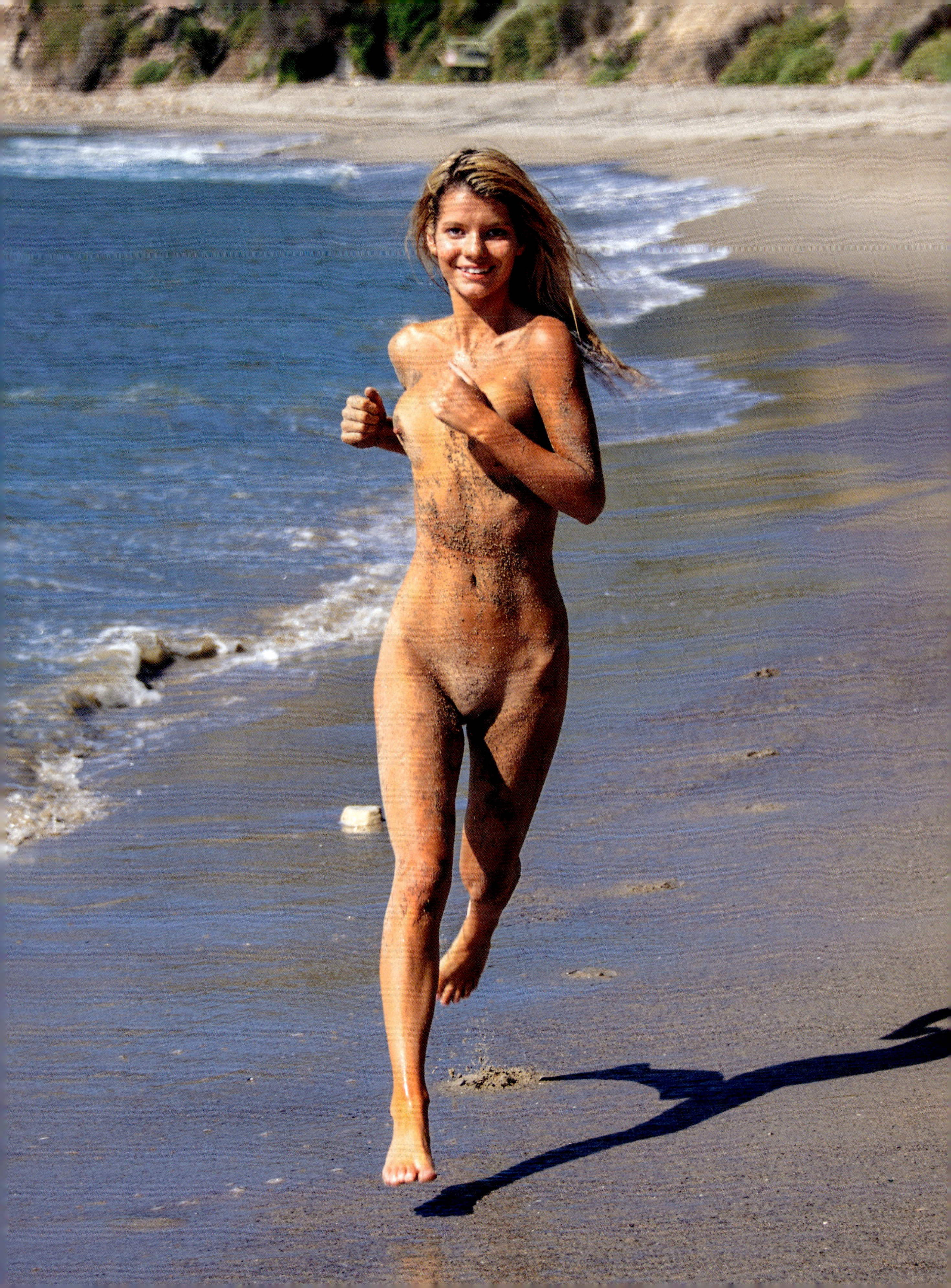

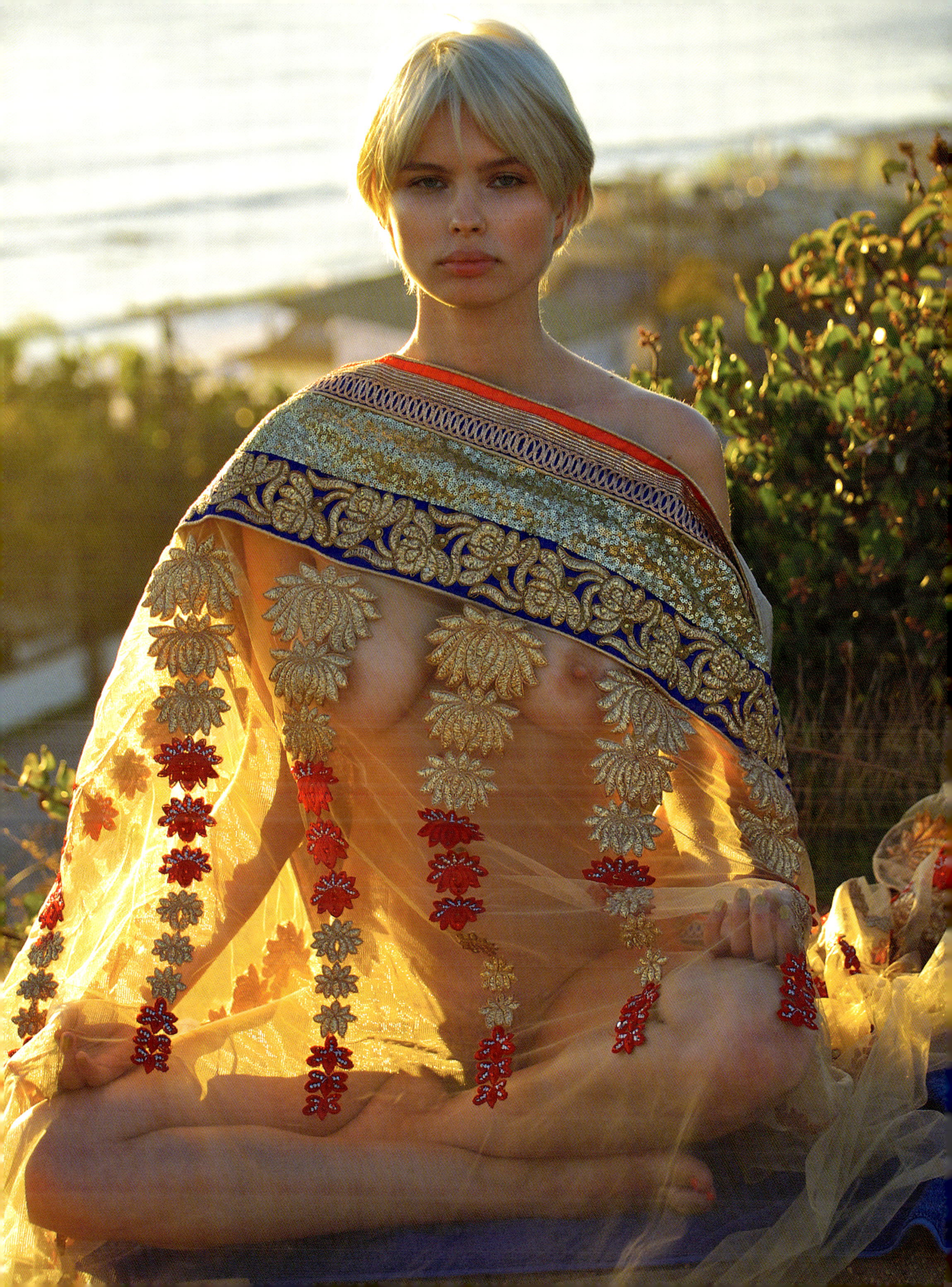

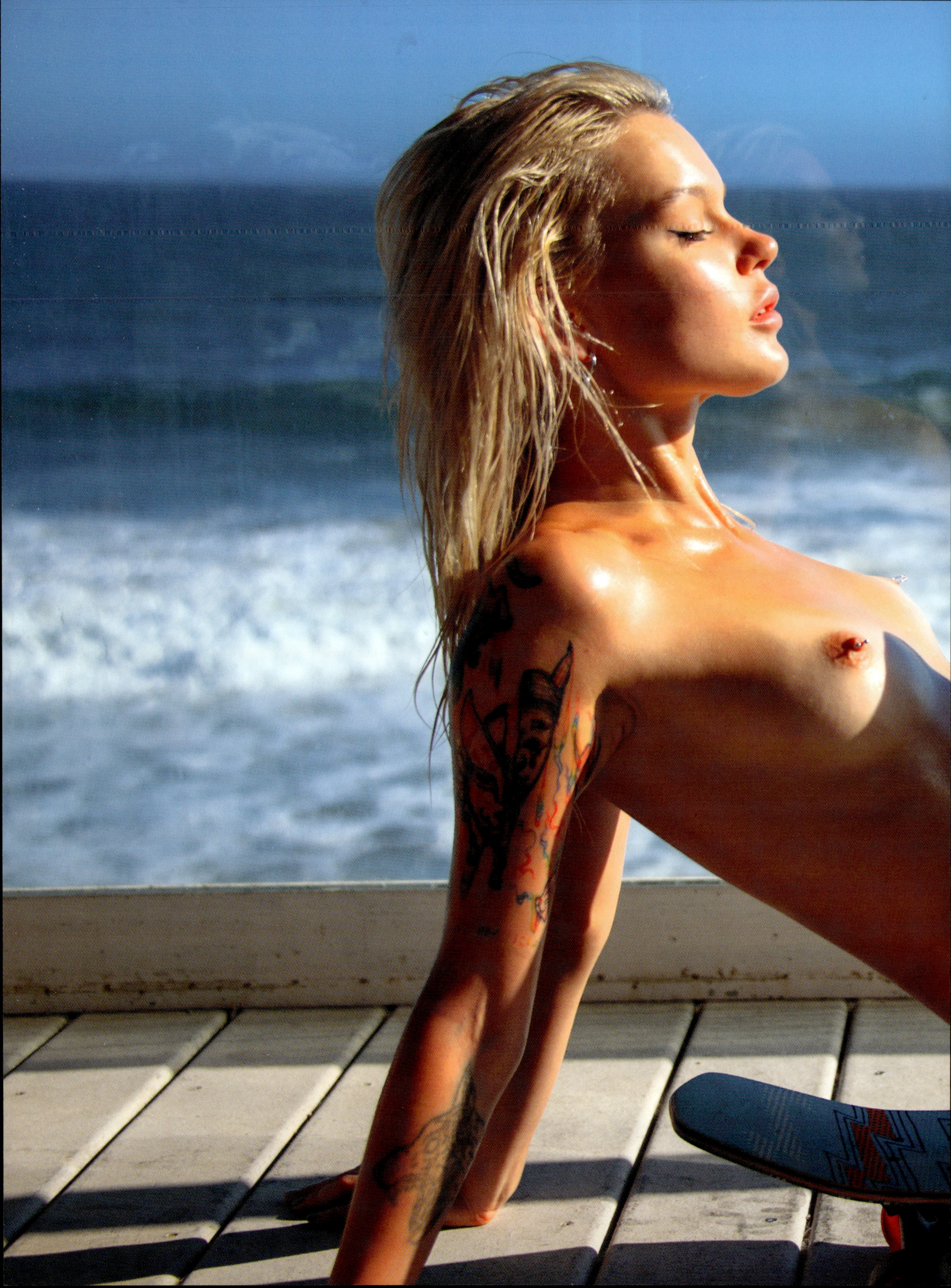

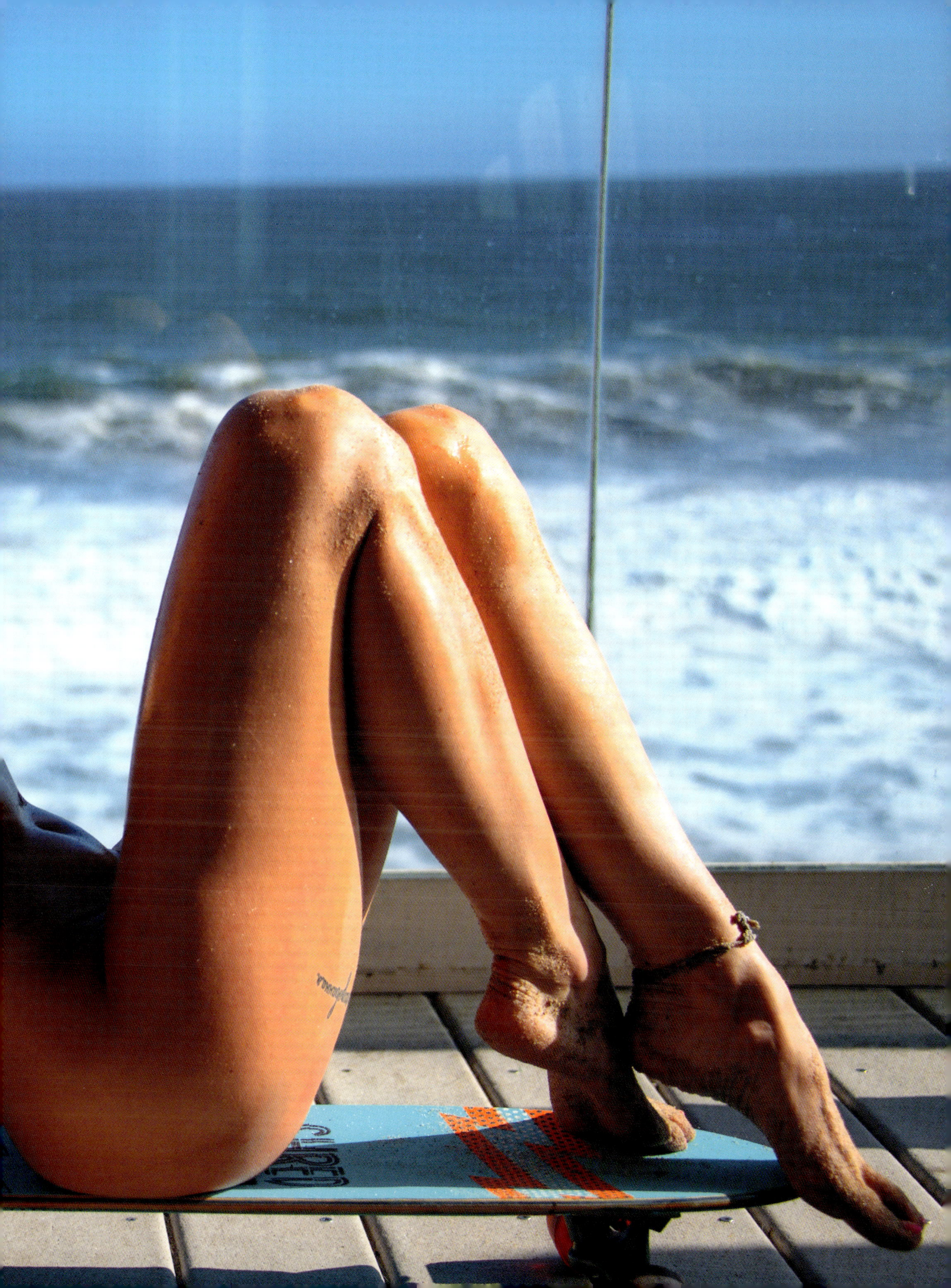

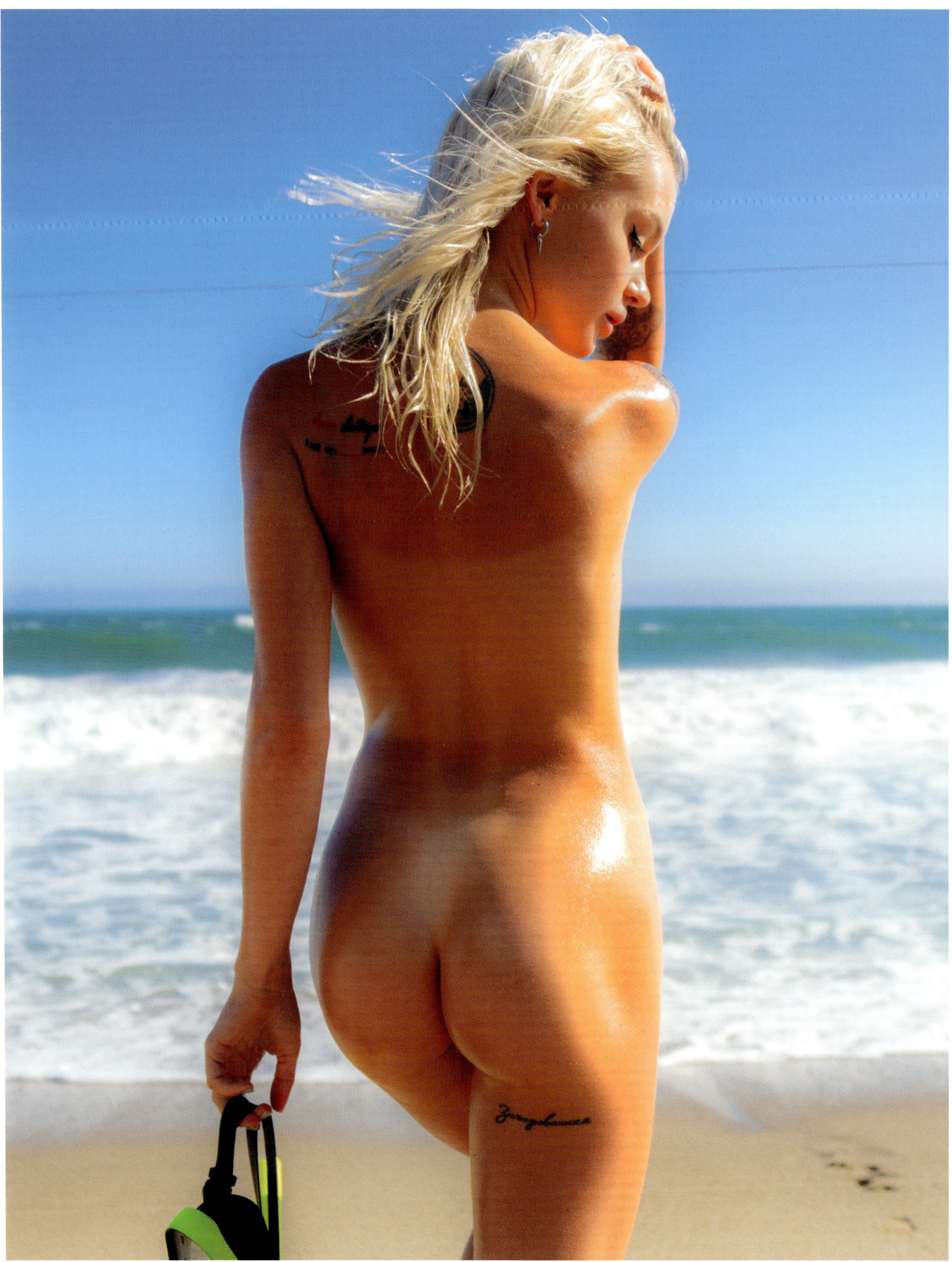

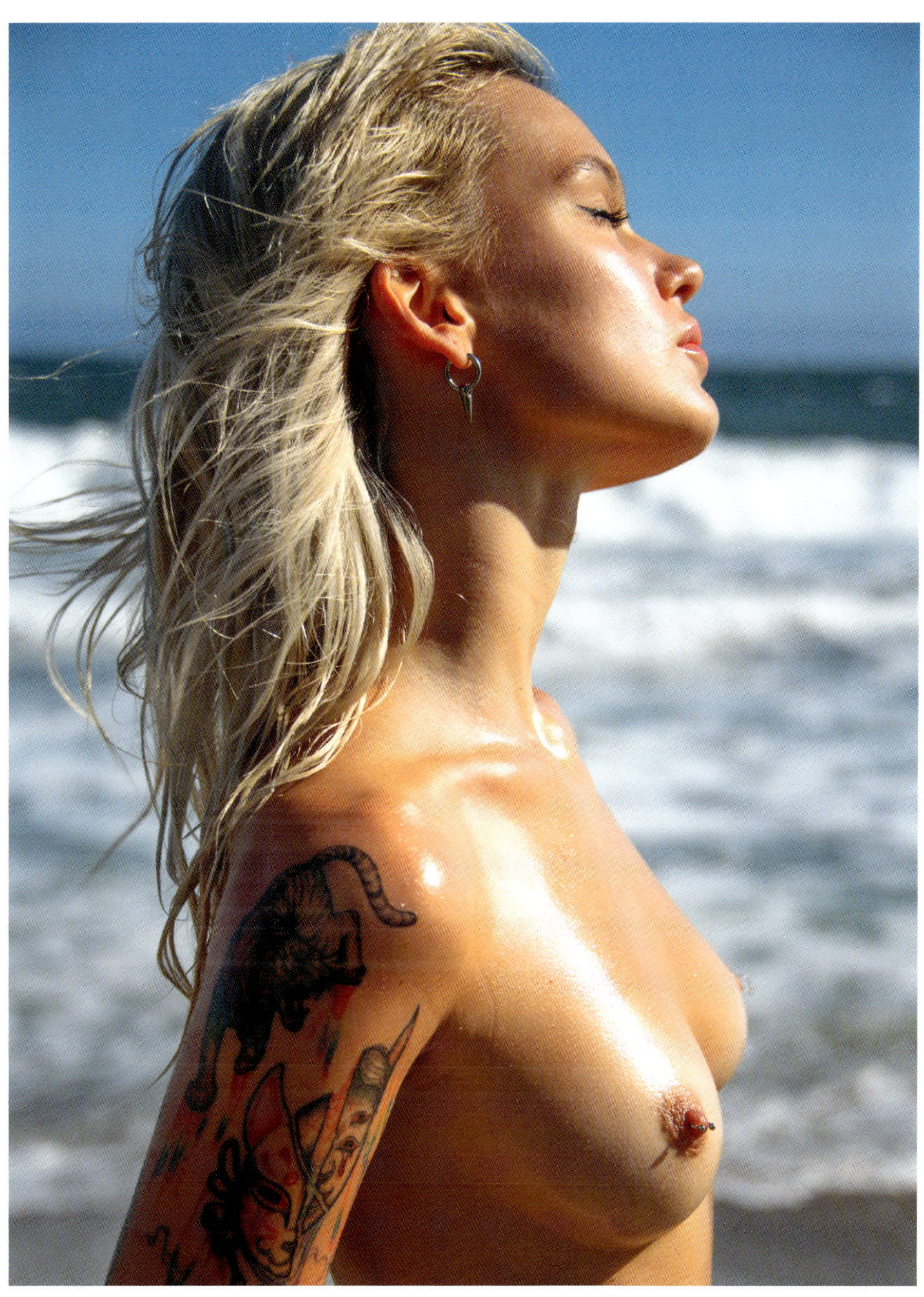

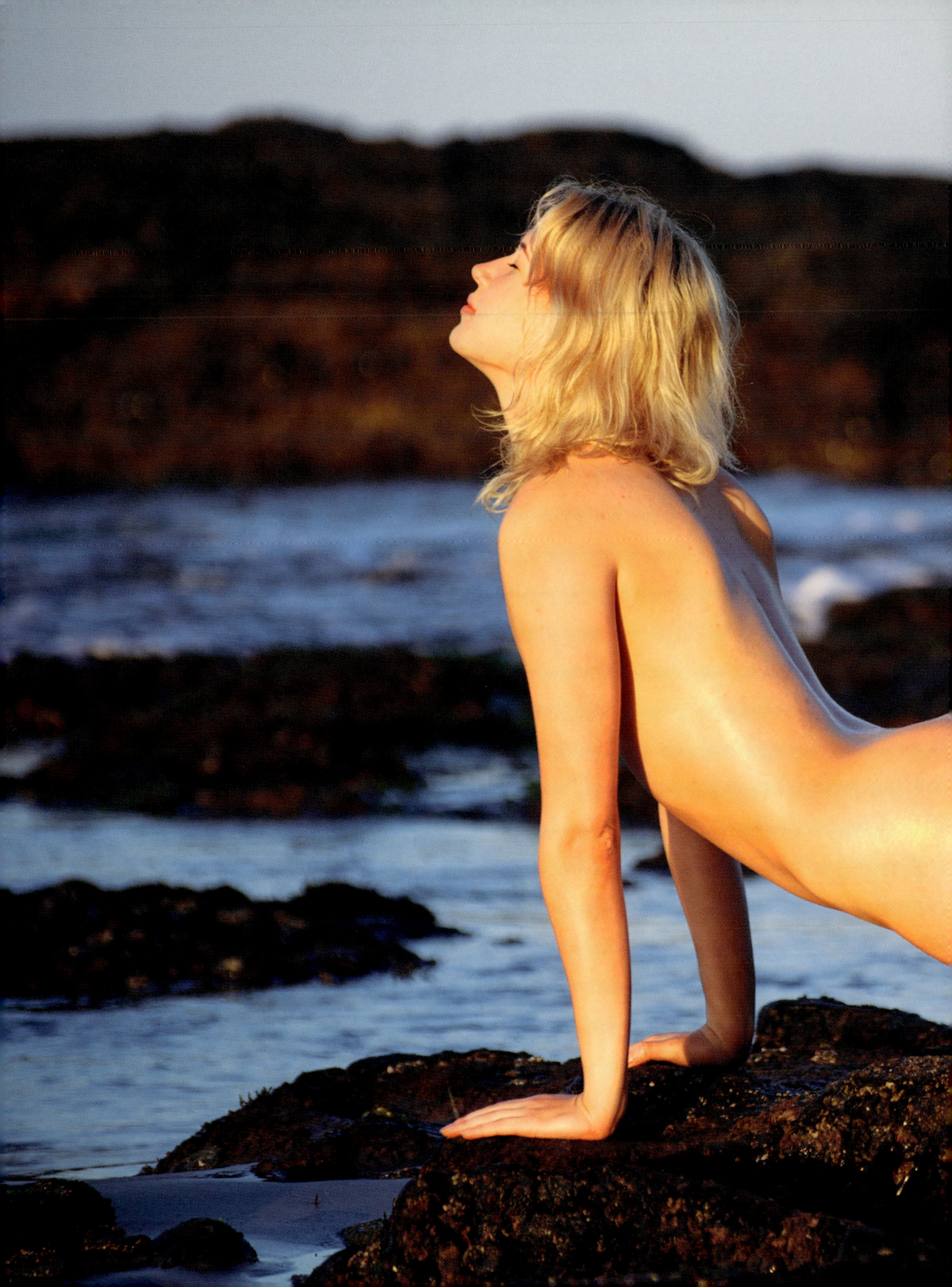

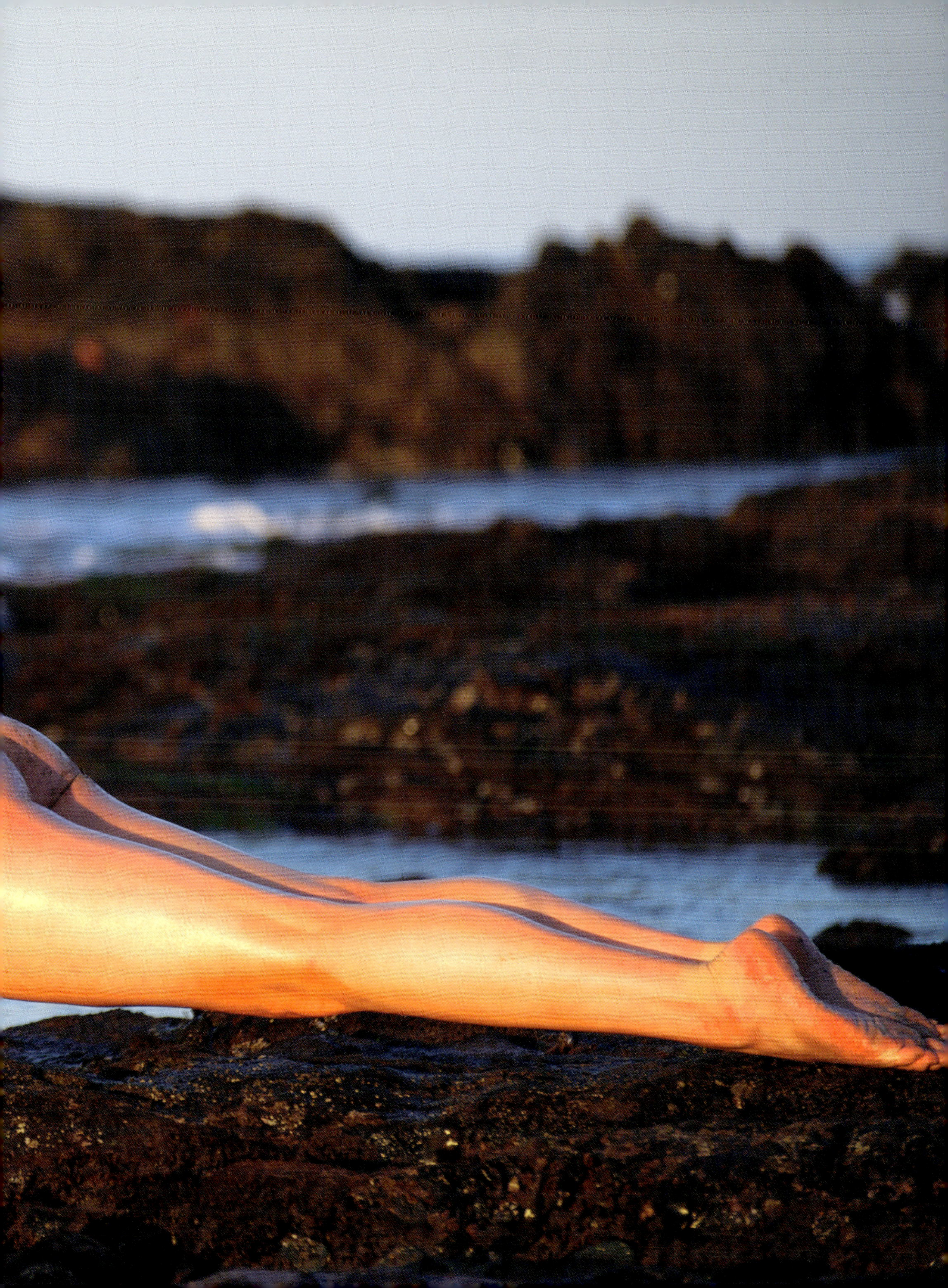

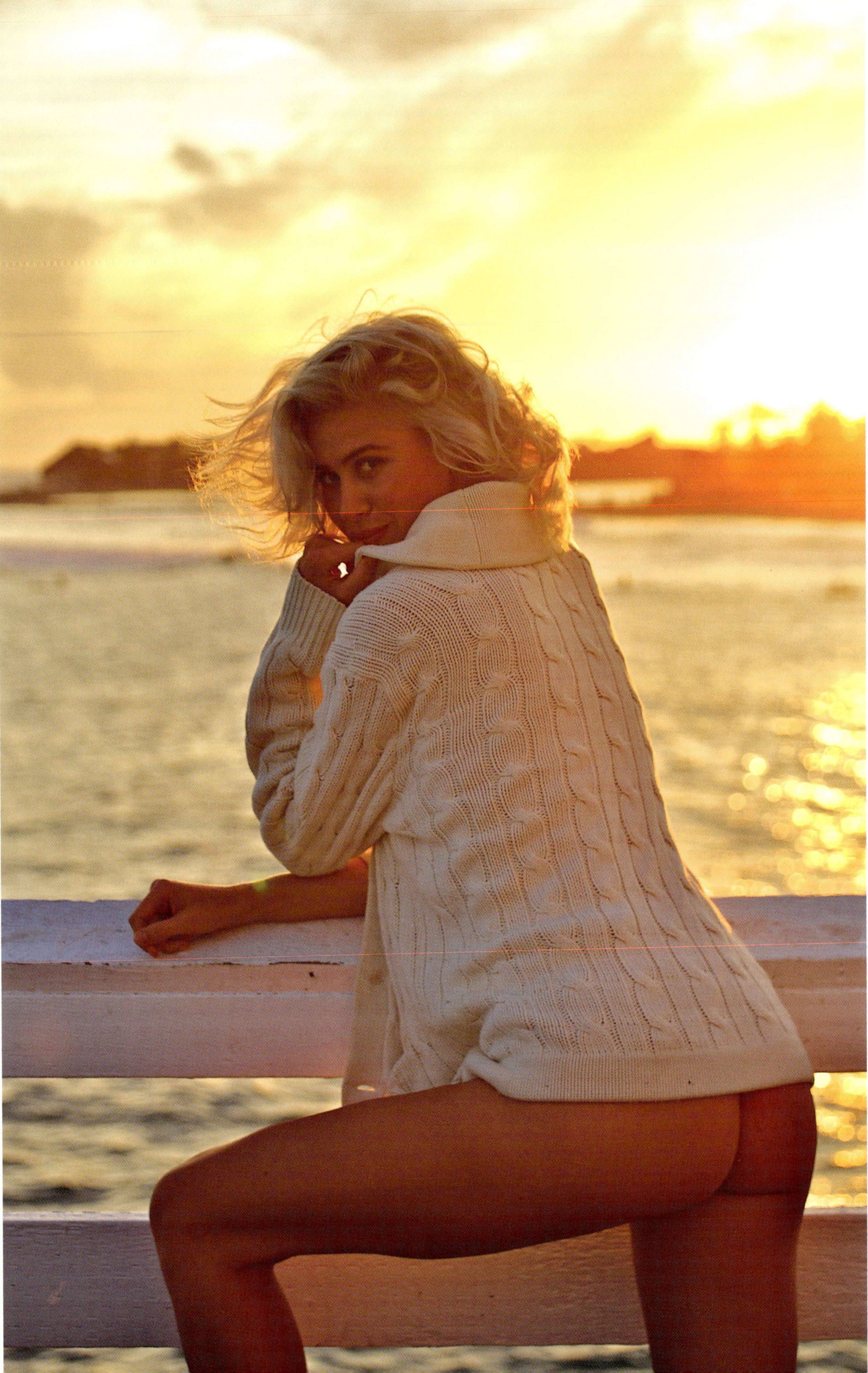

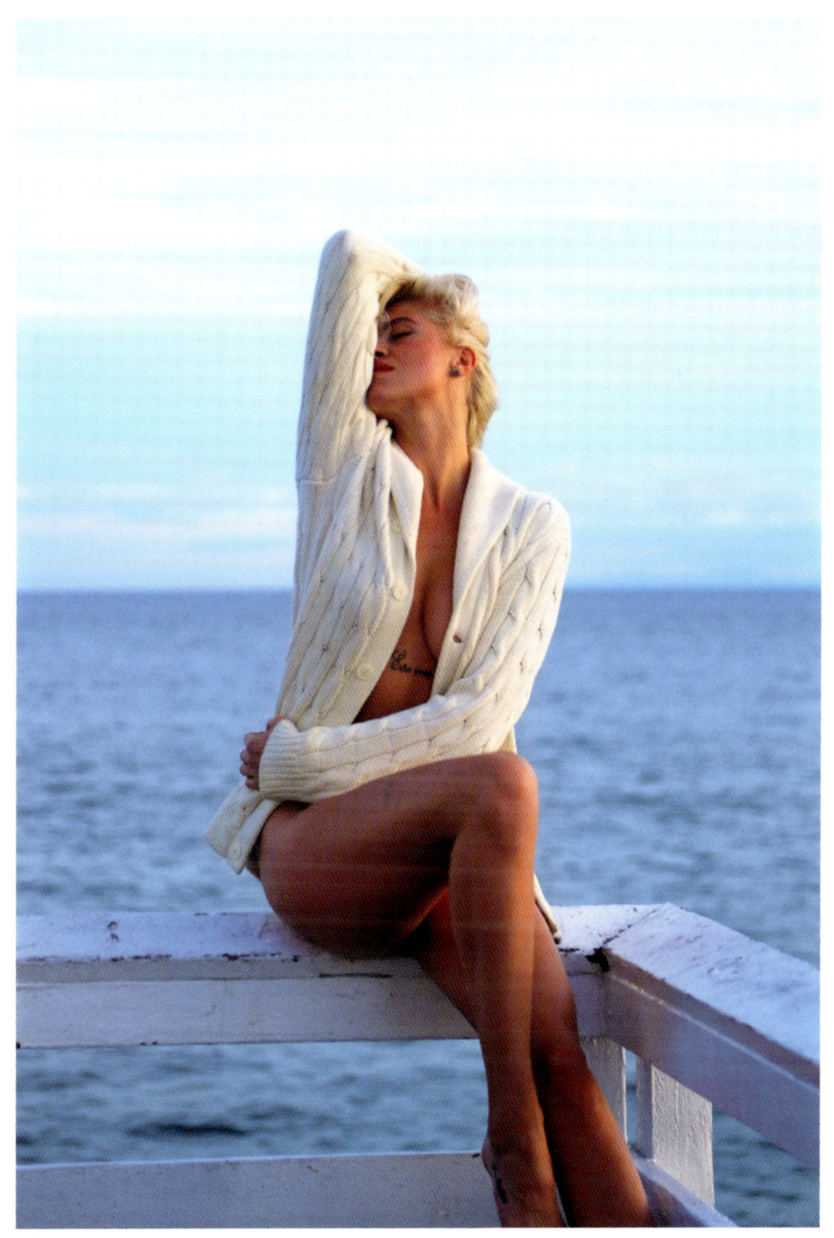

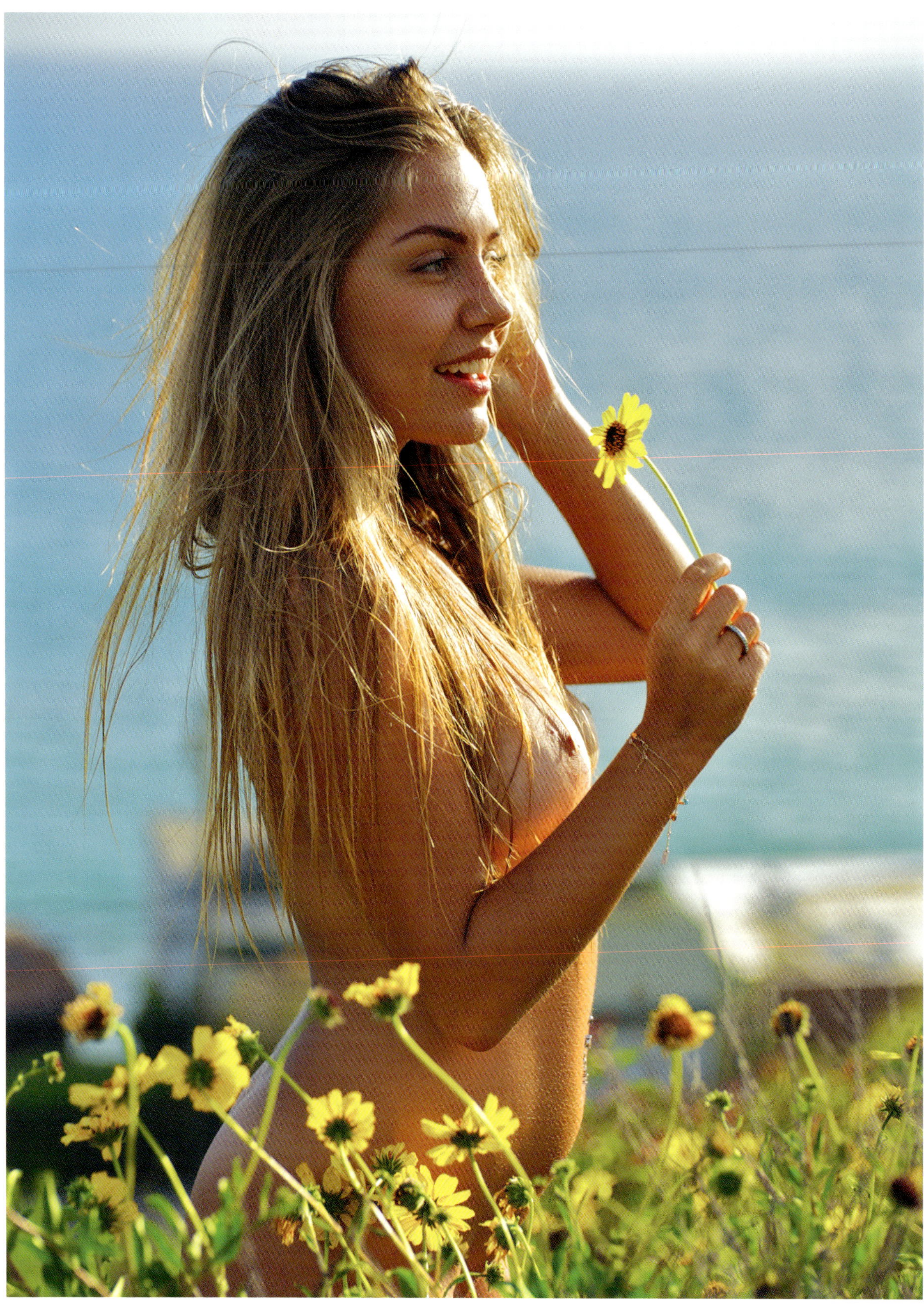

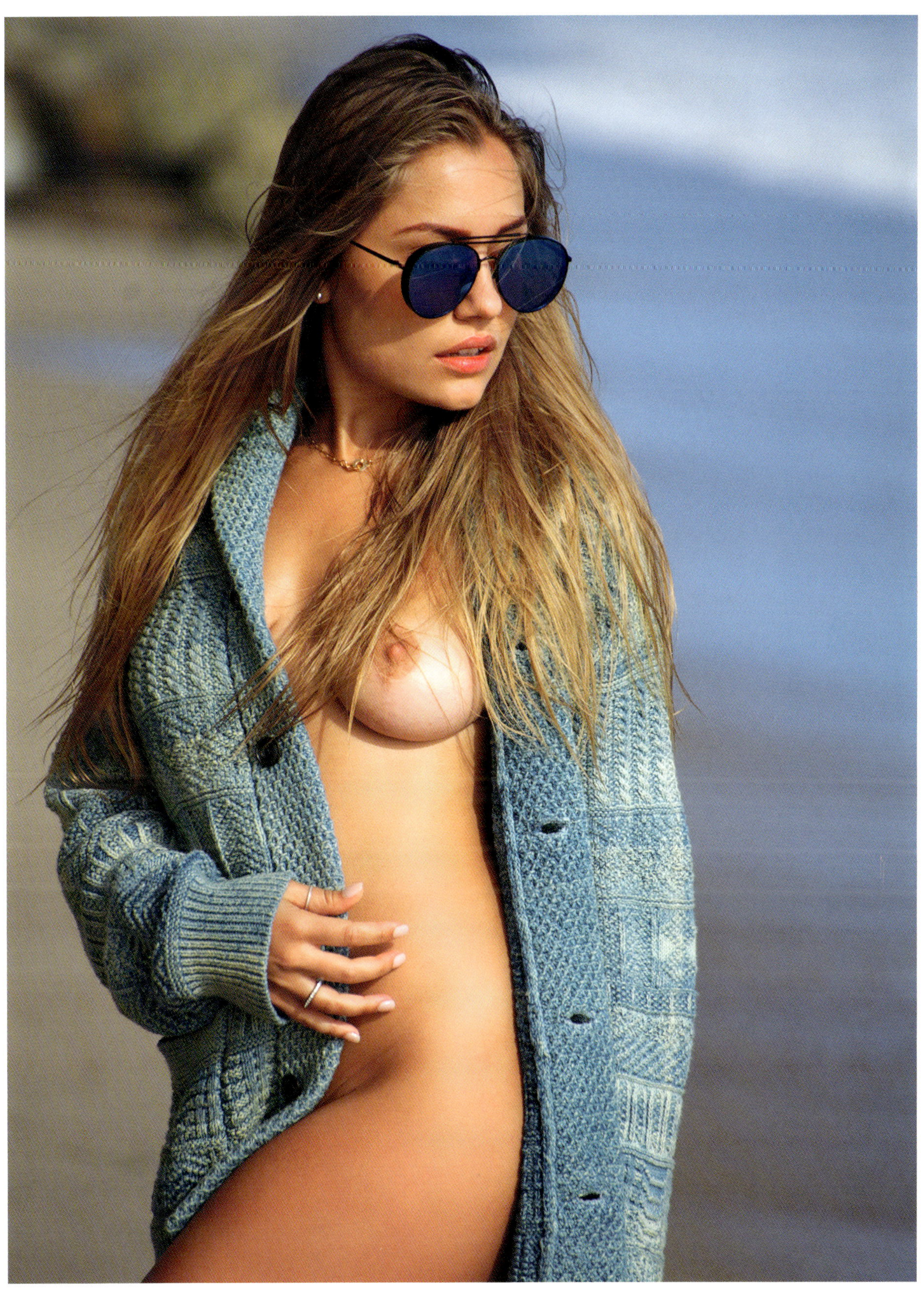

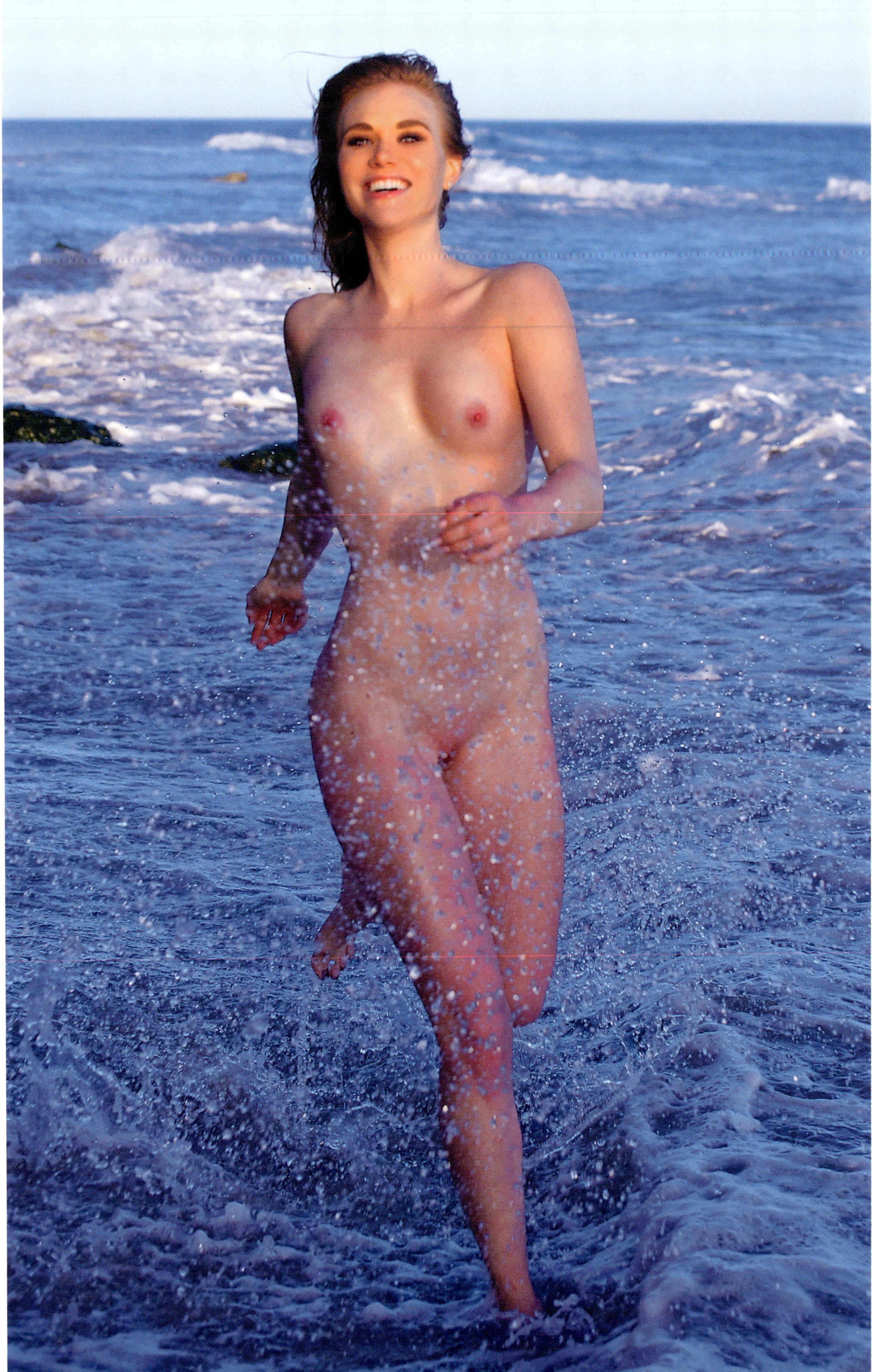

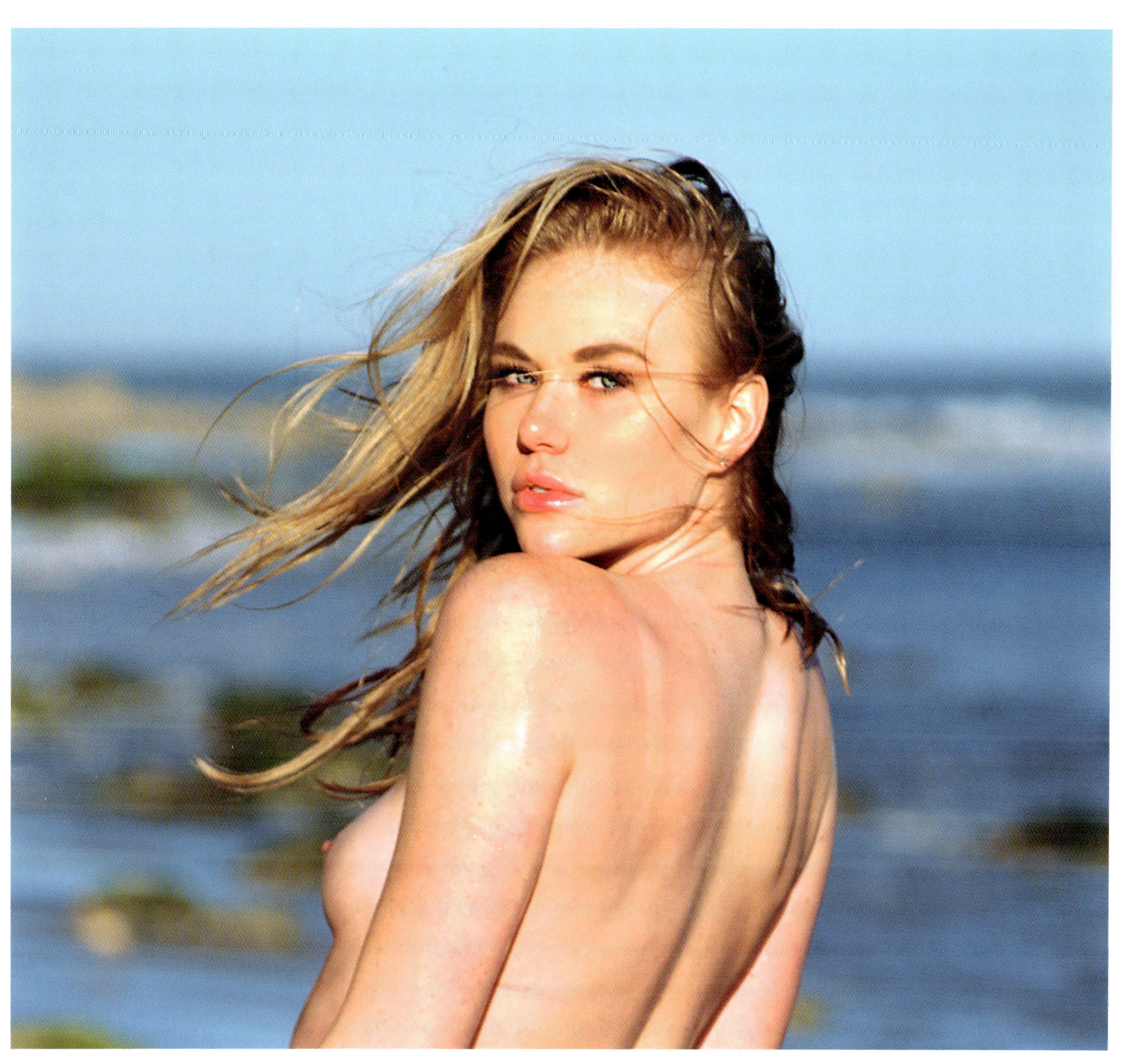

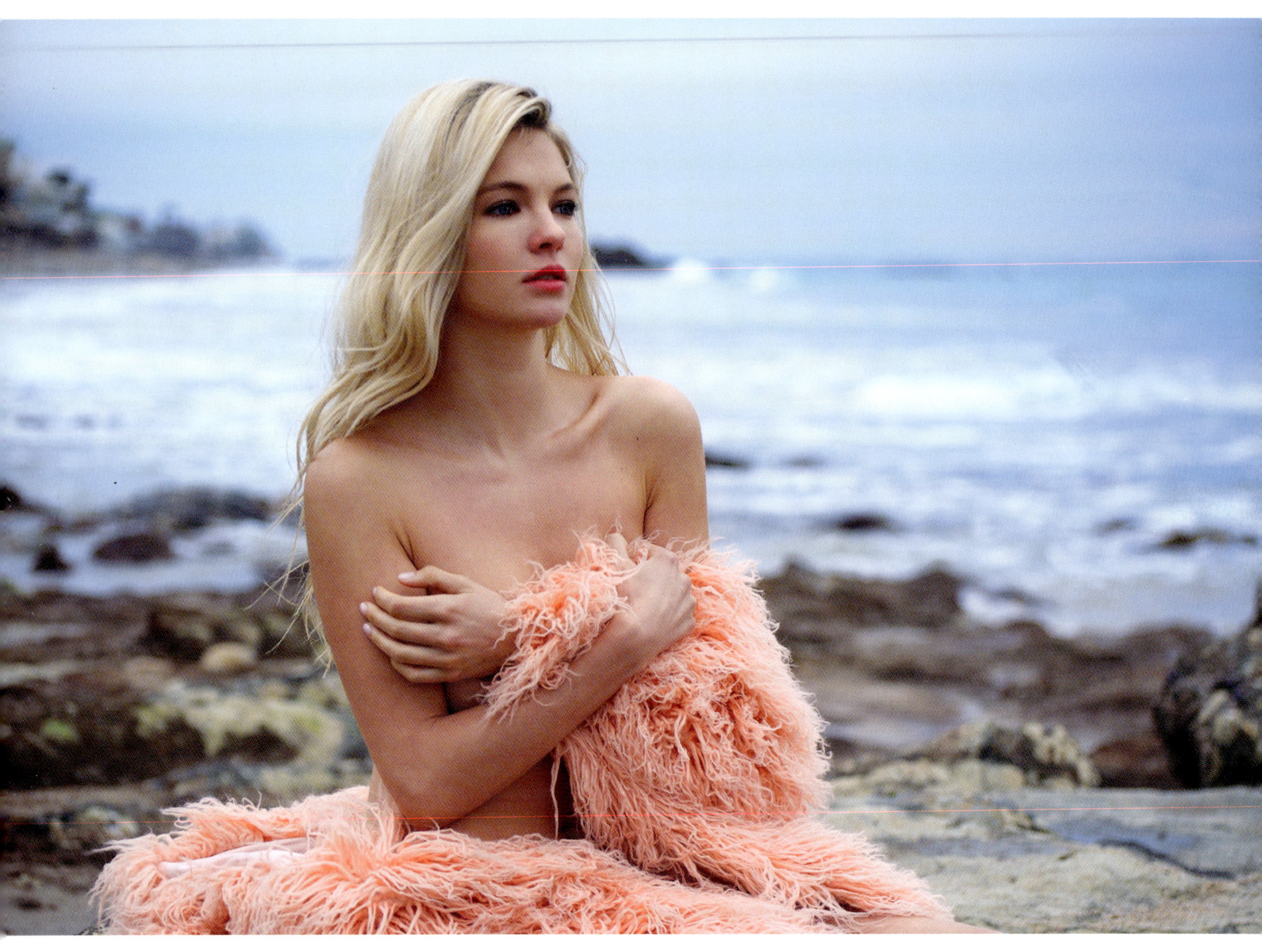

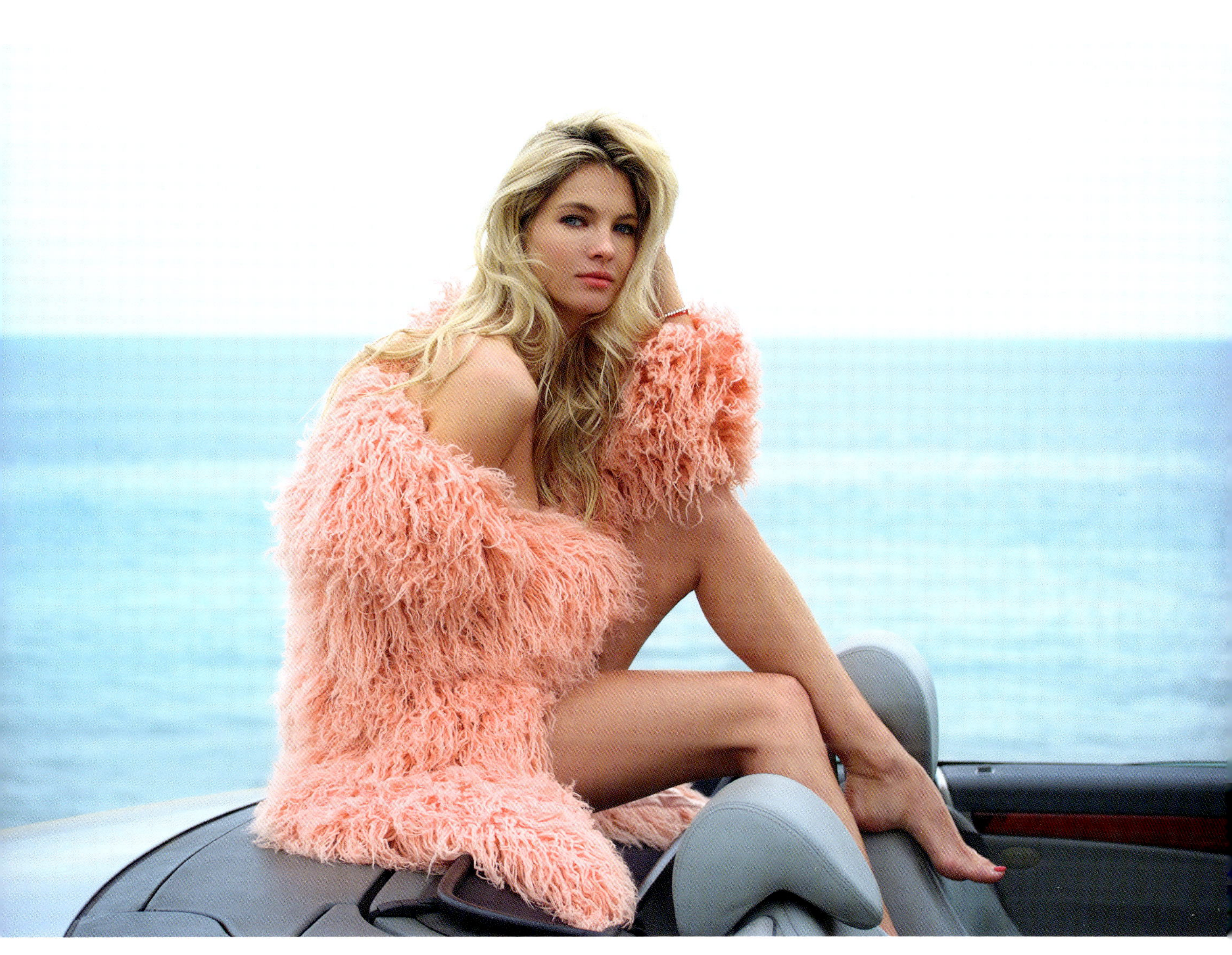

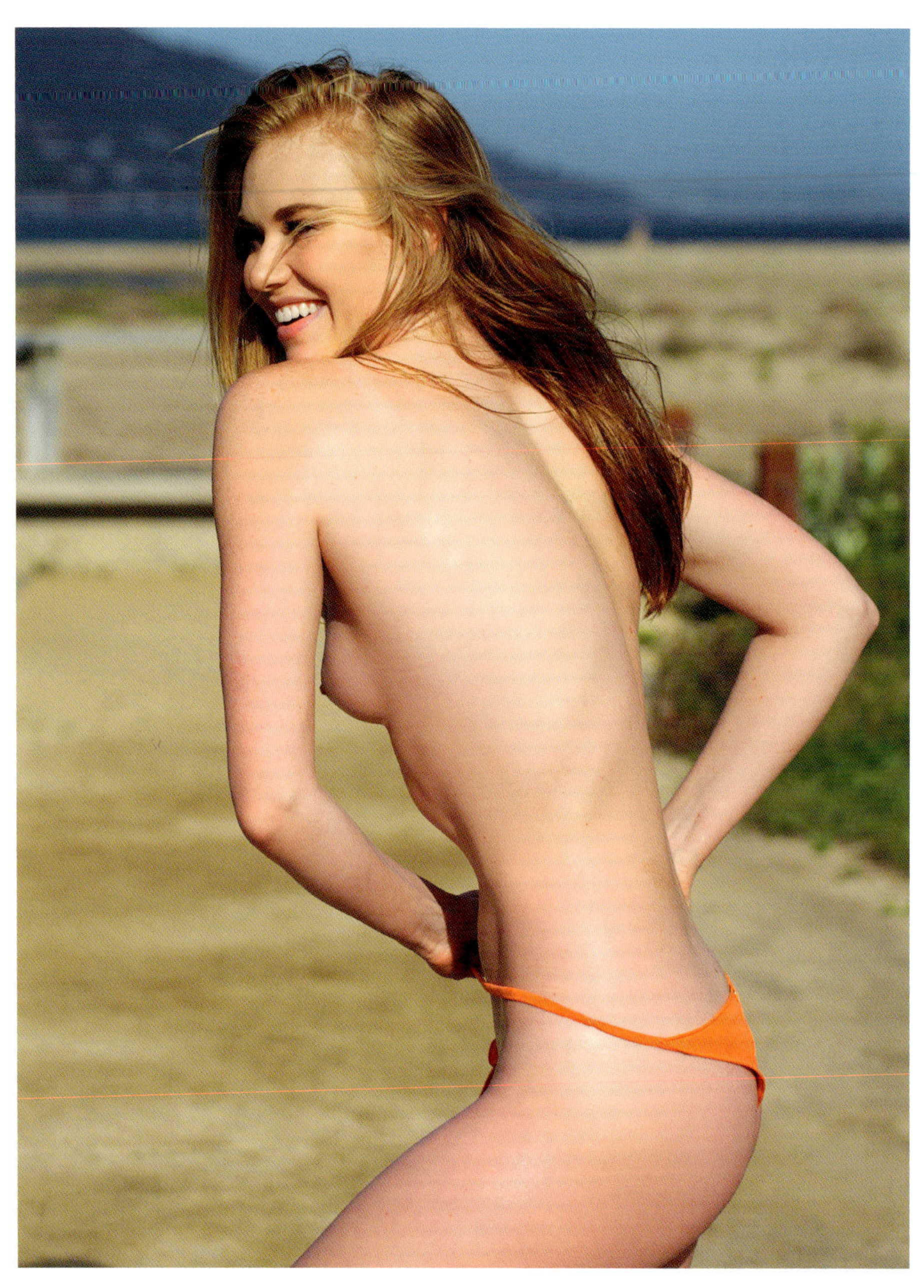

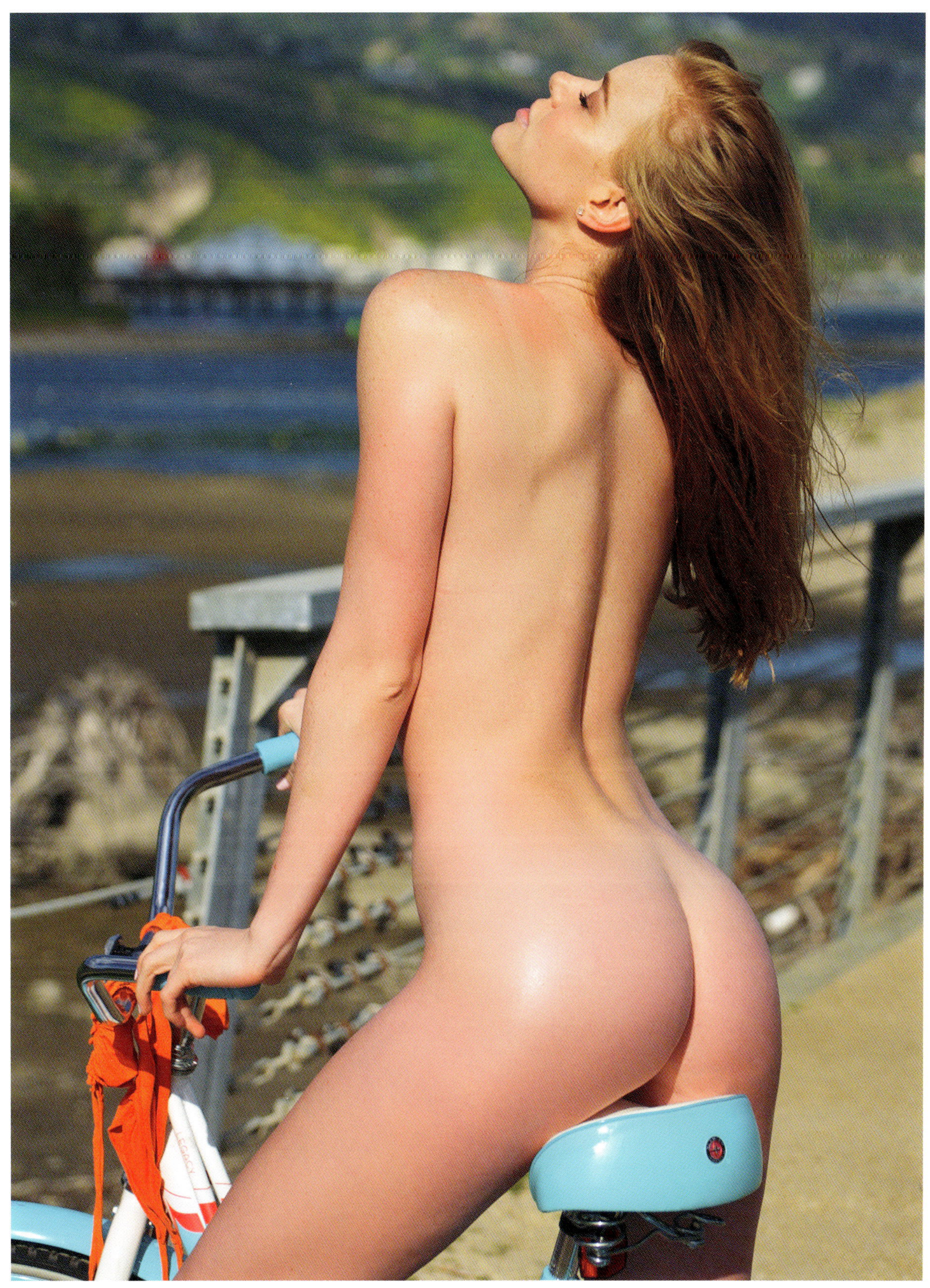

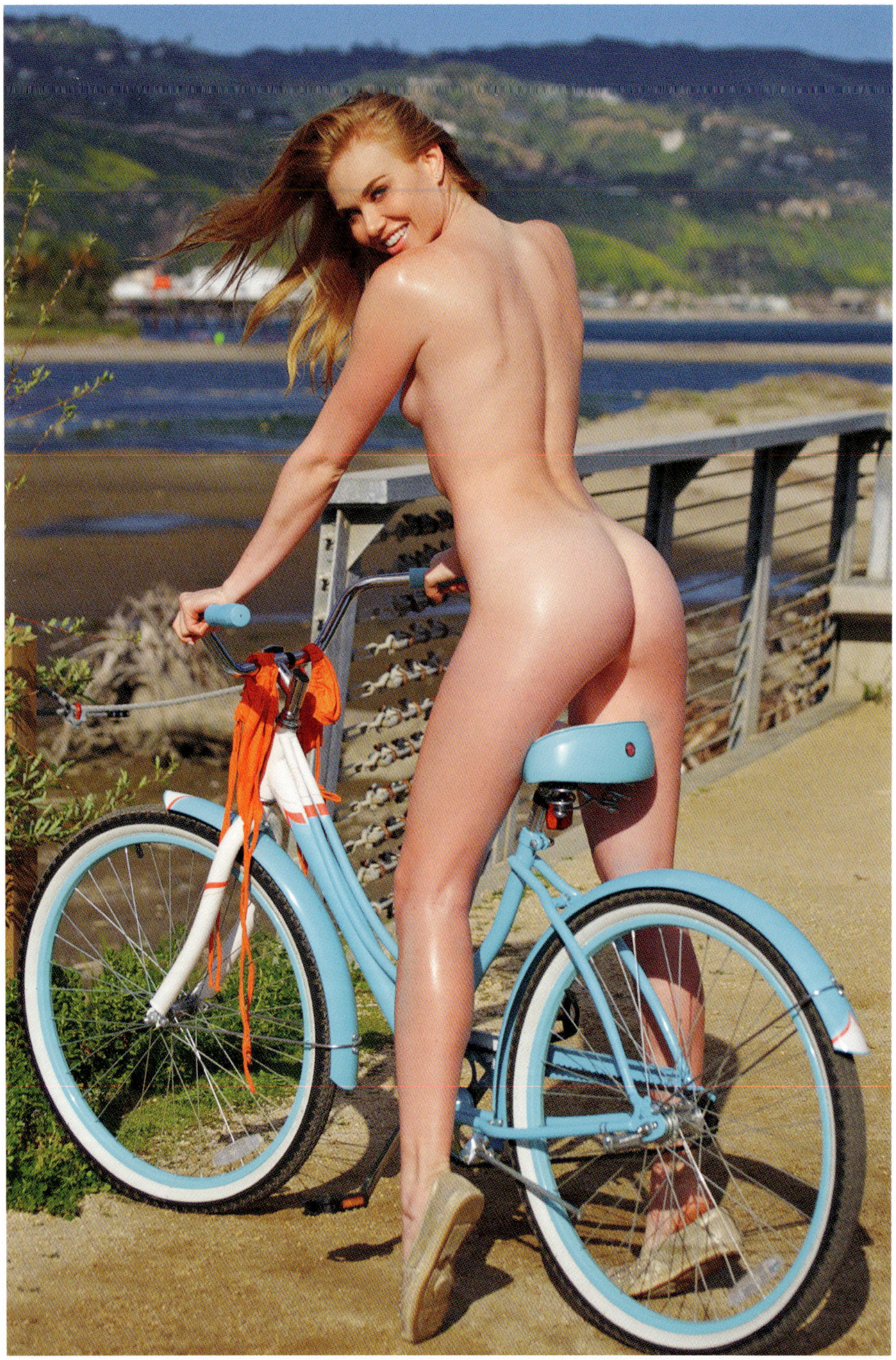

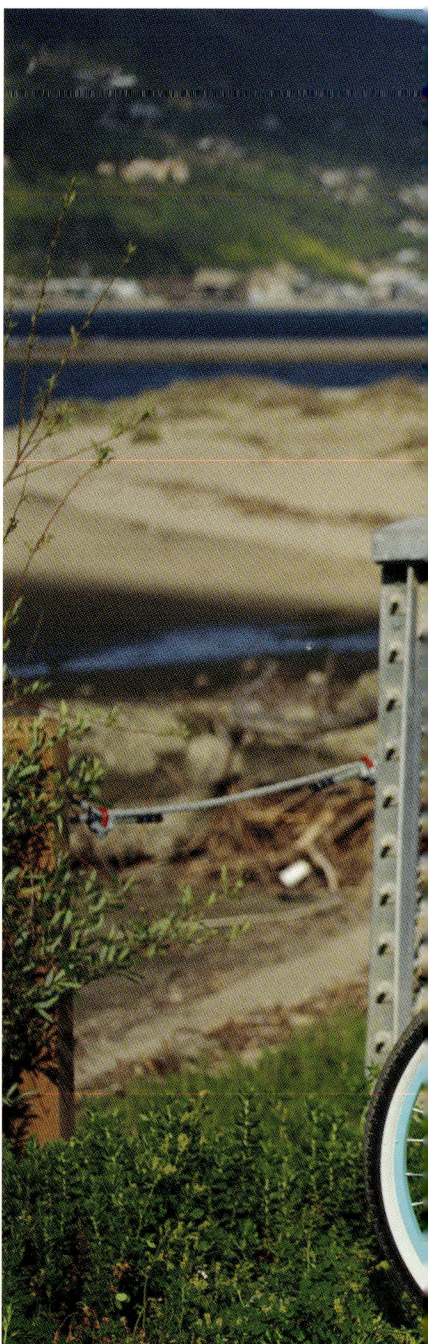

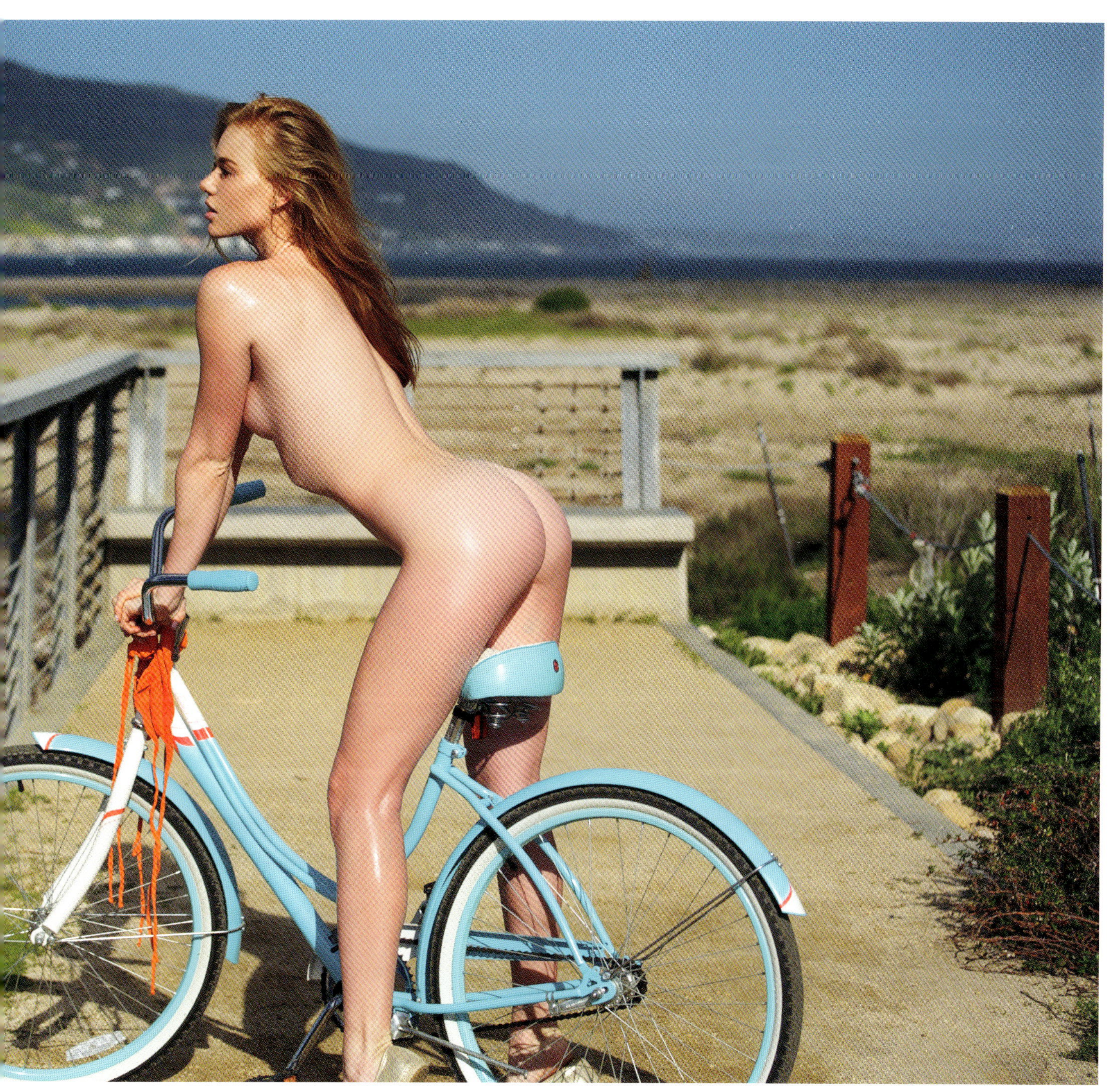

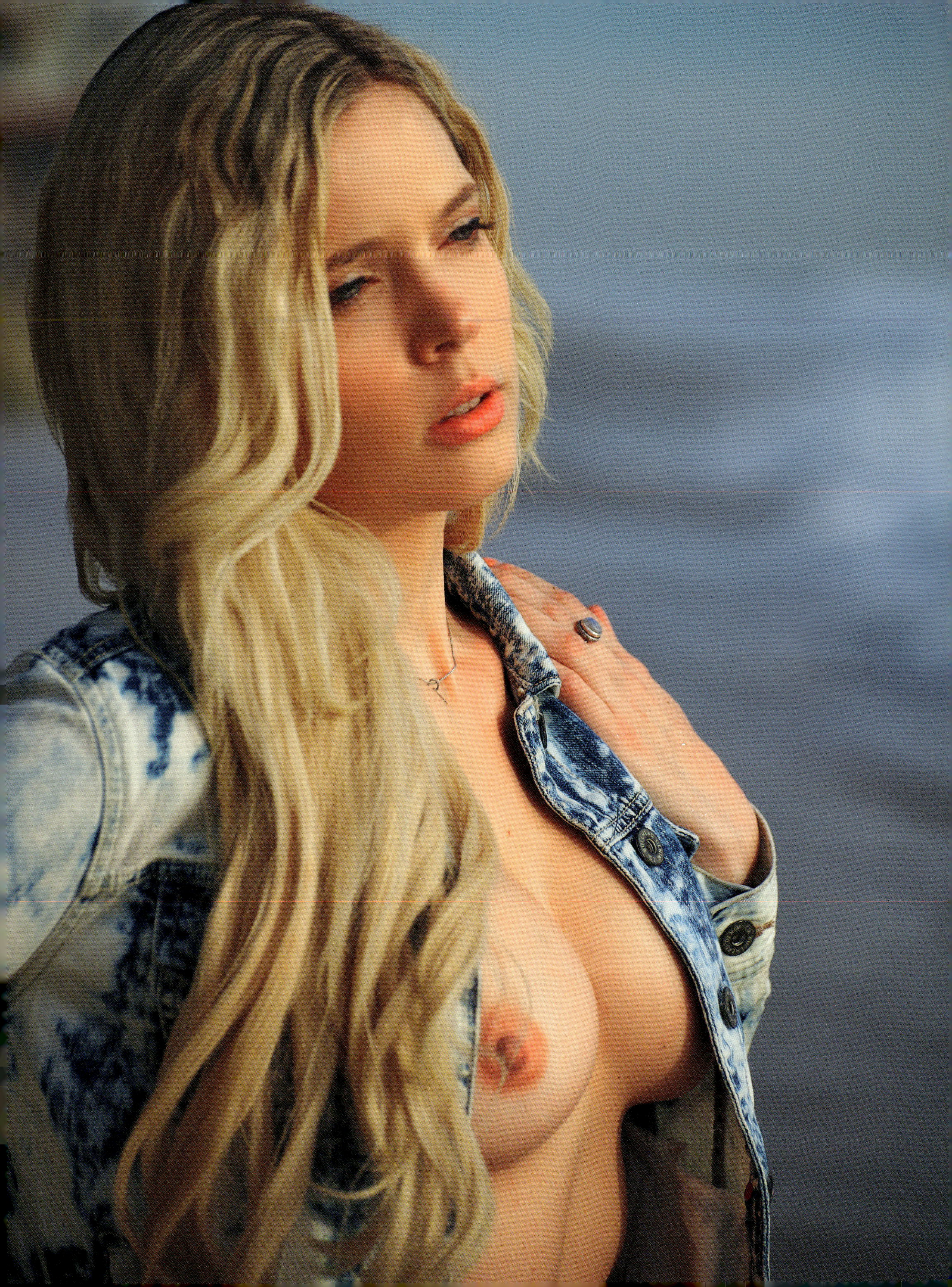

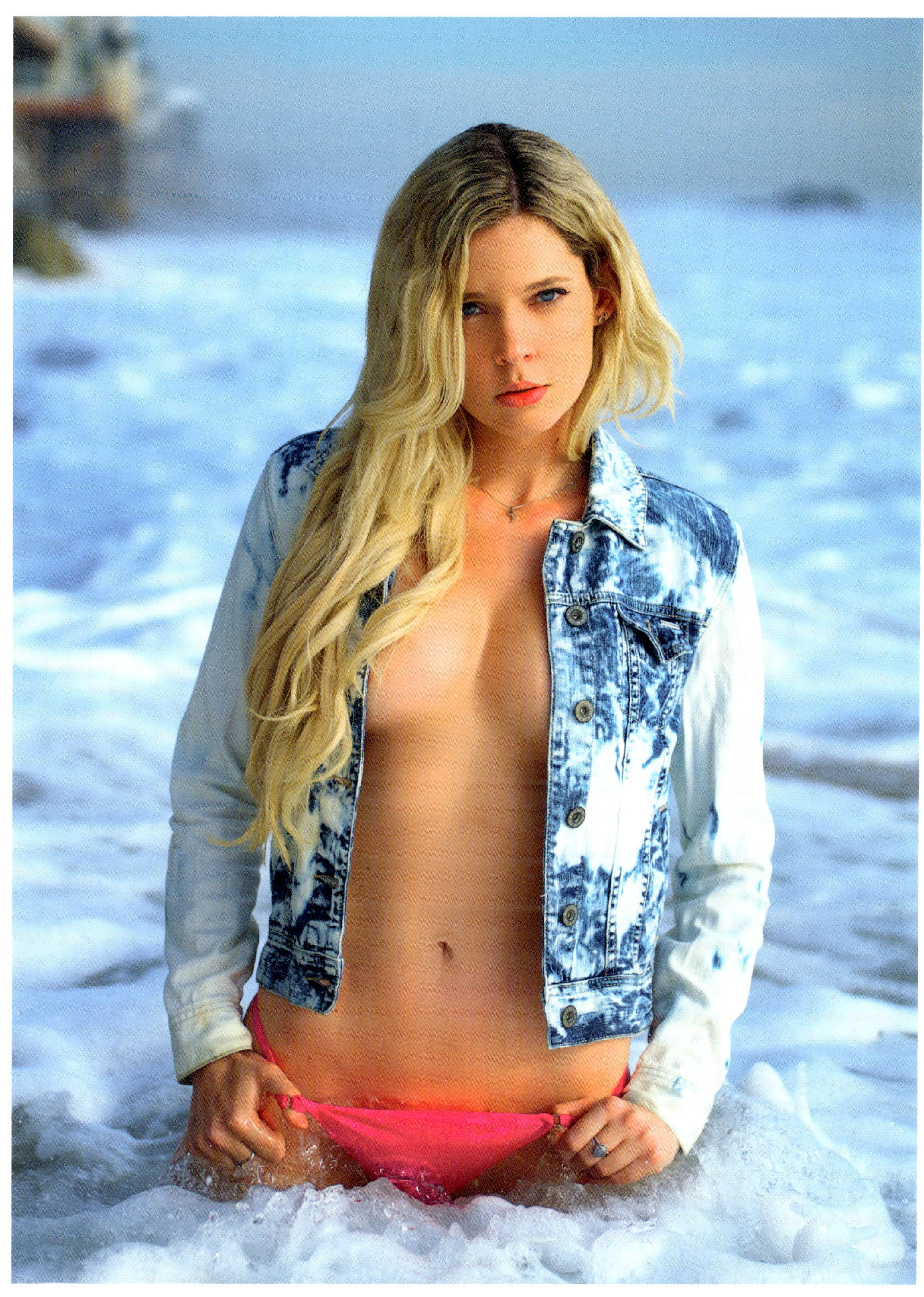

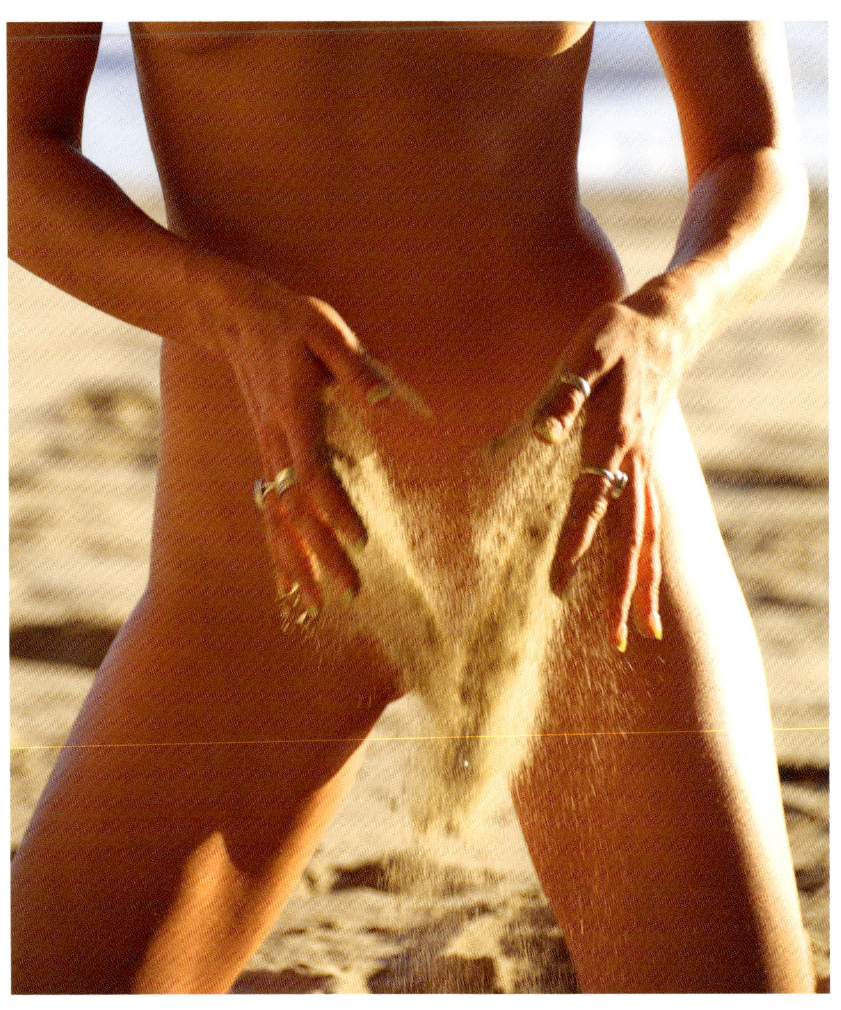

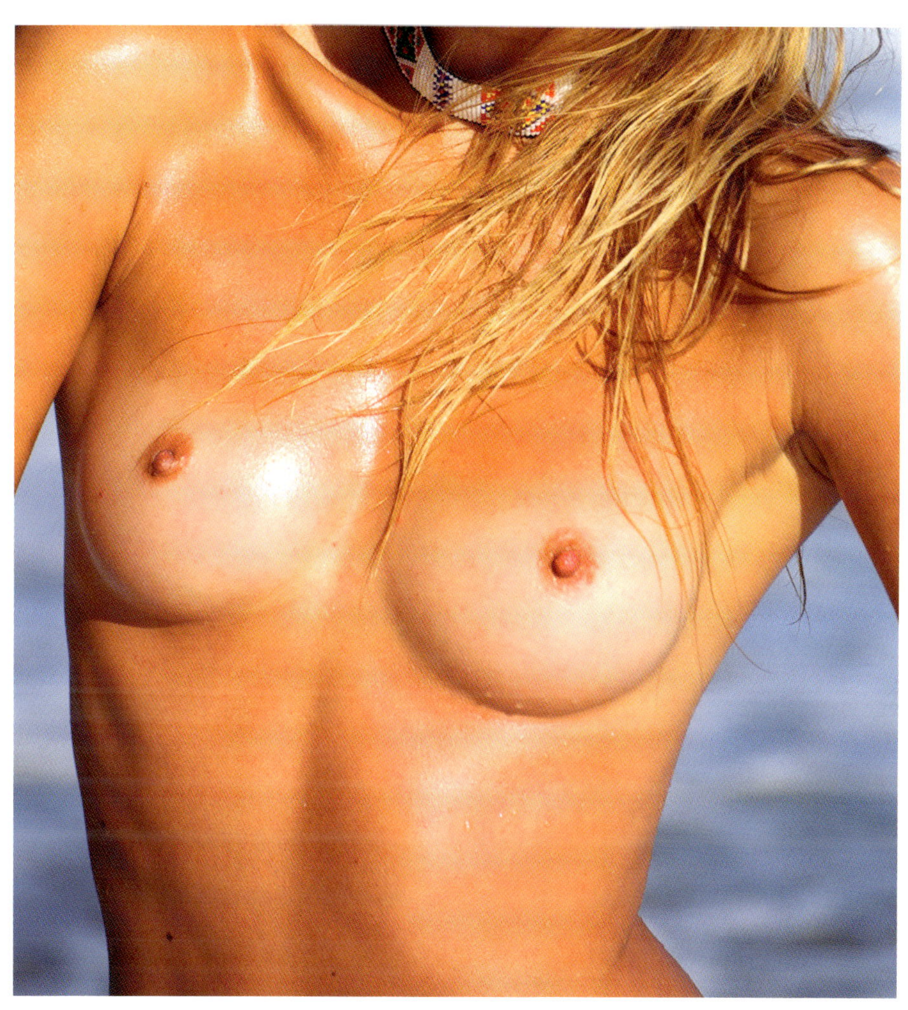

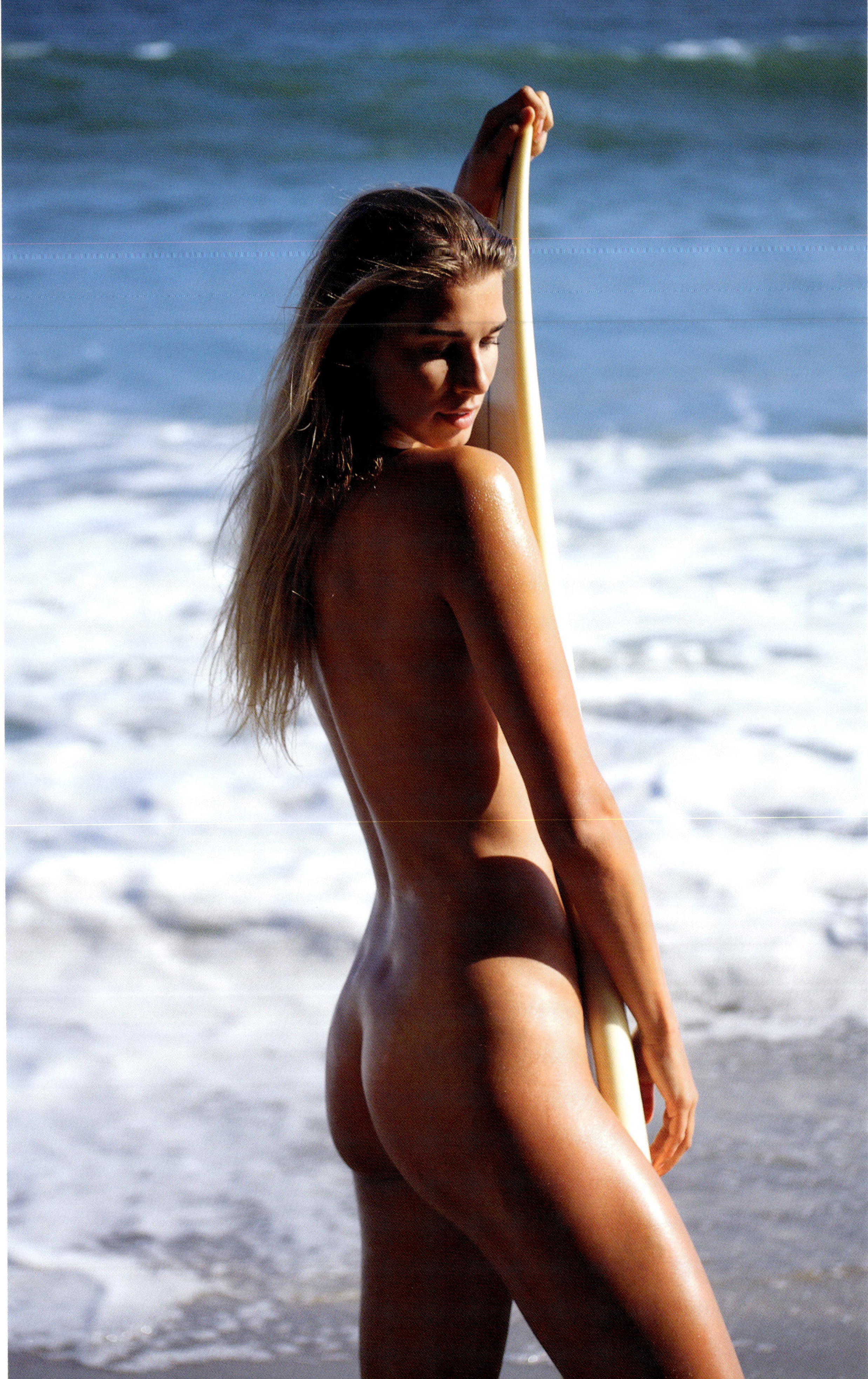

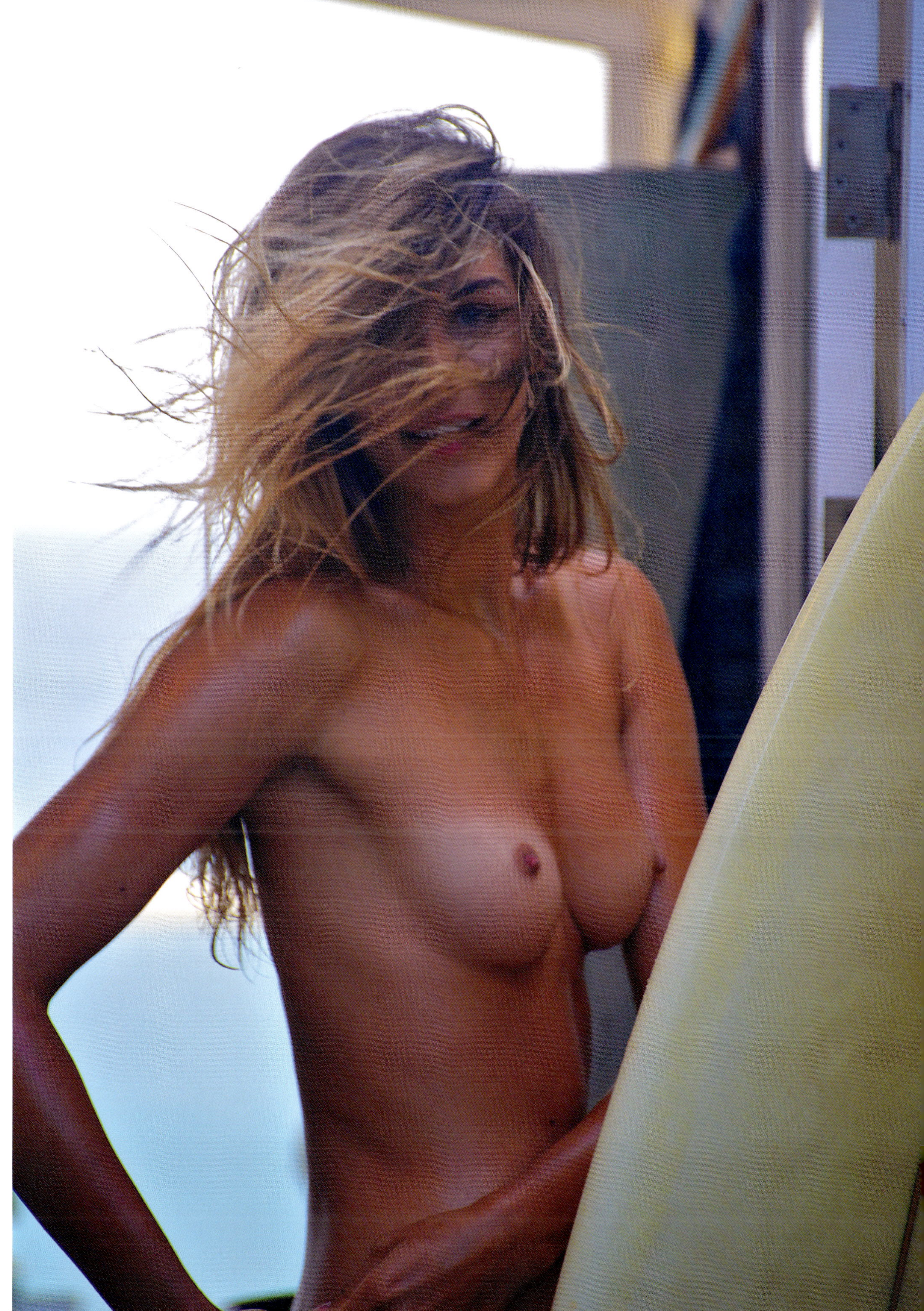

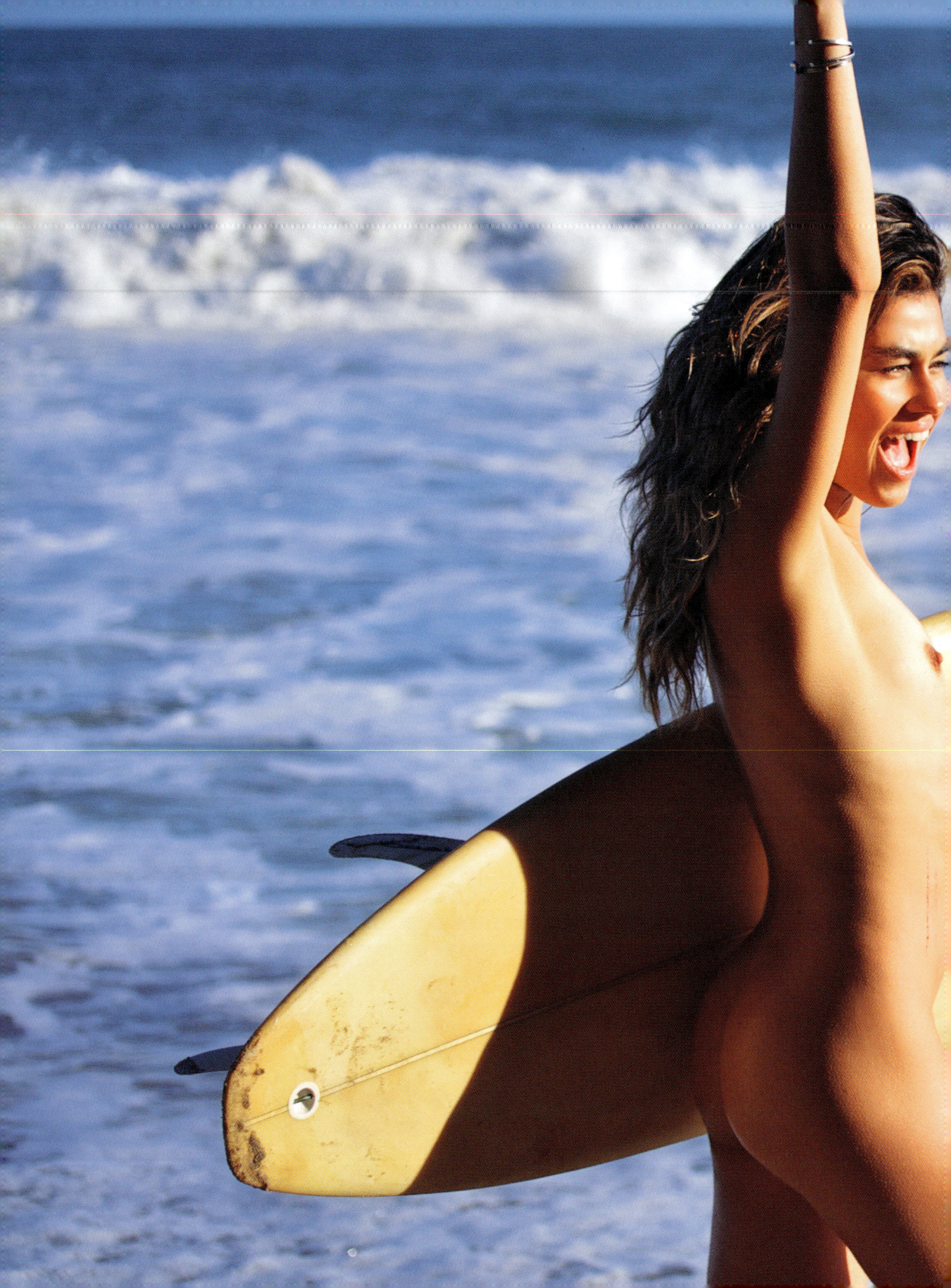

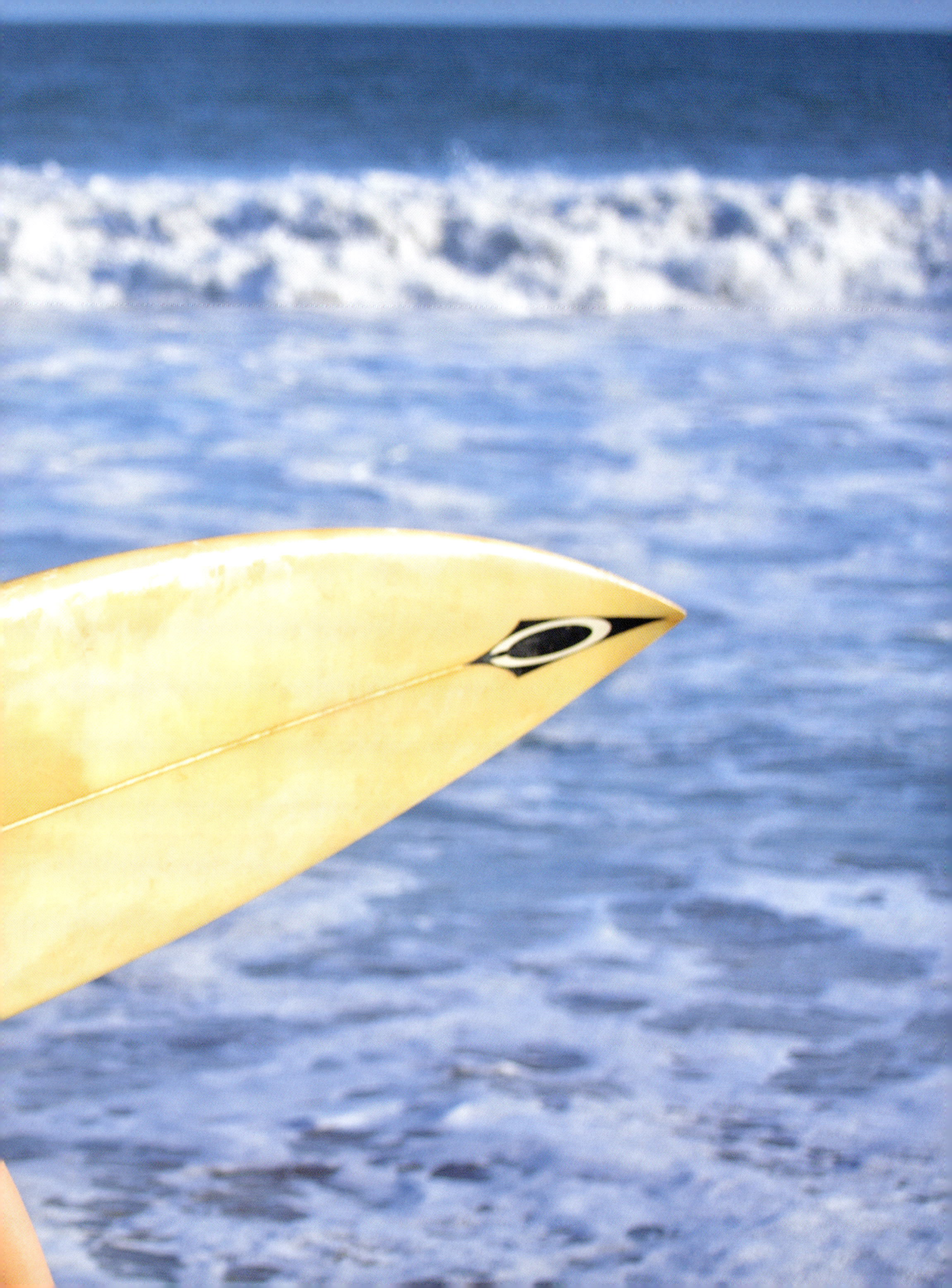

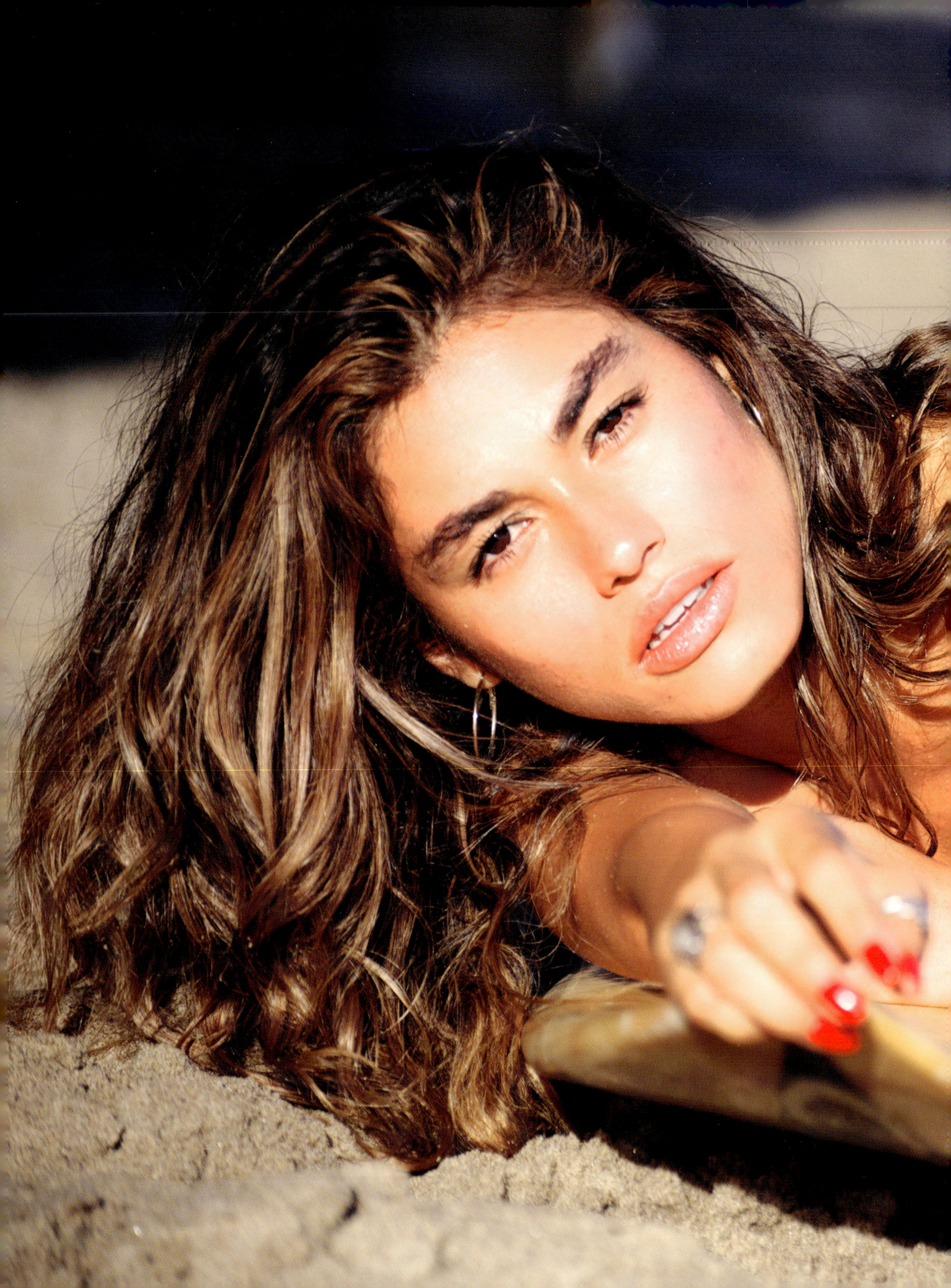

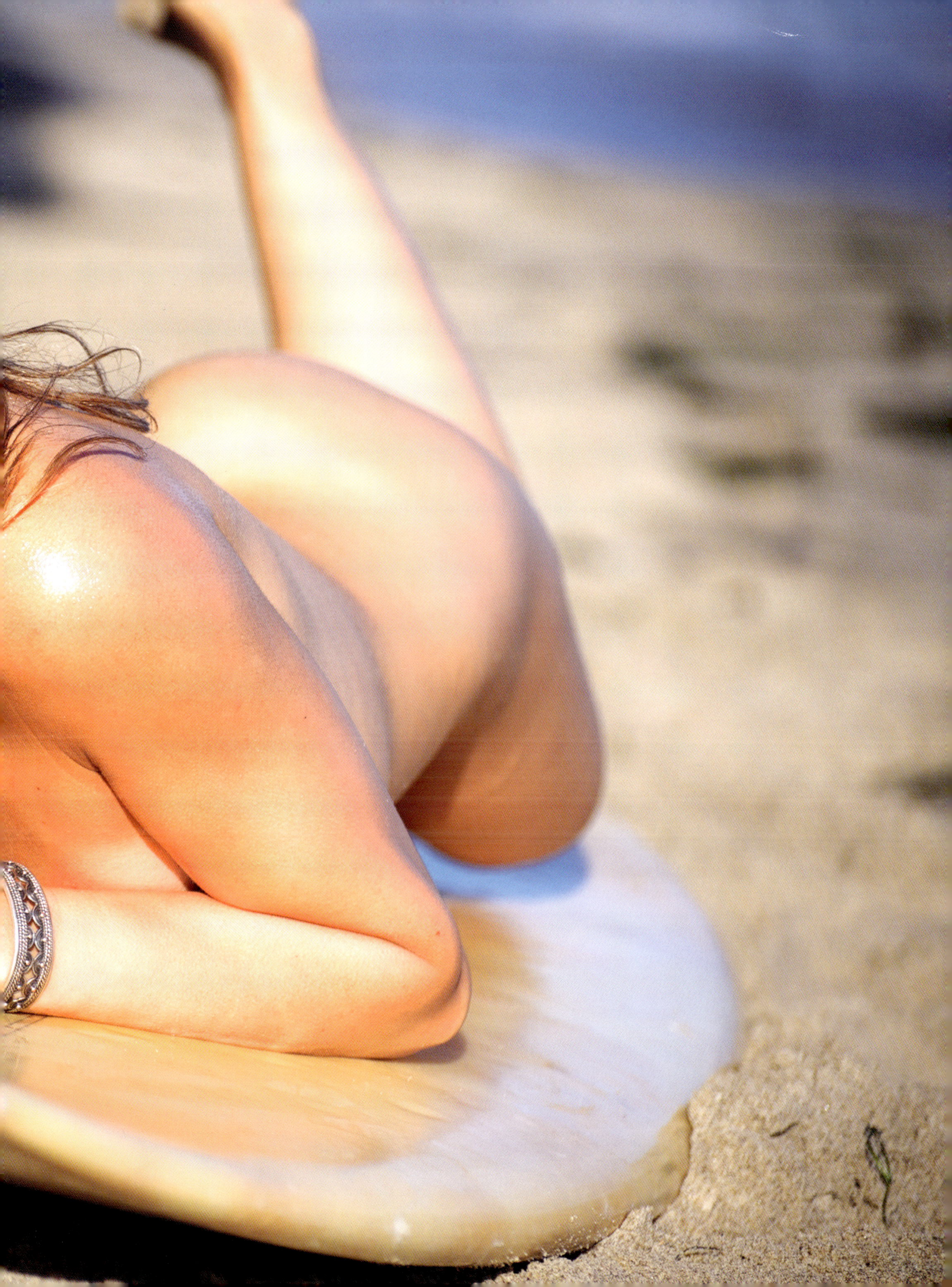

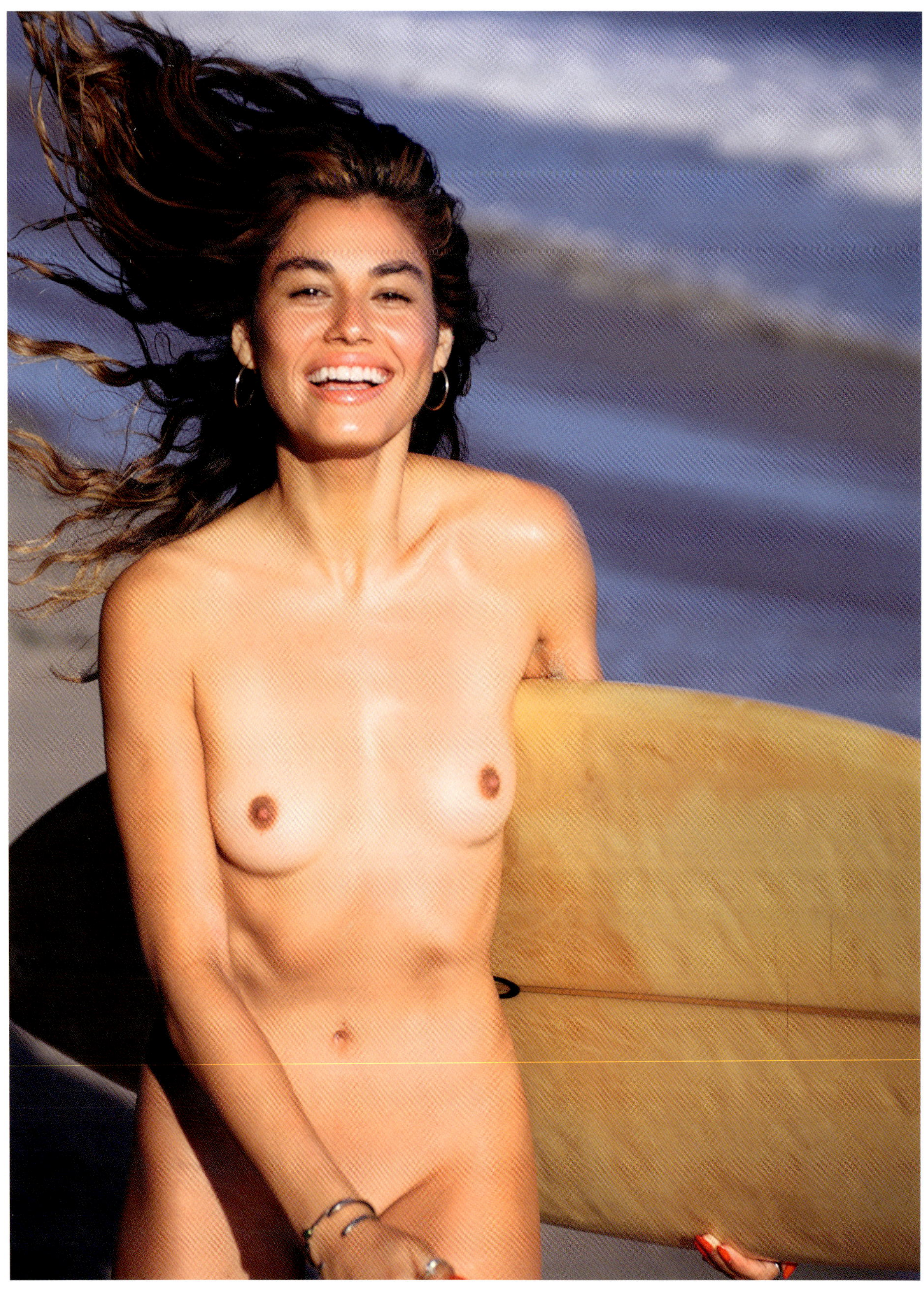

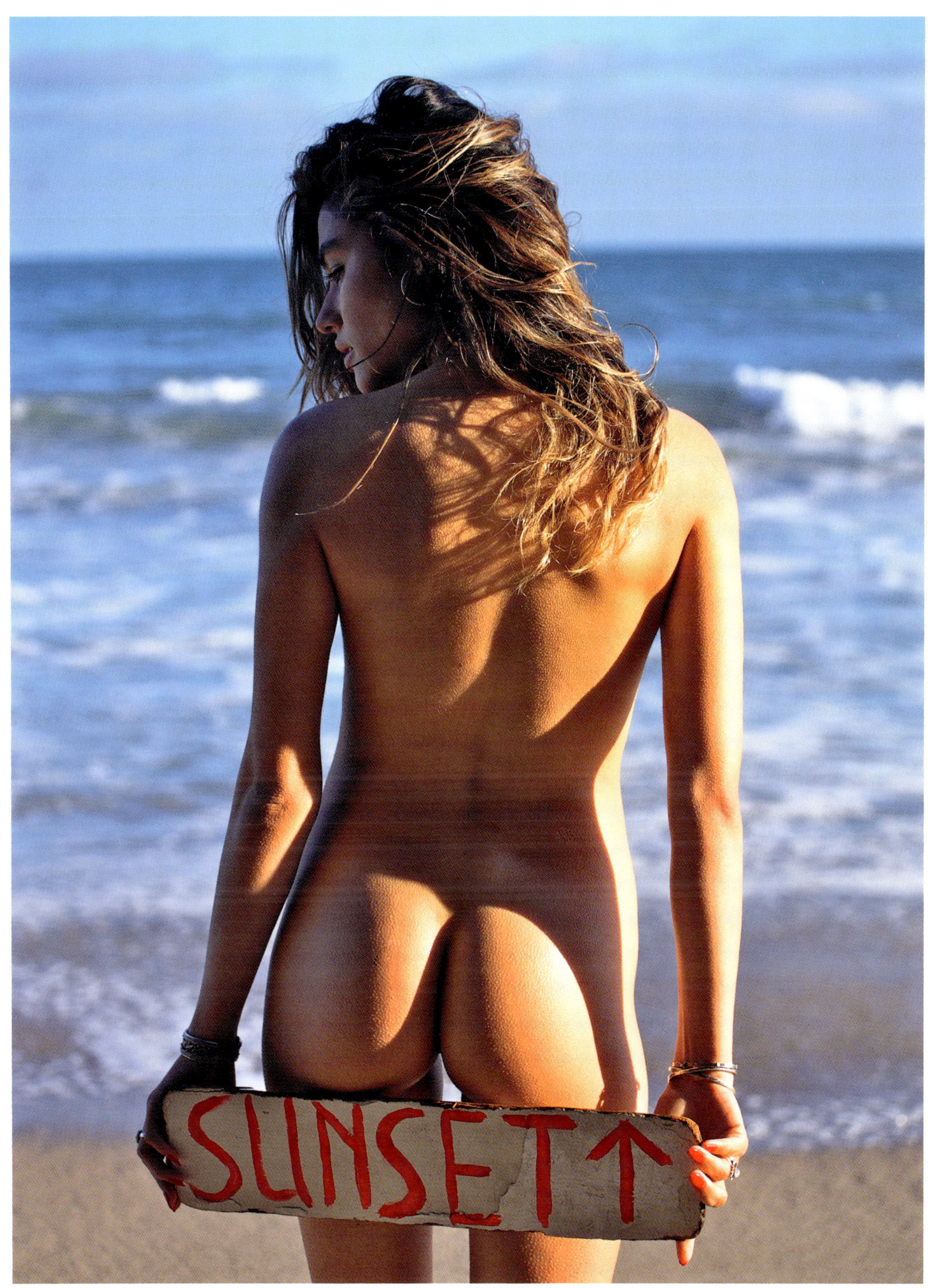
SUNSET ↑

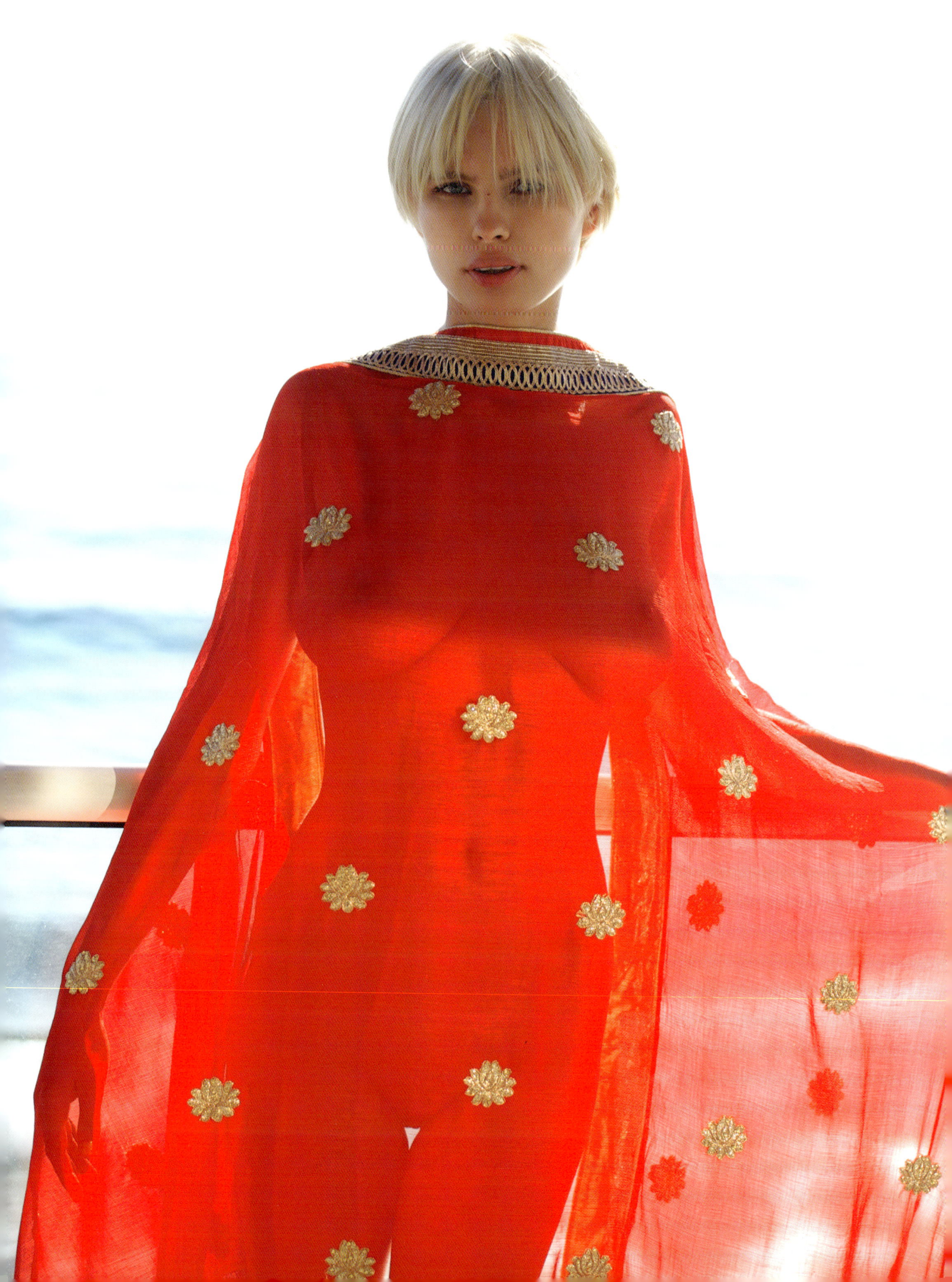

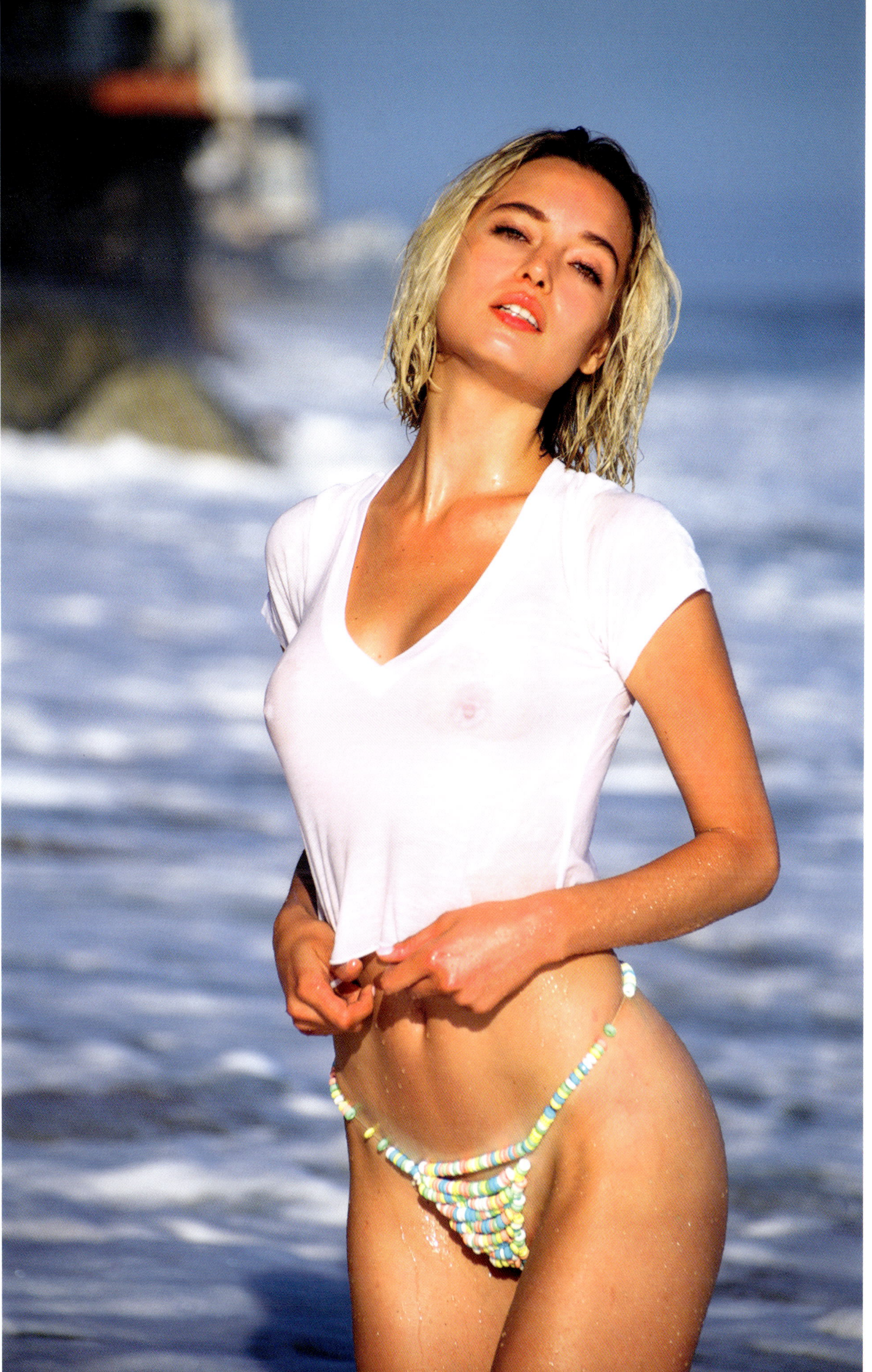

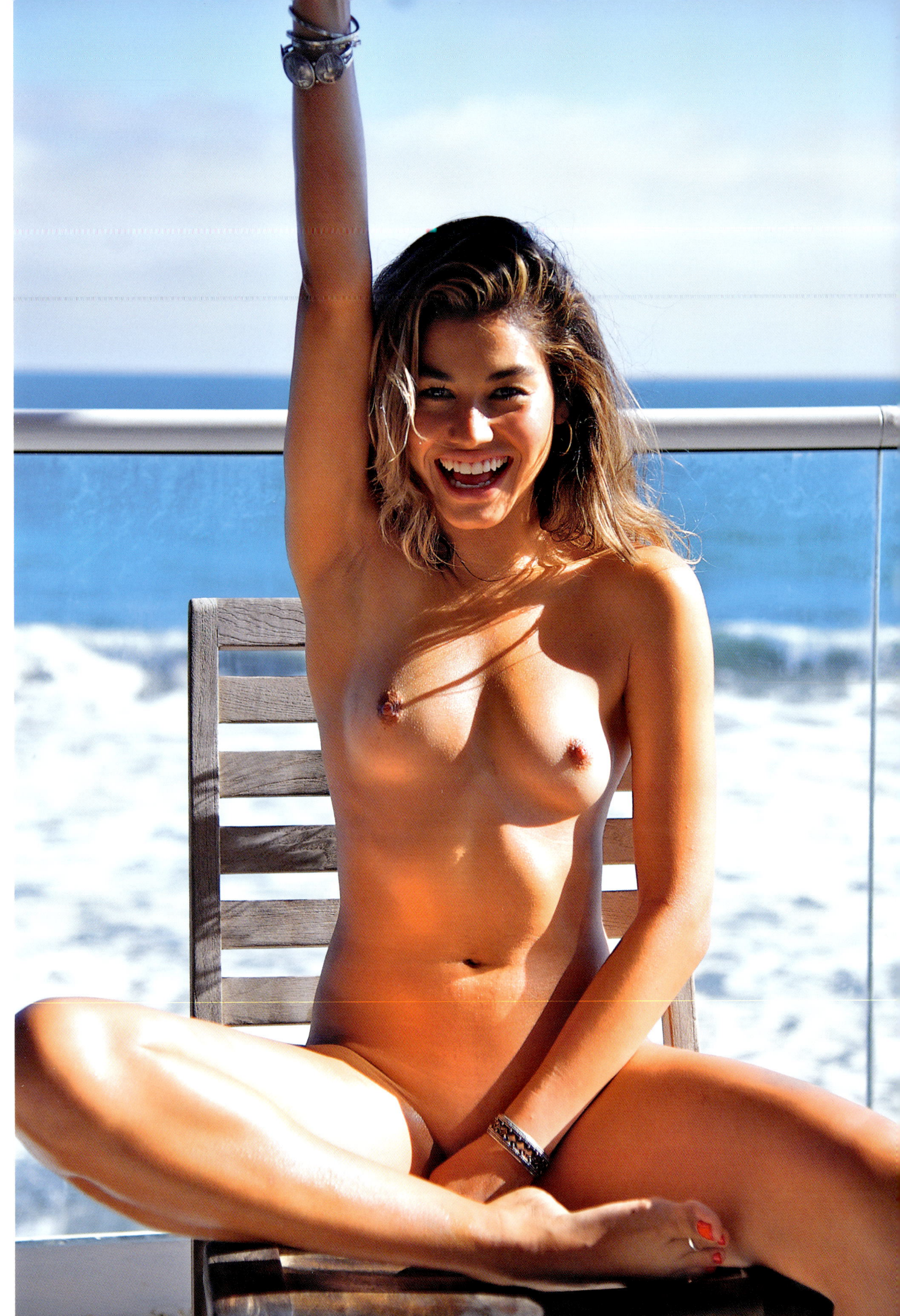

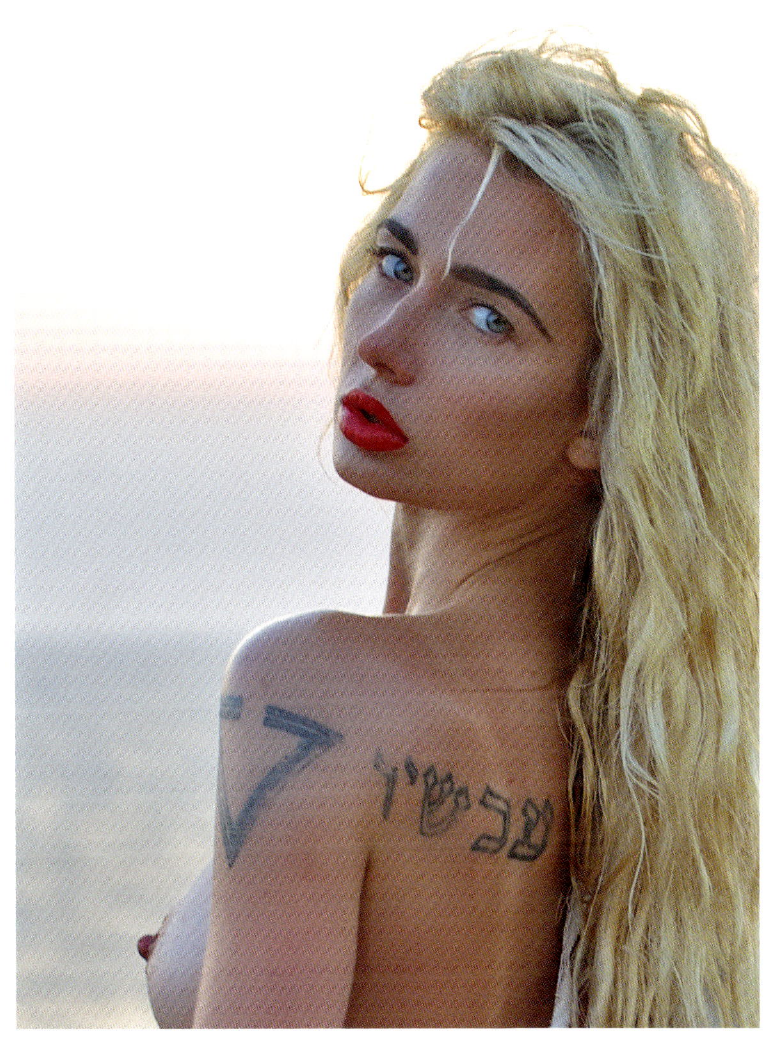

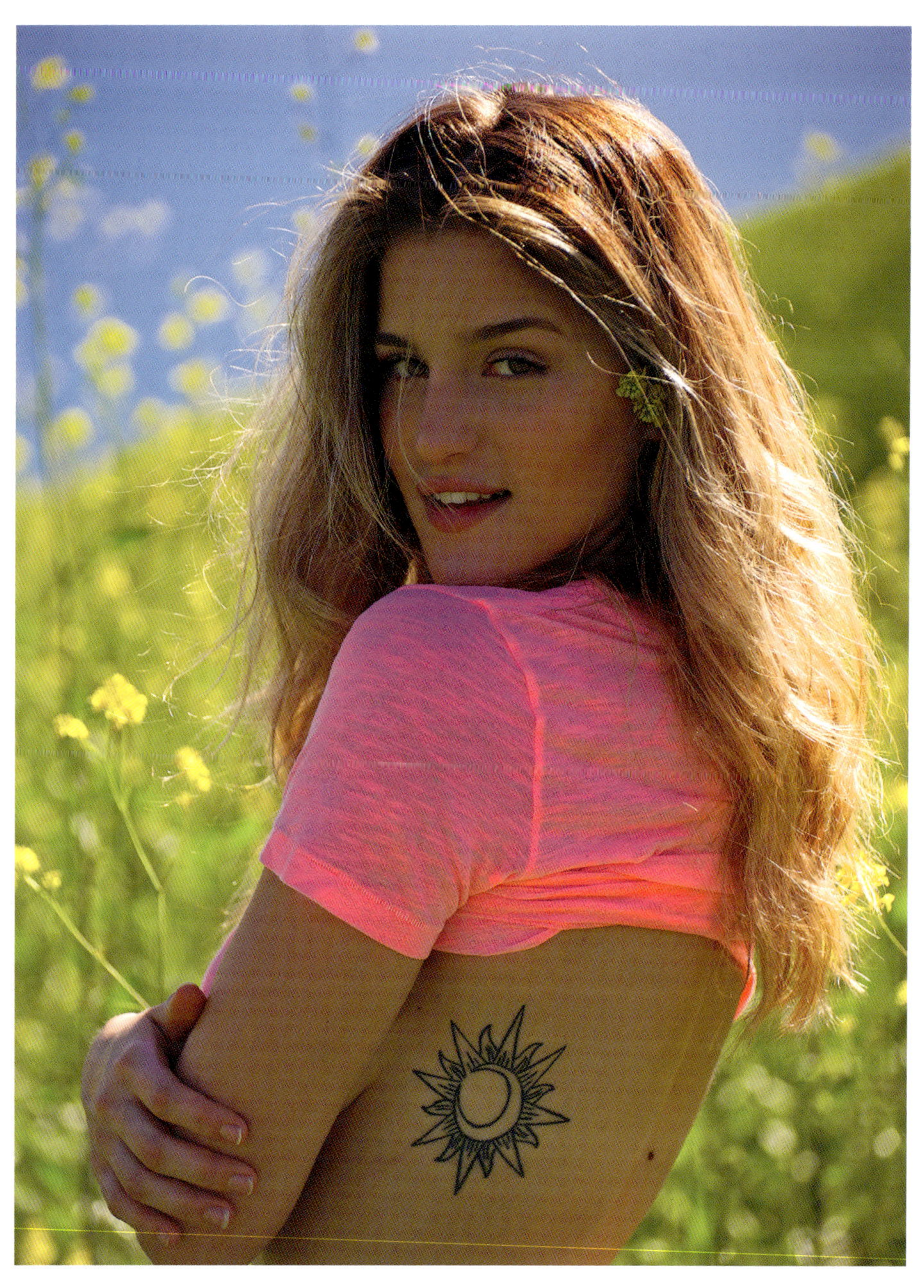

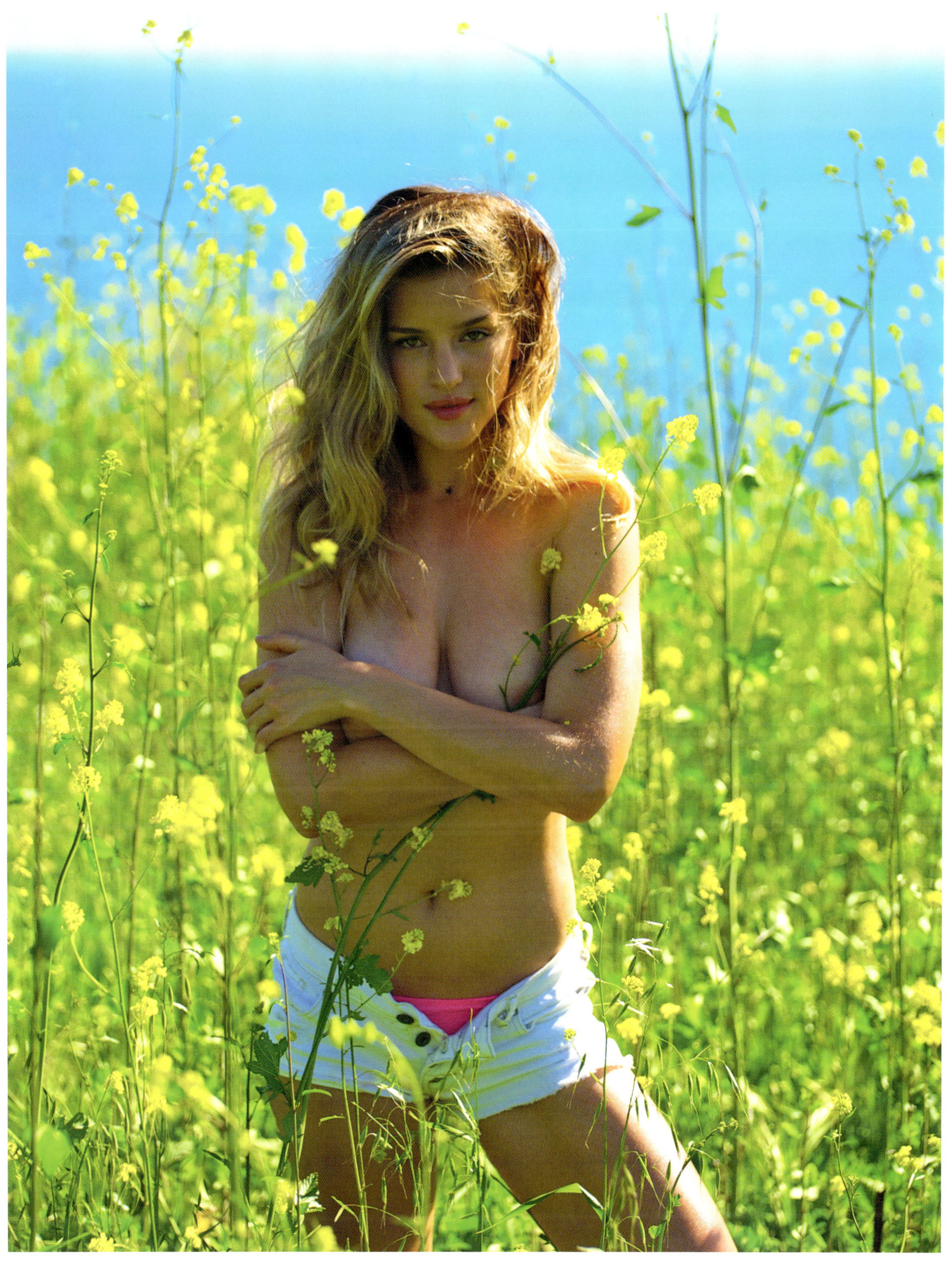

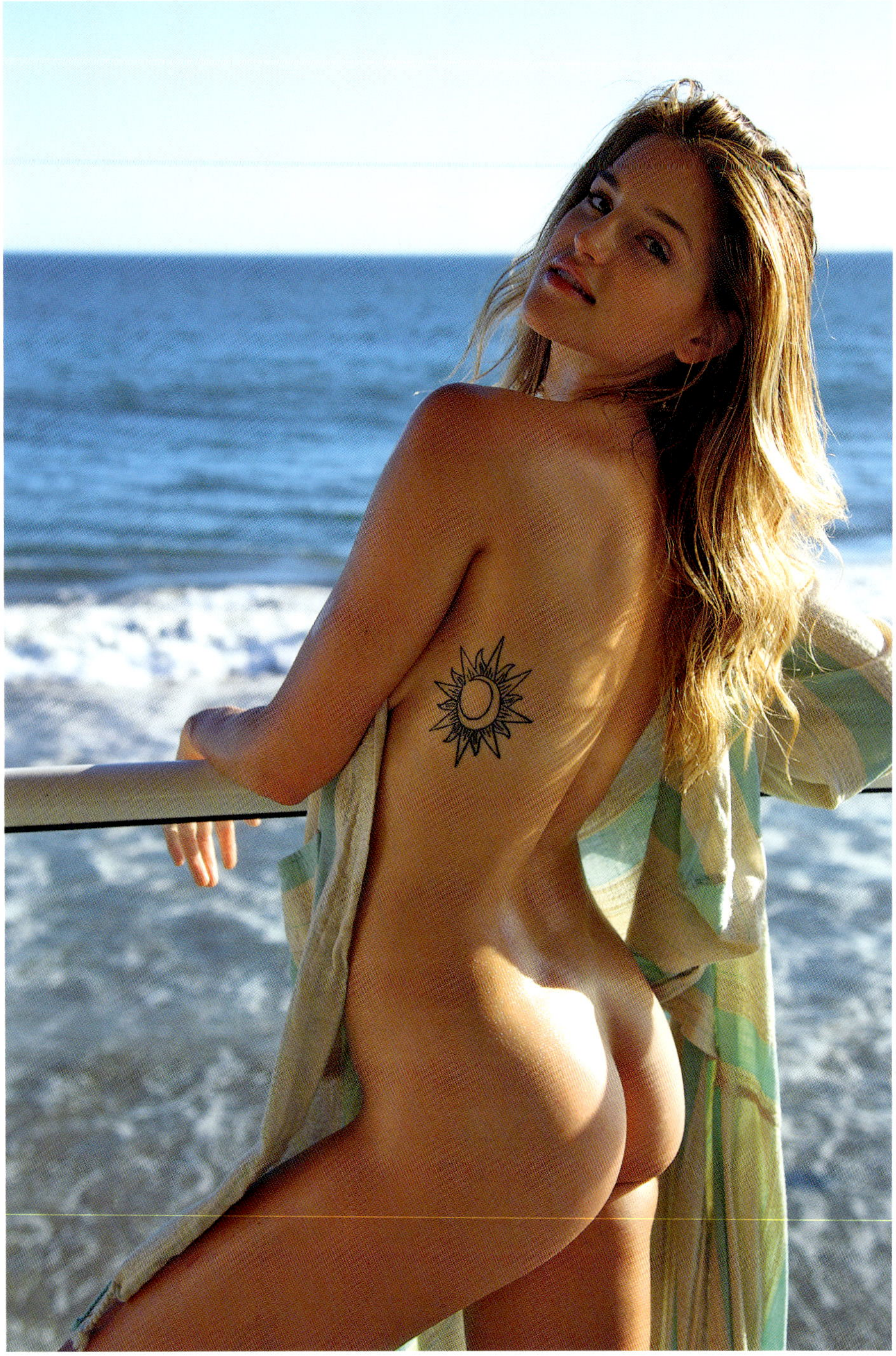

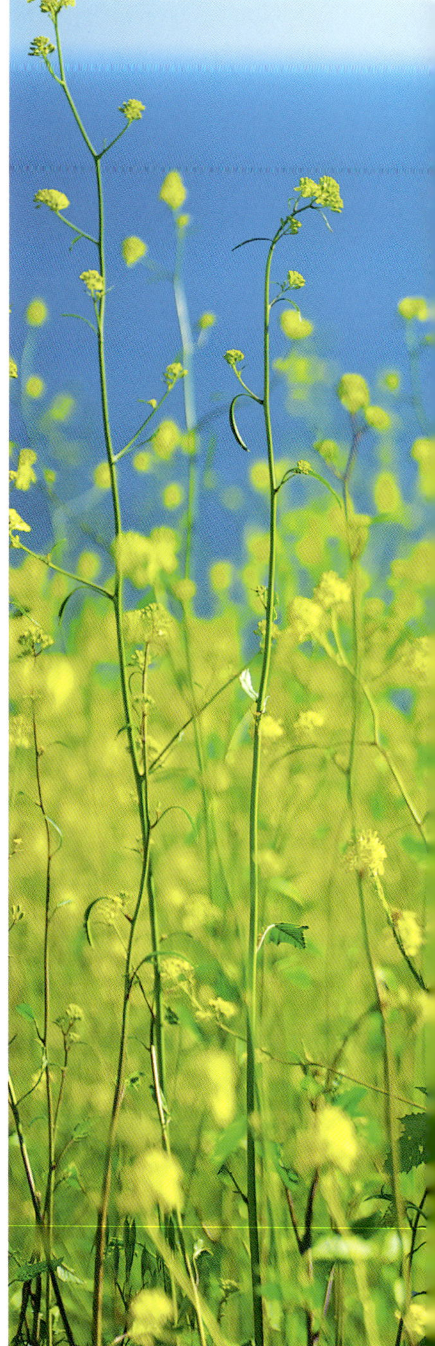

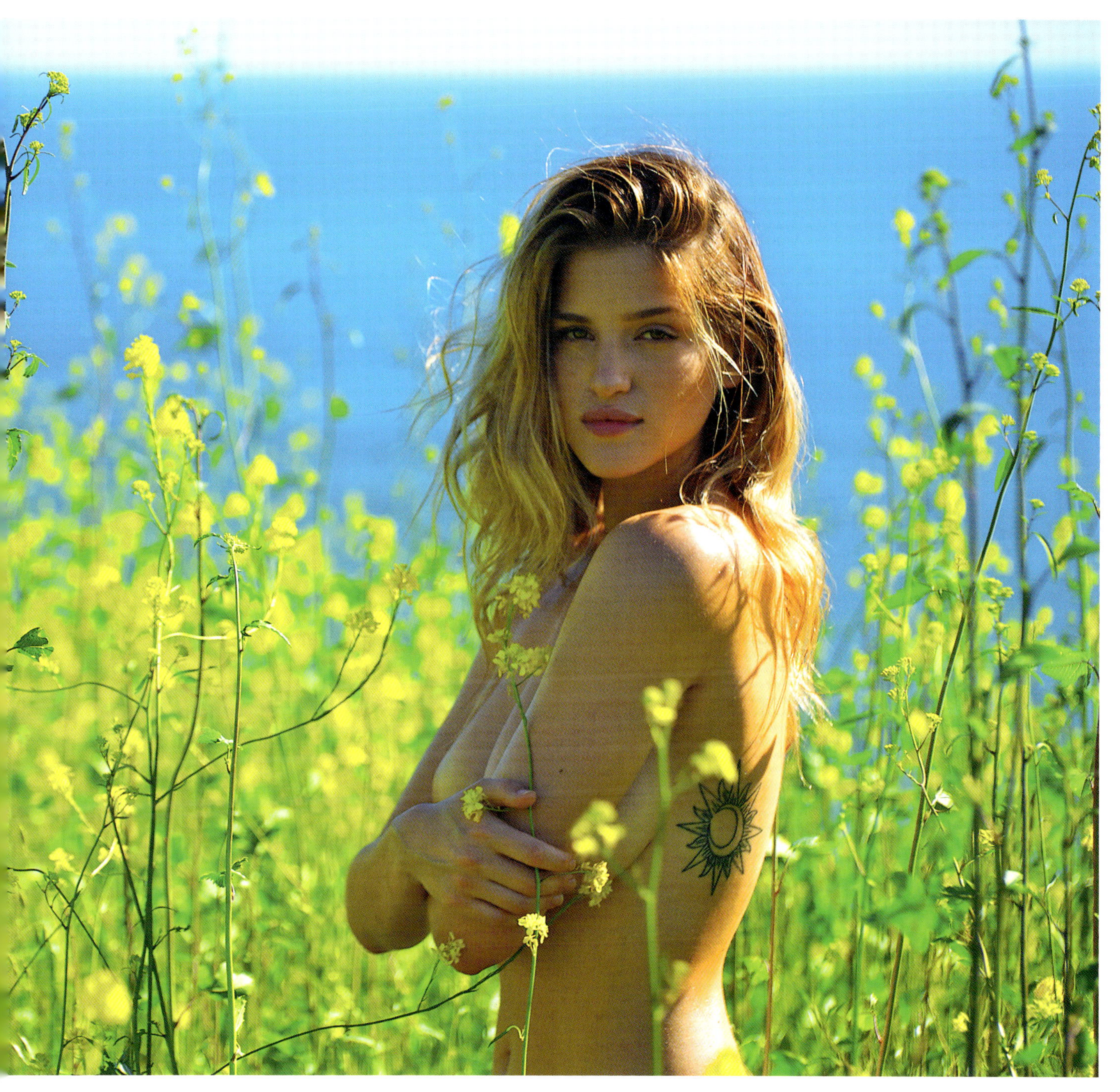

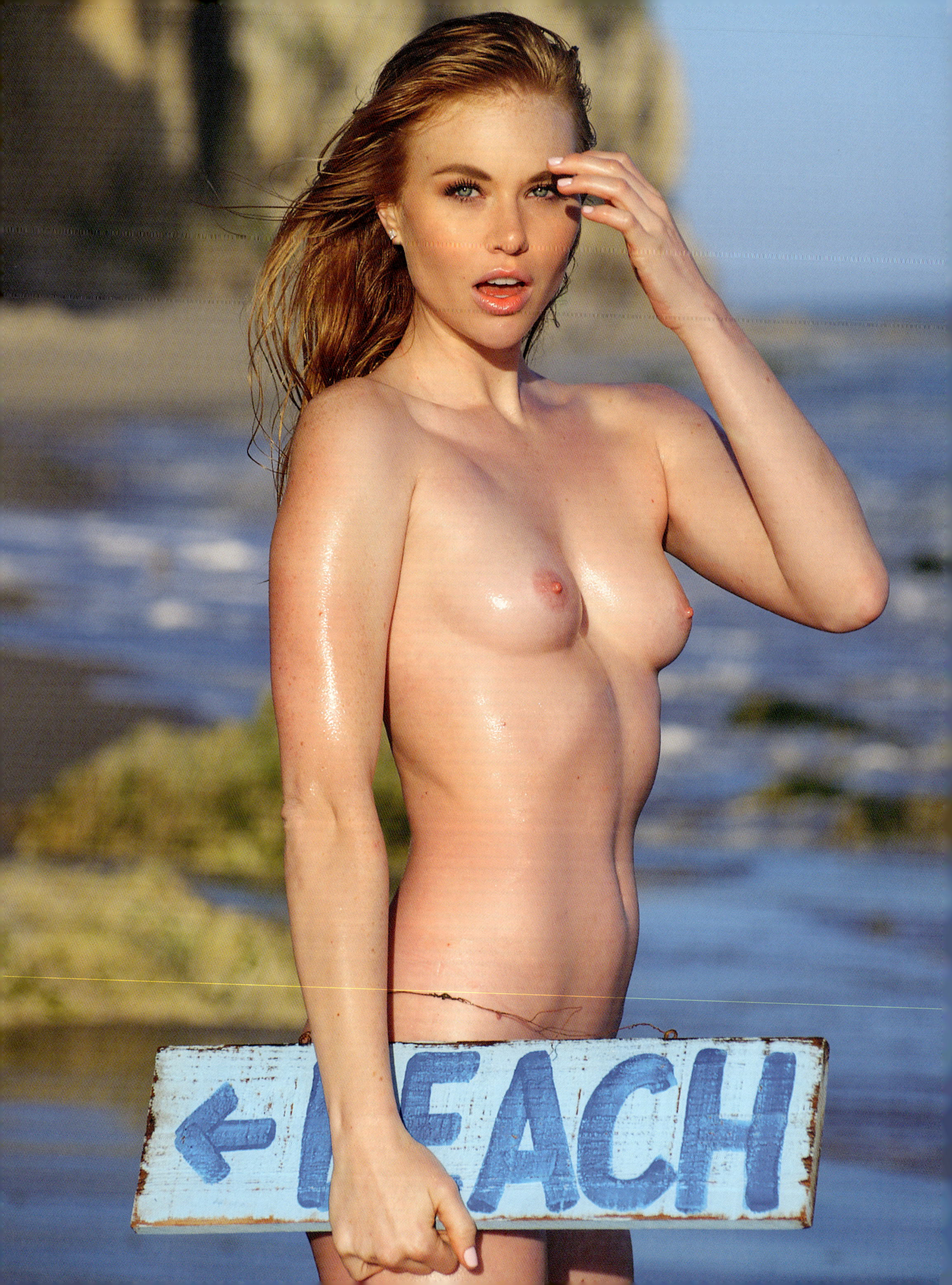

← EACH

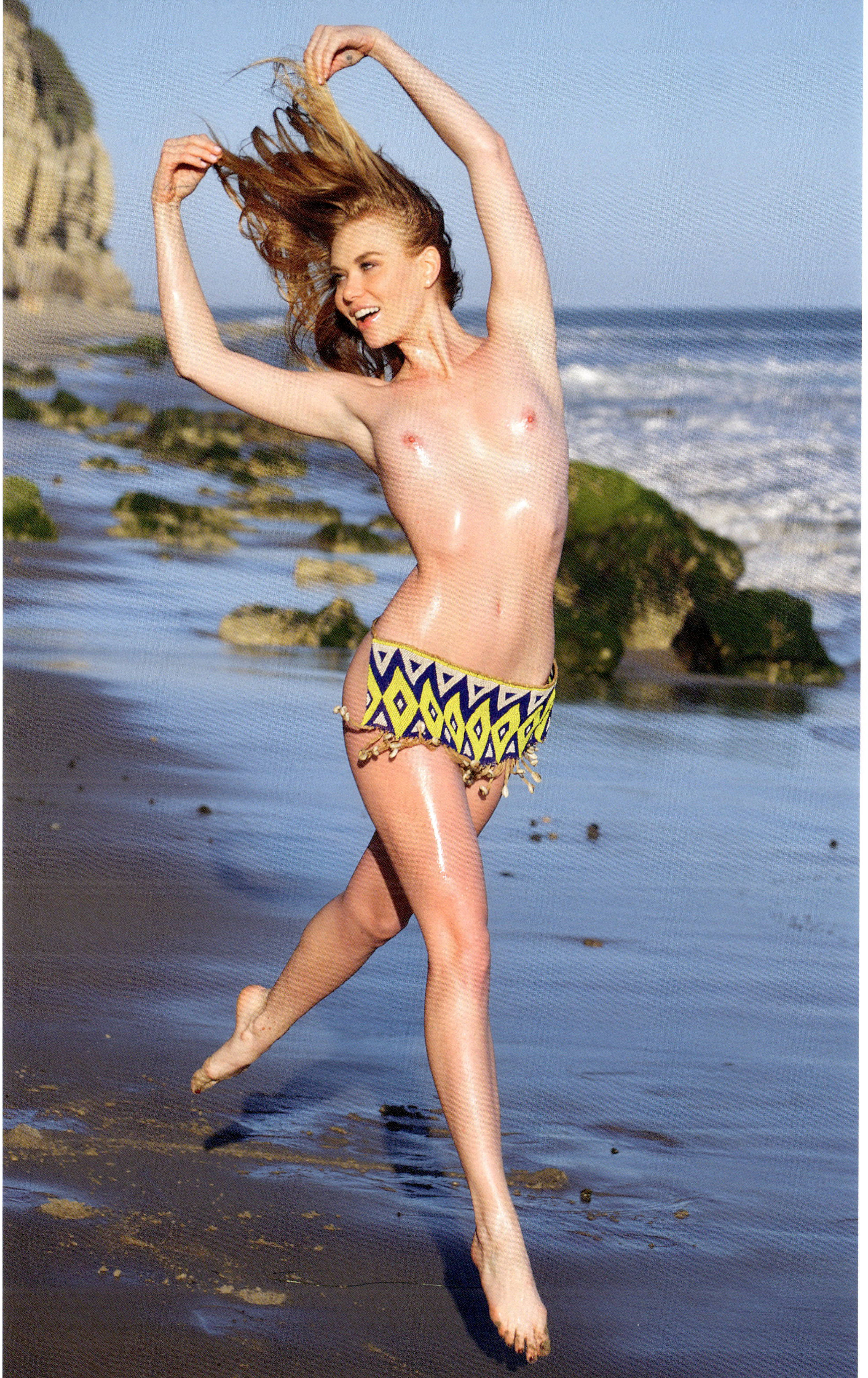

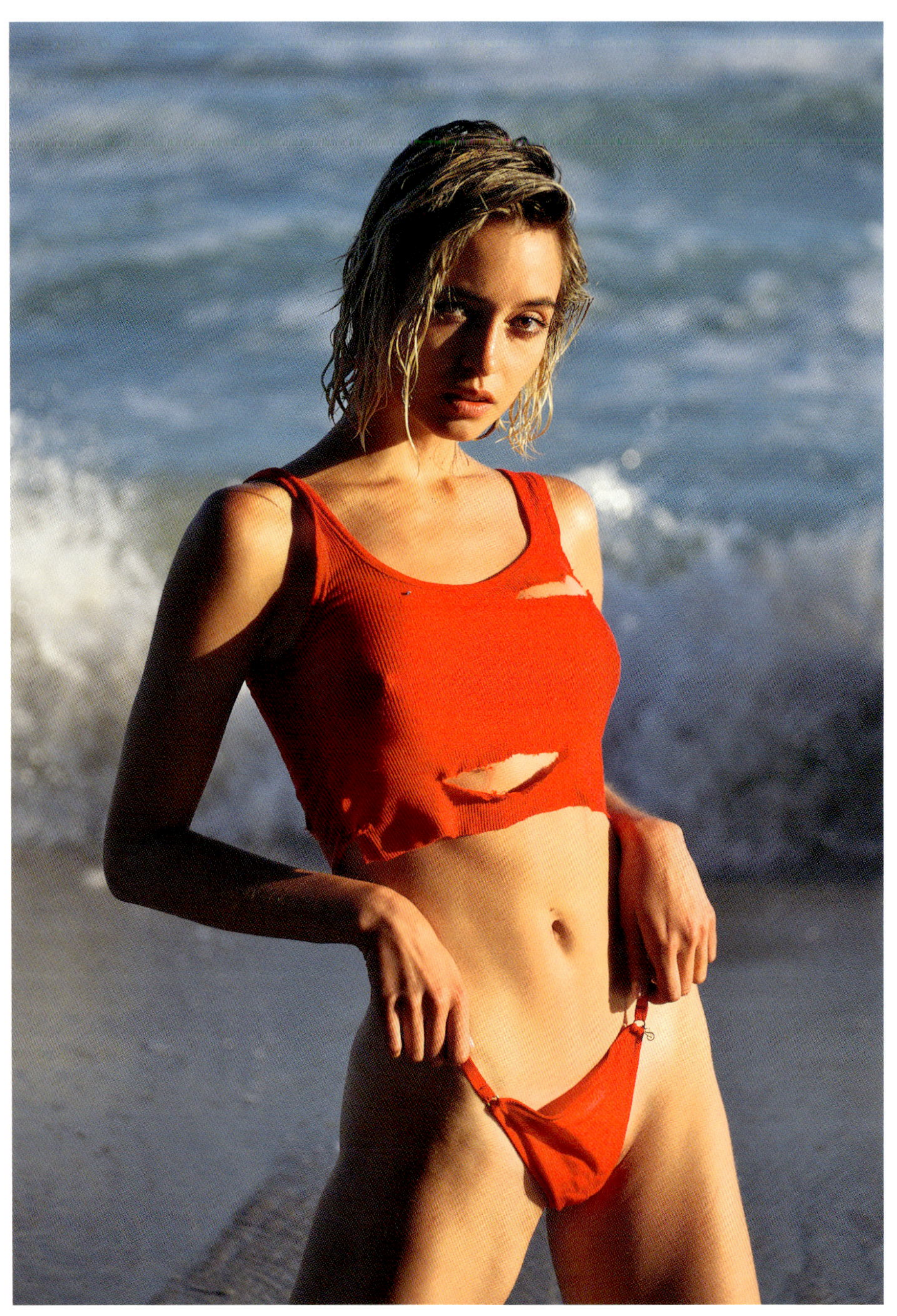

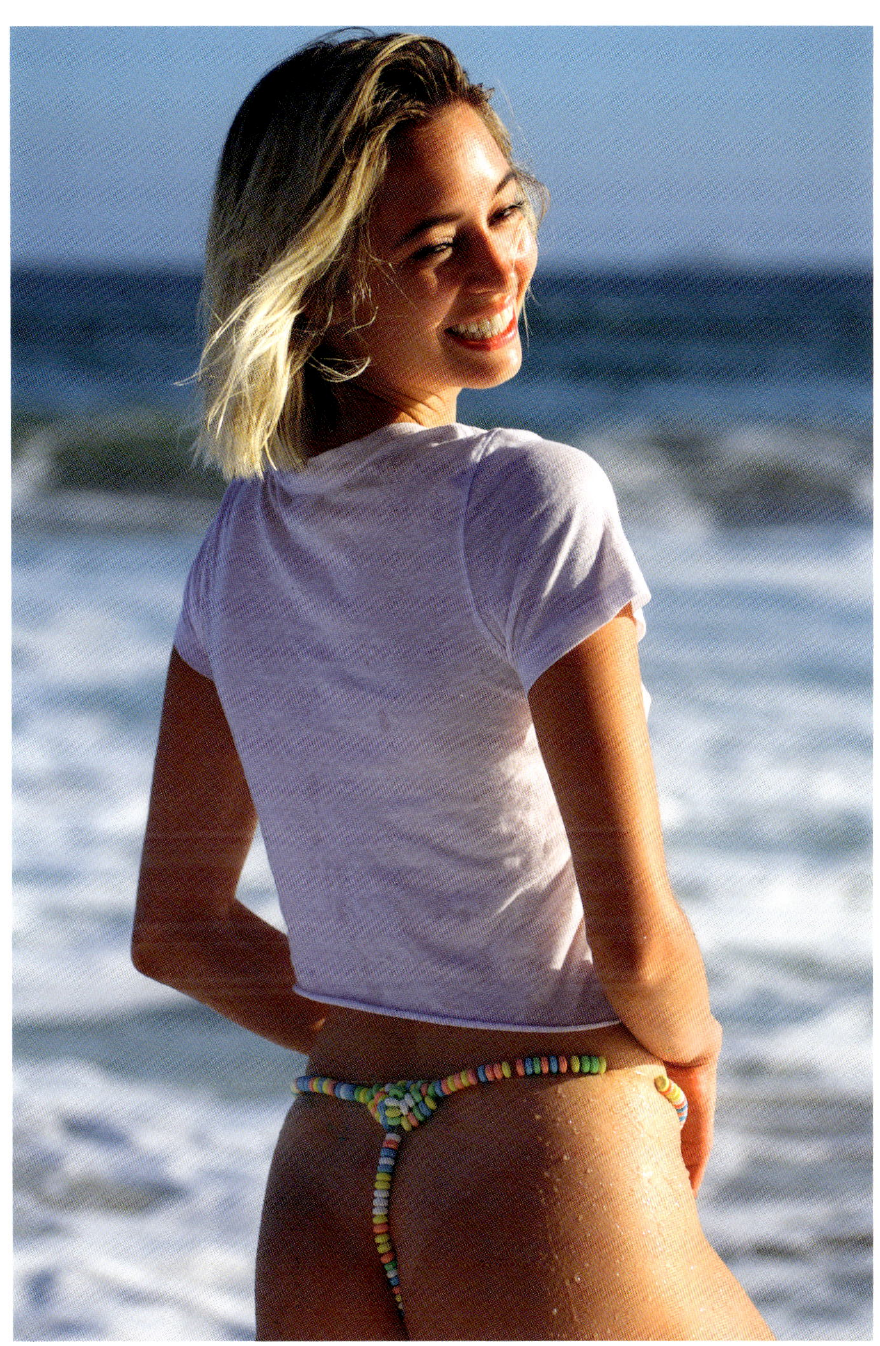

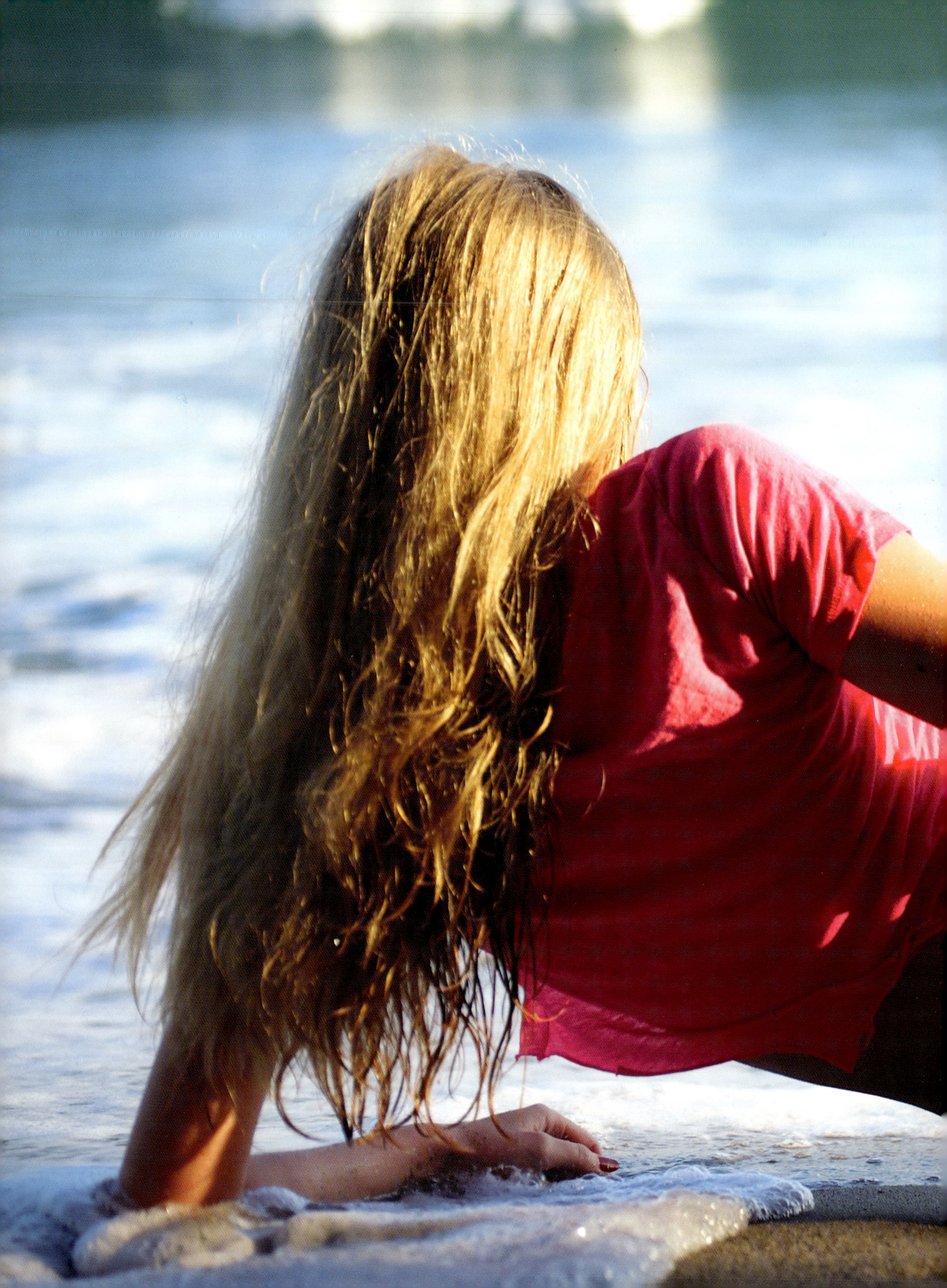

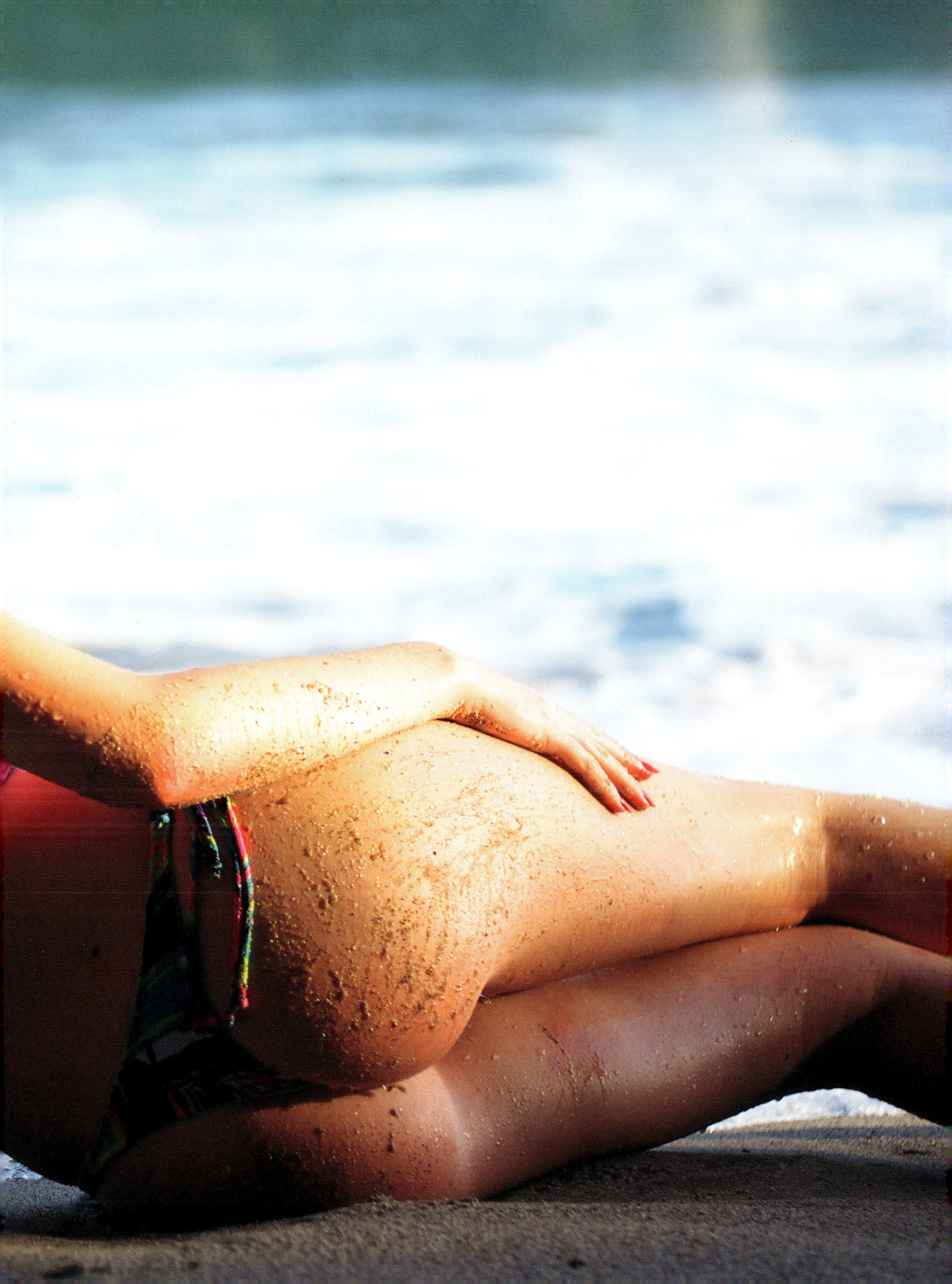

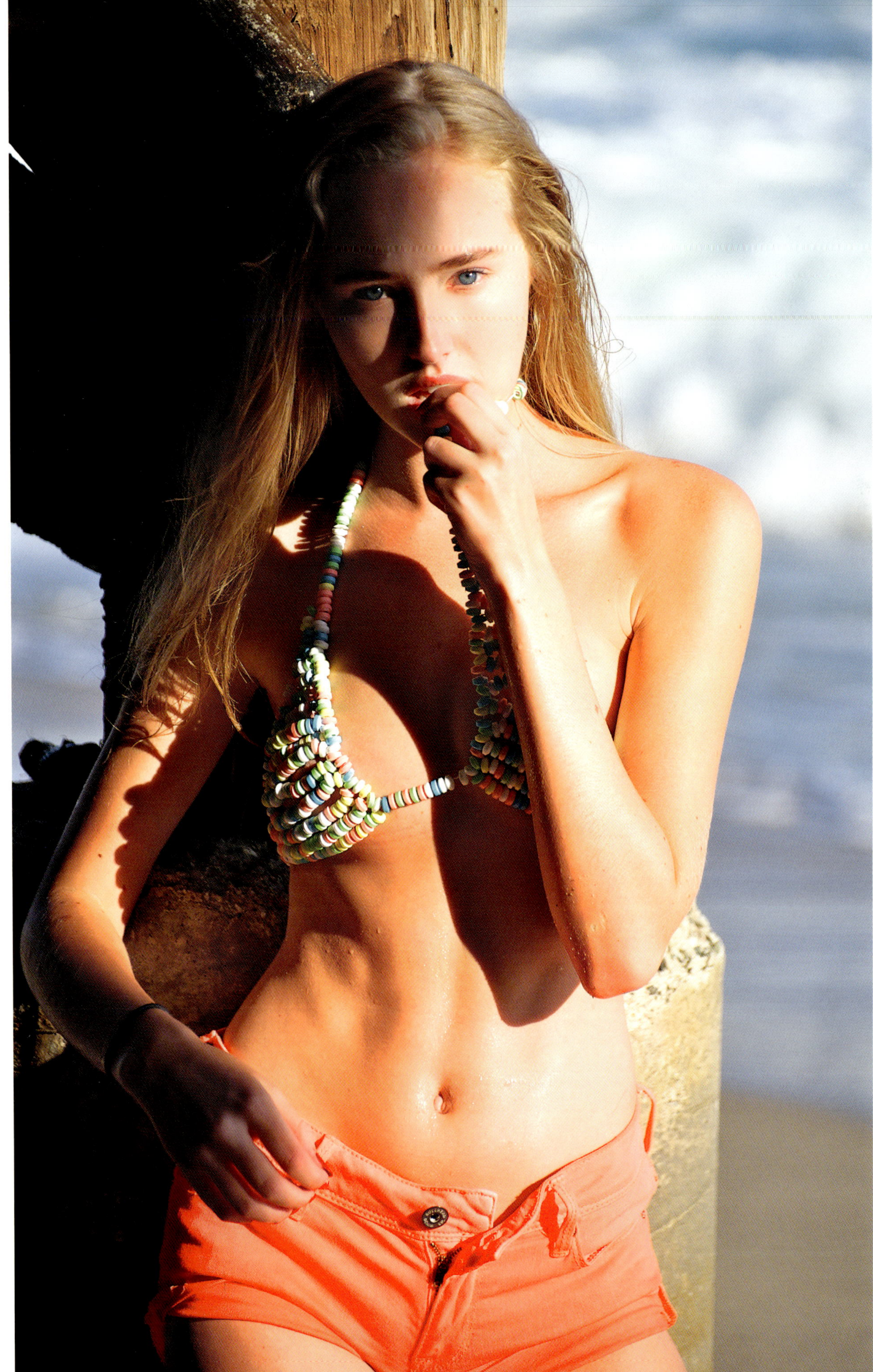

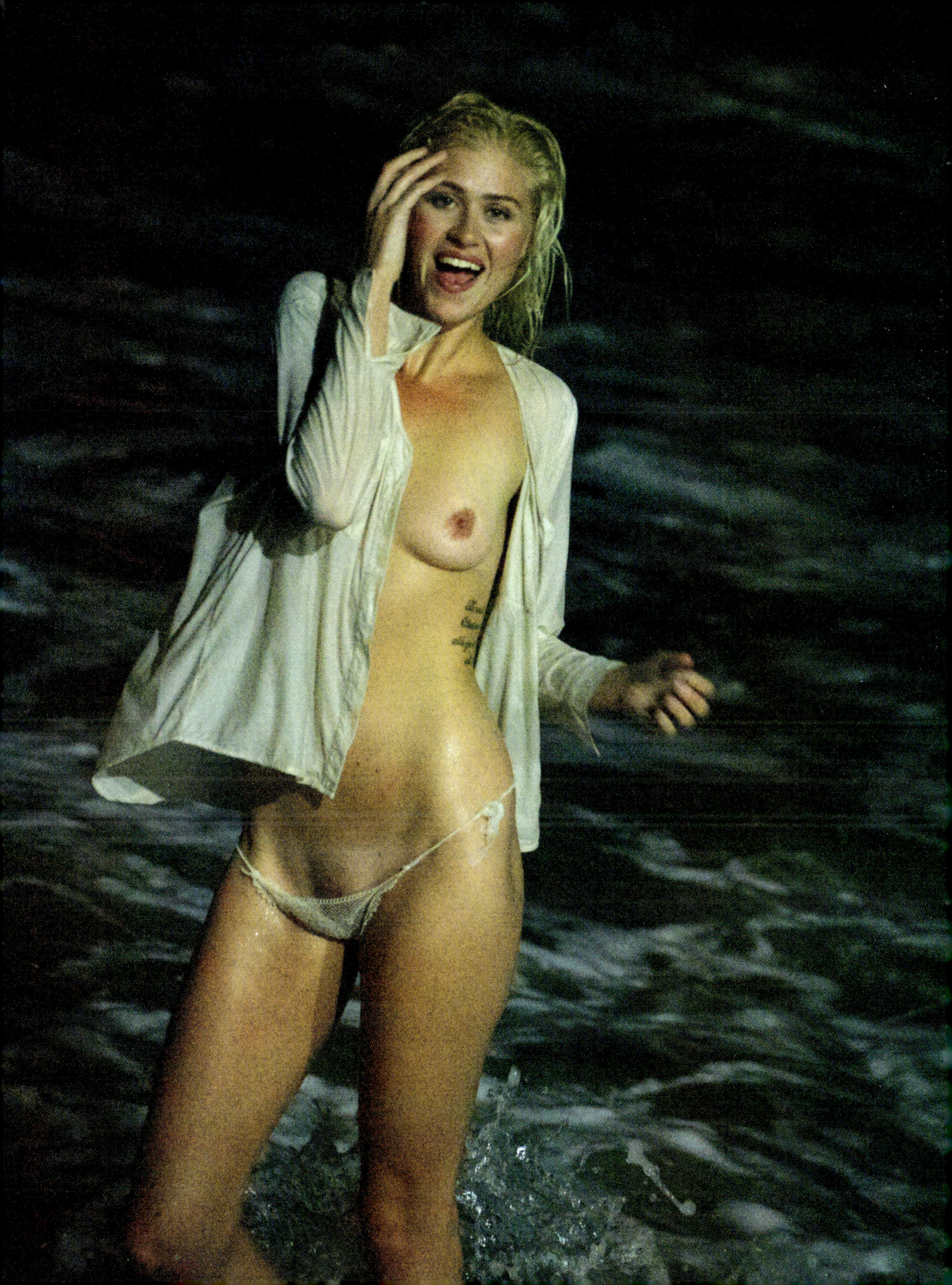

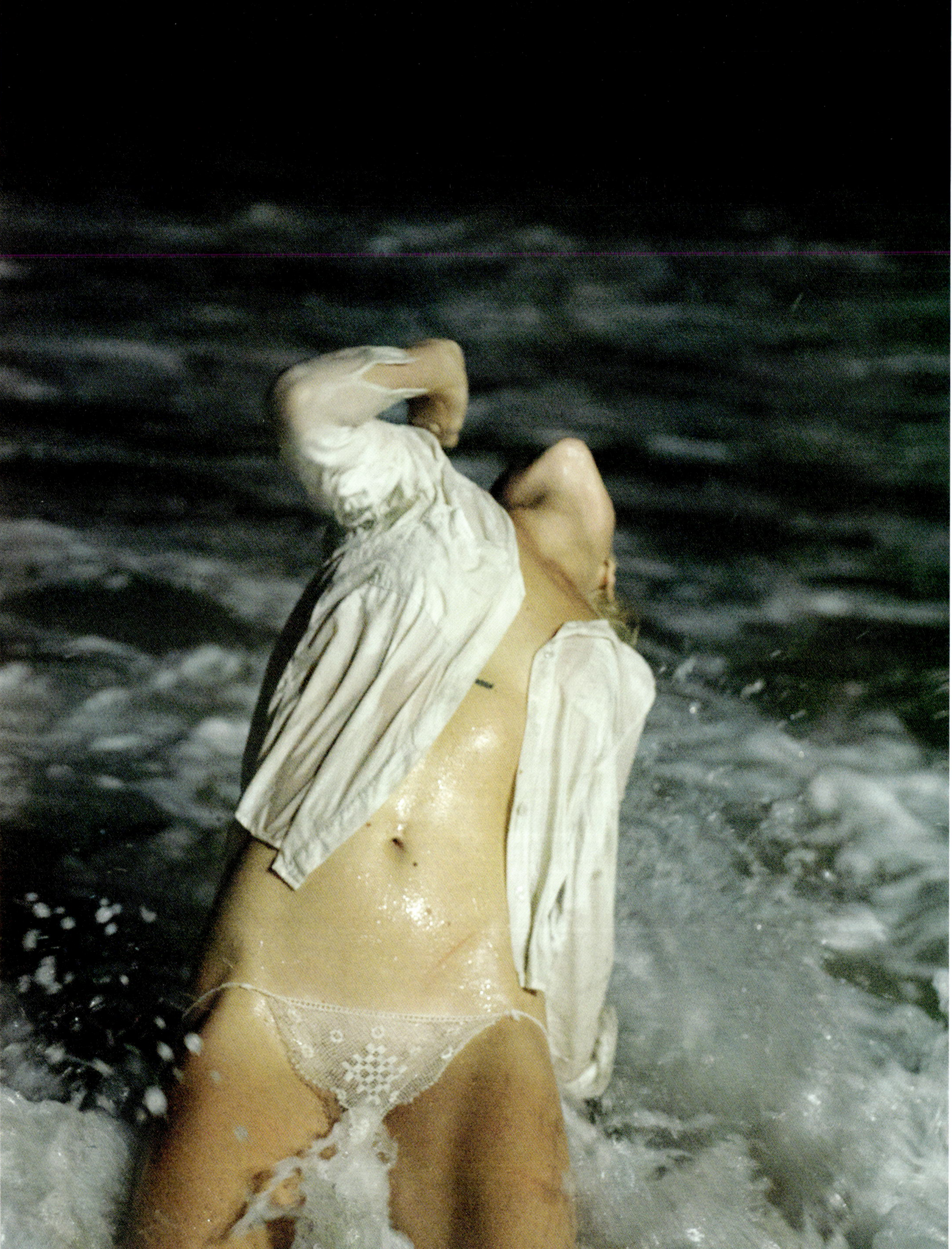

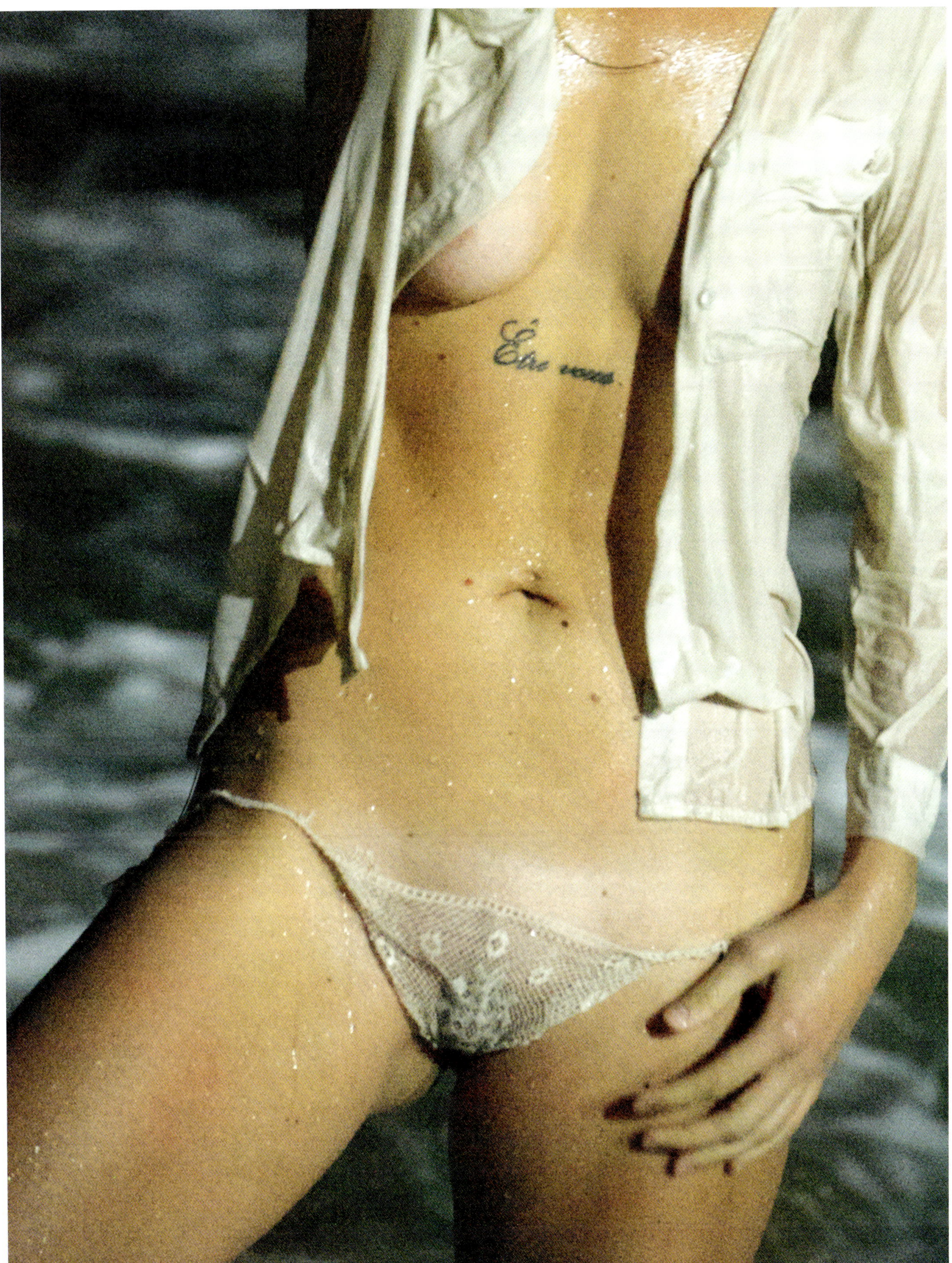

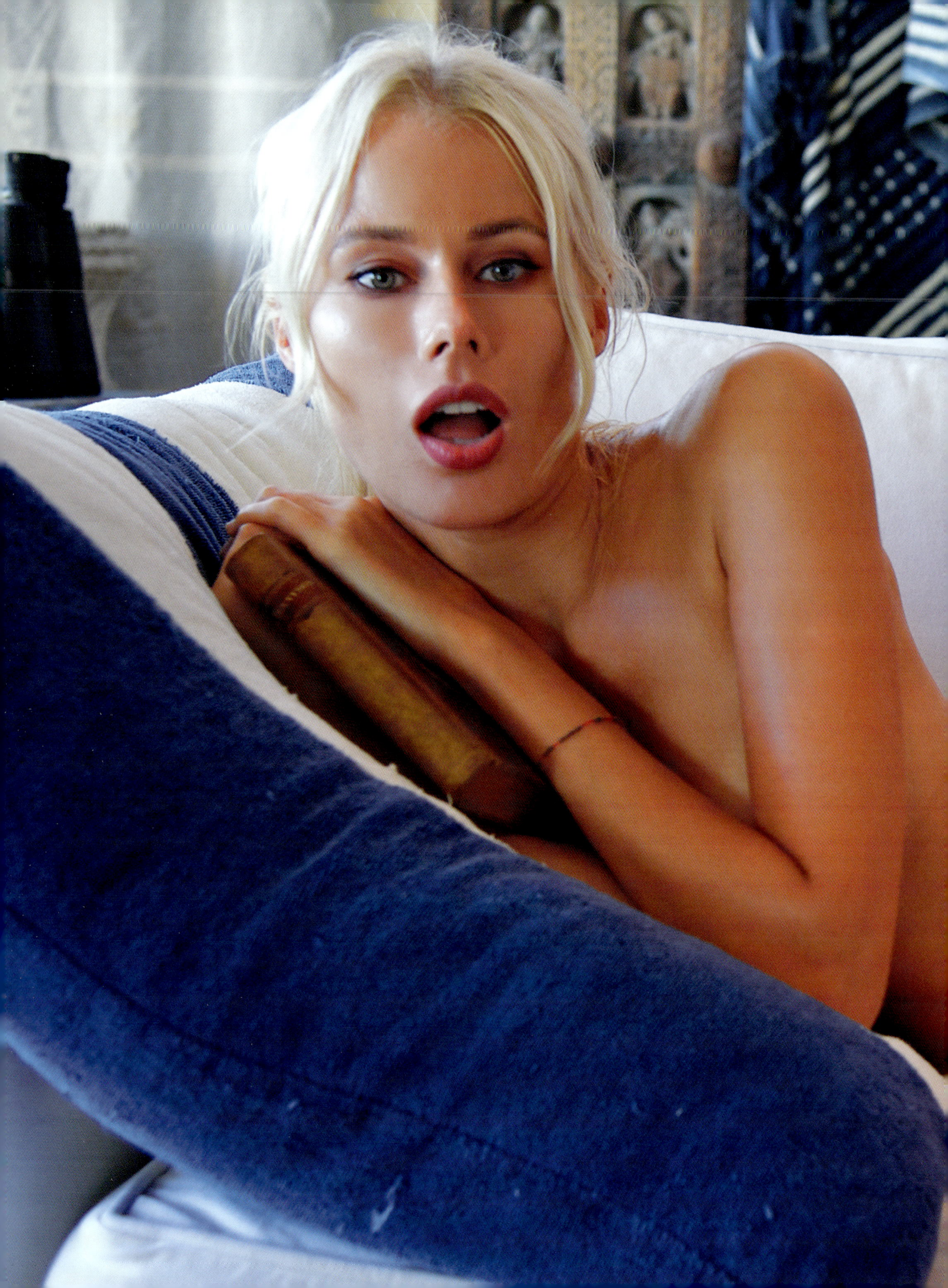

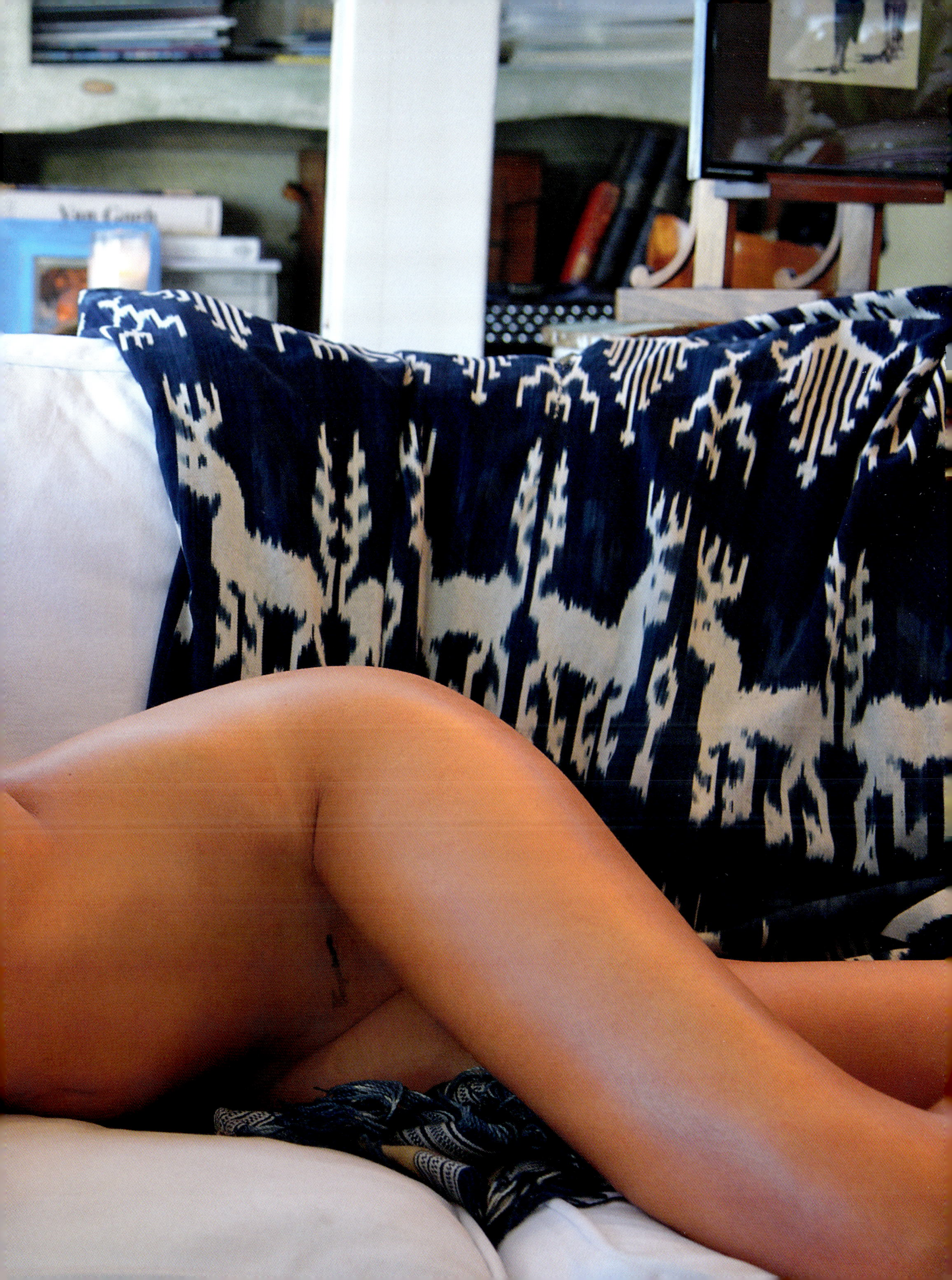

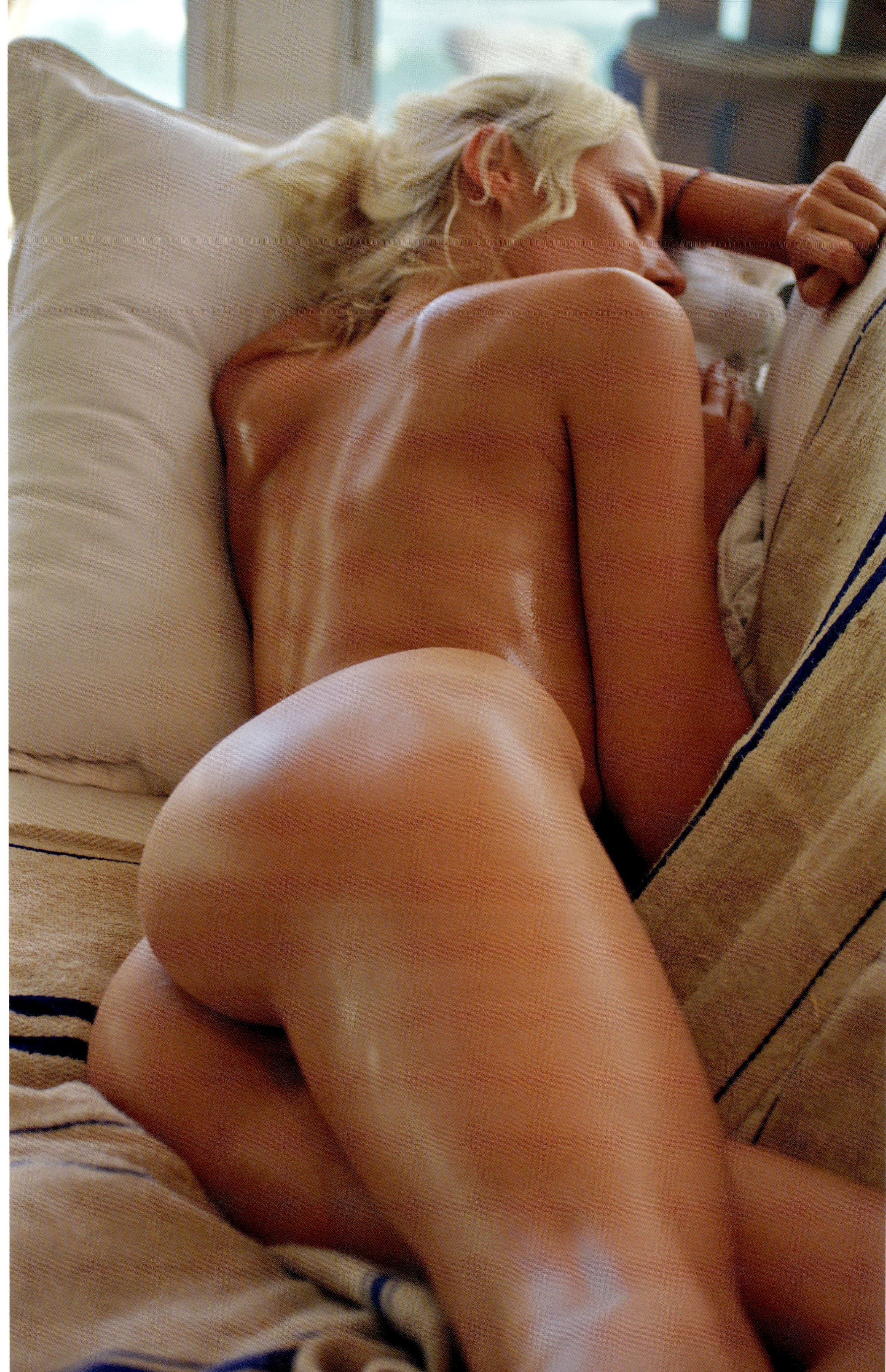

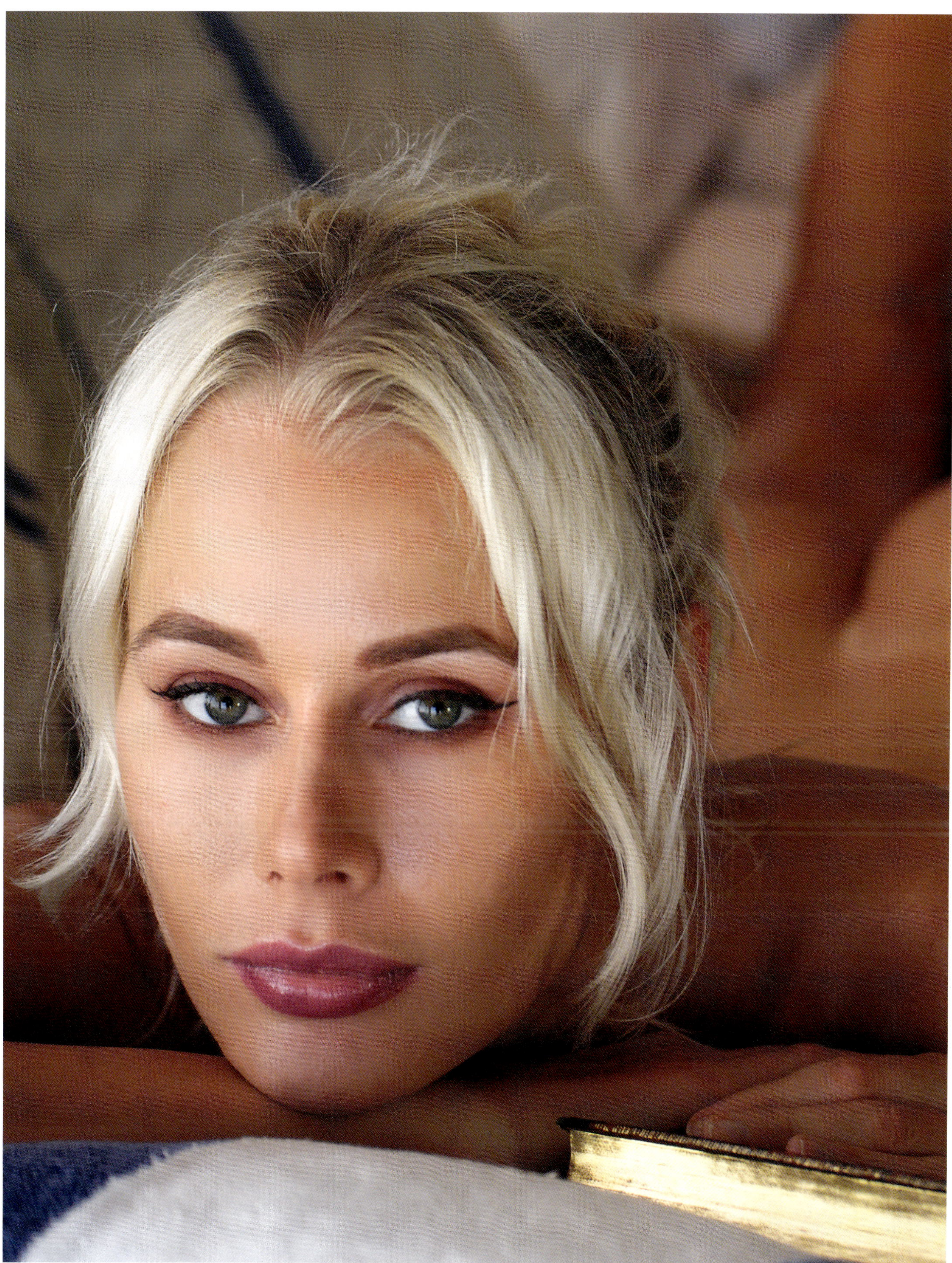

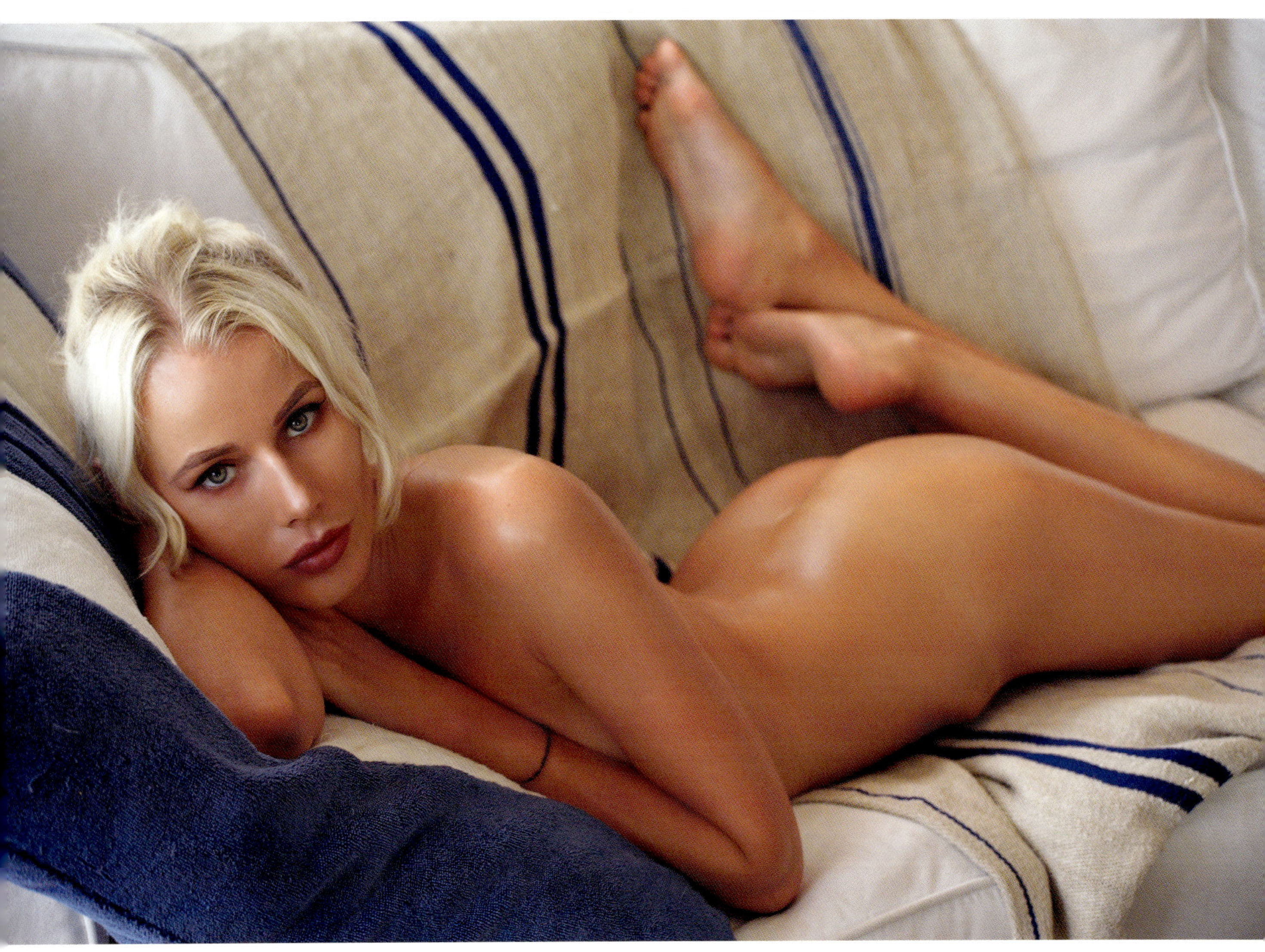

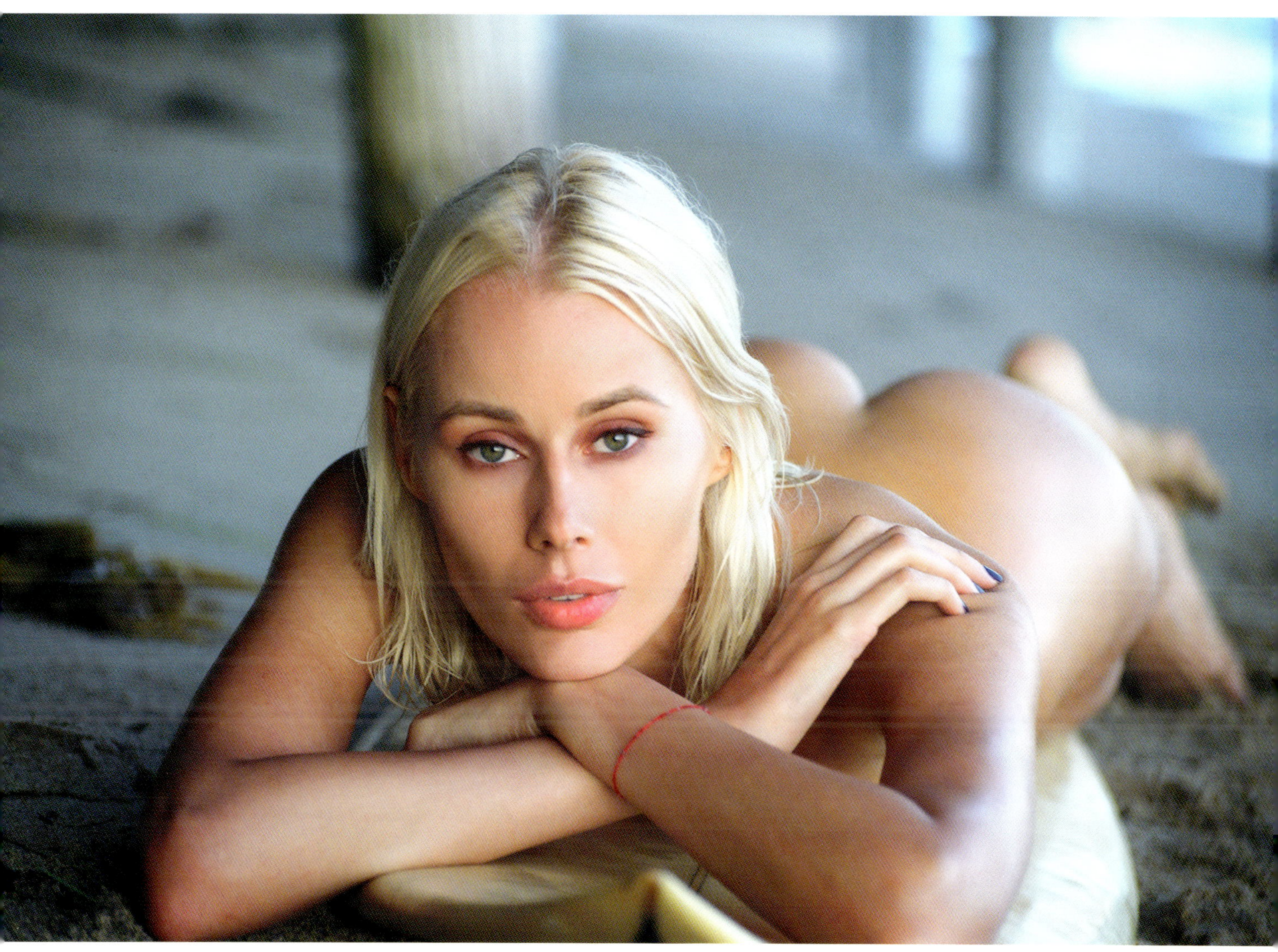

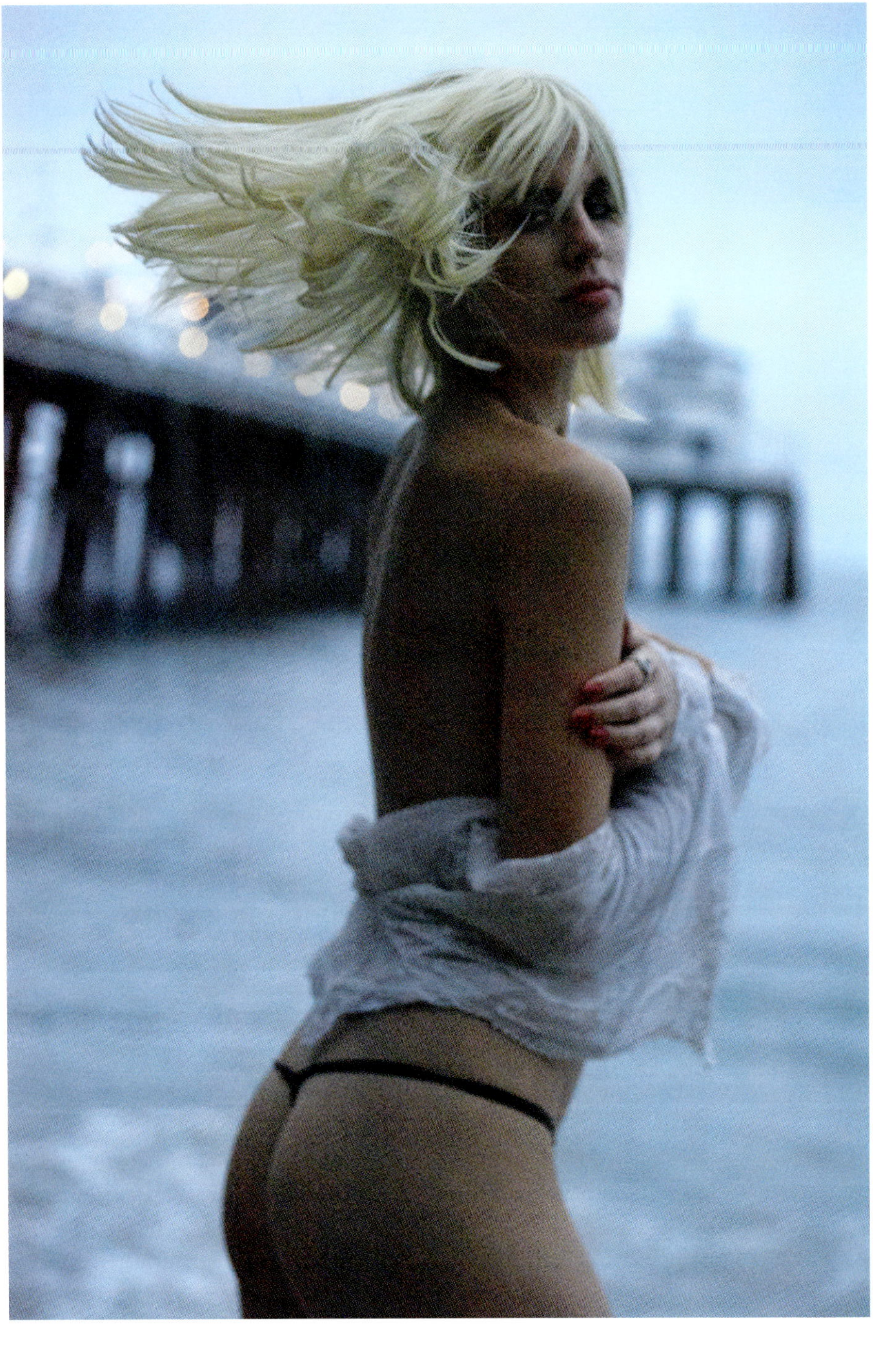

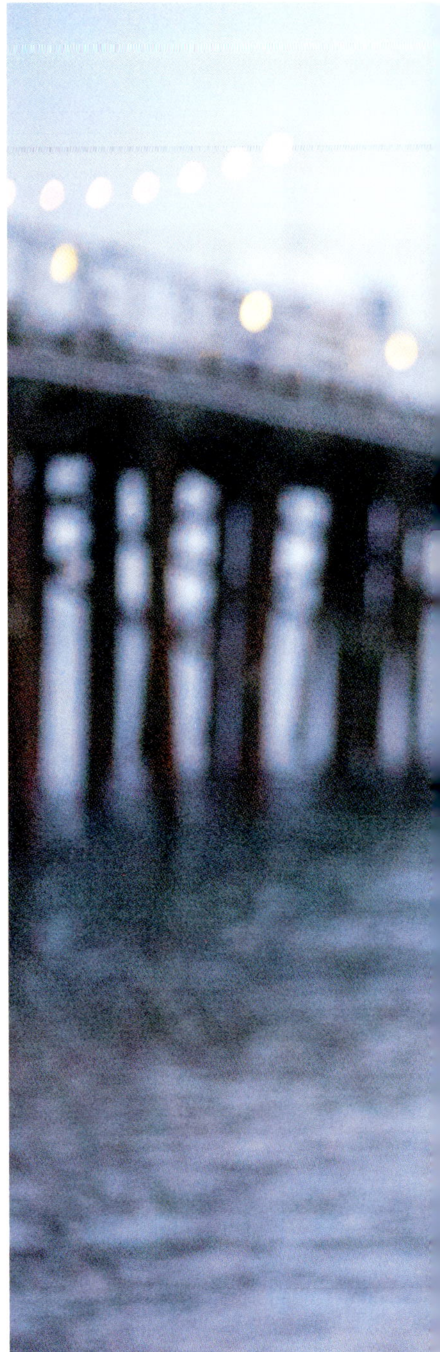

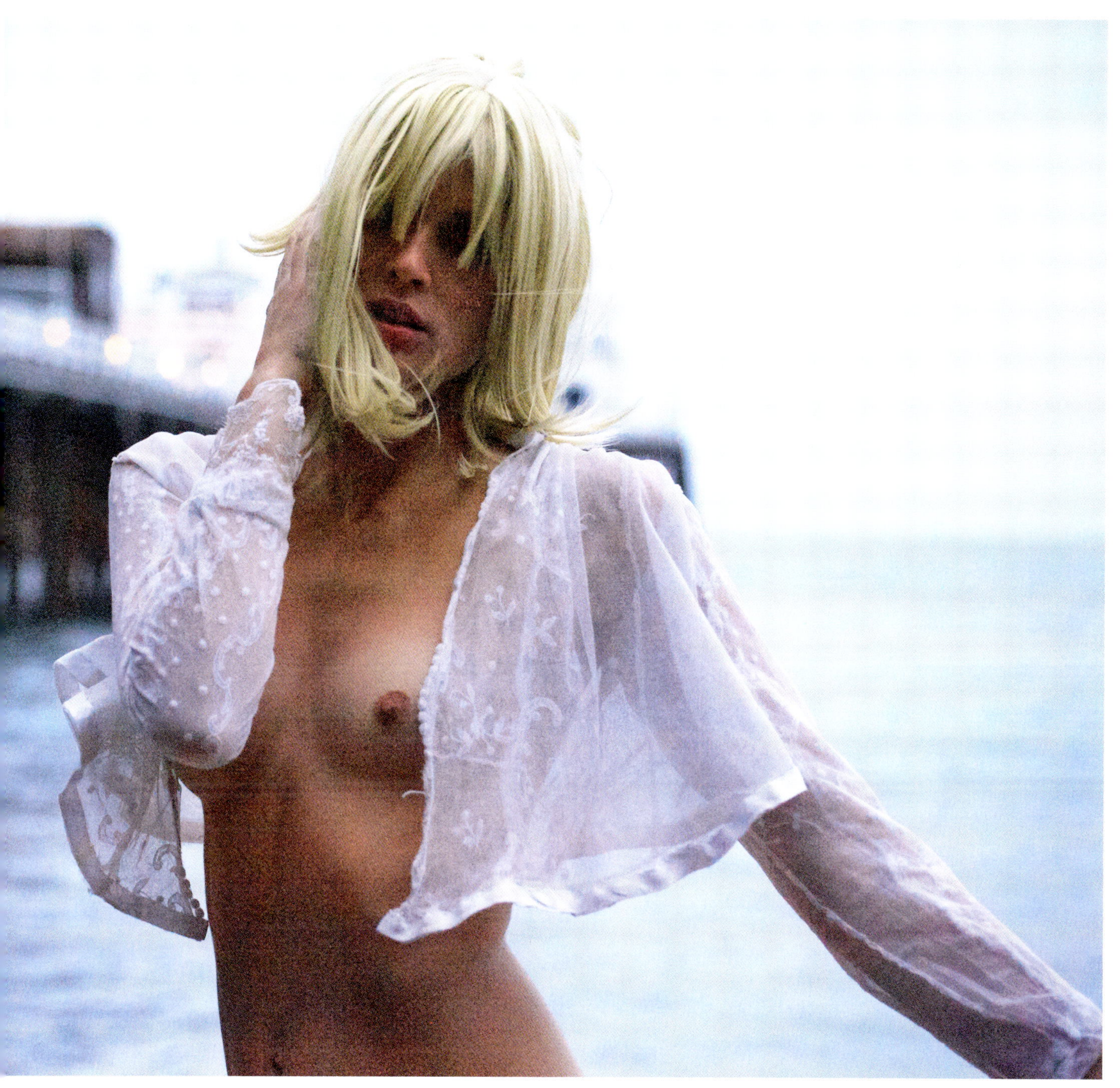

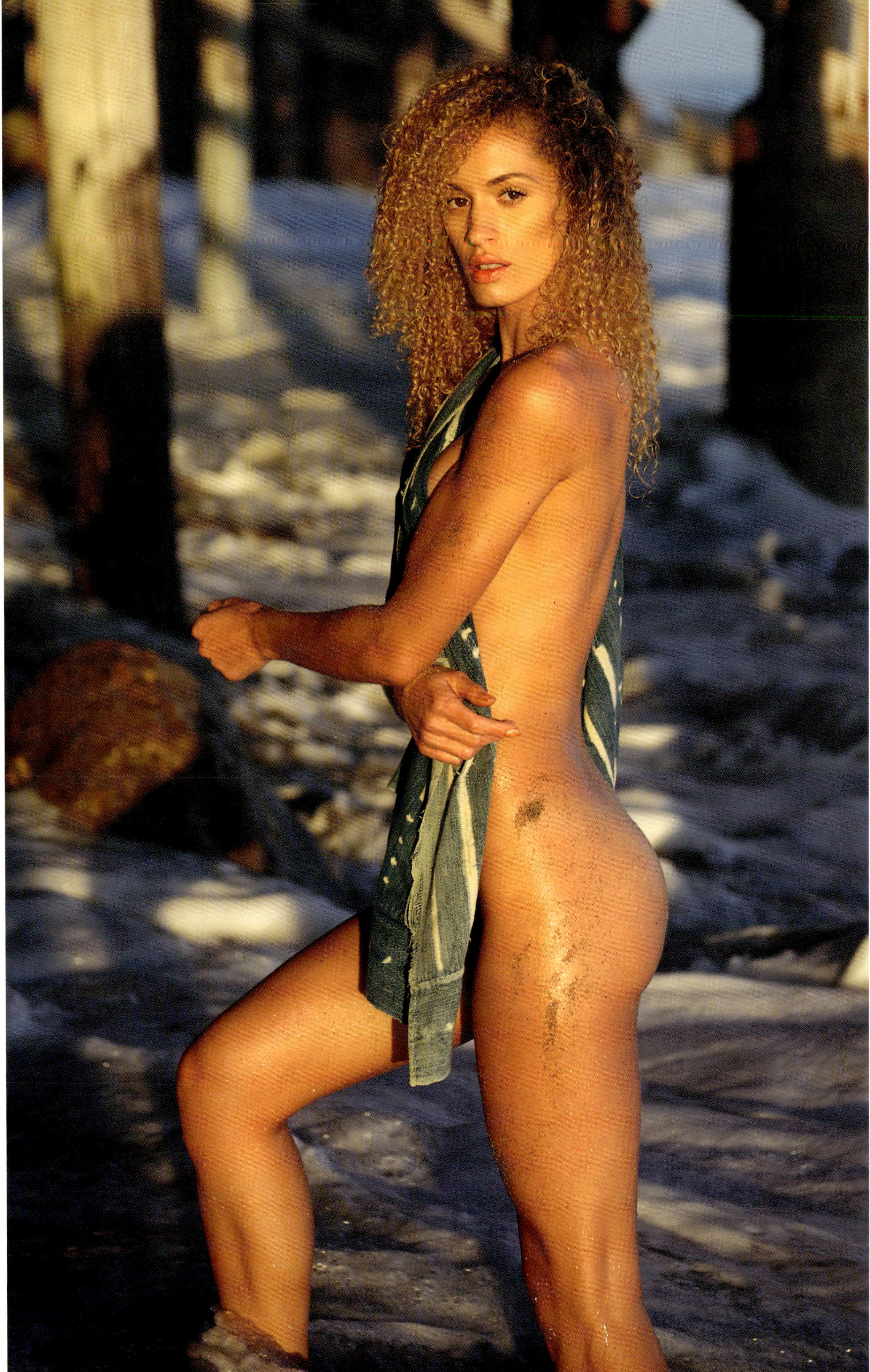

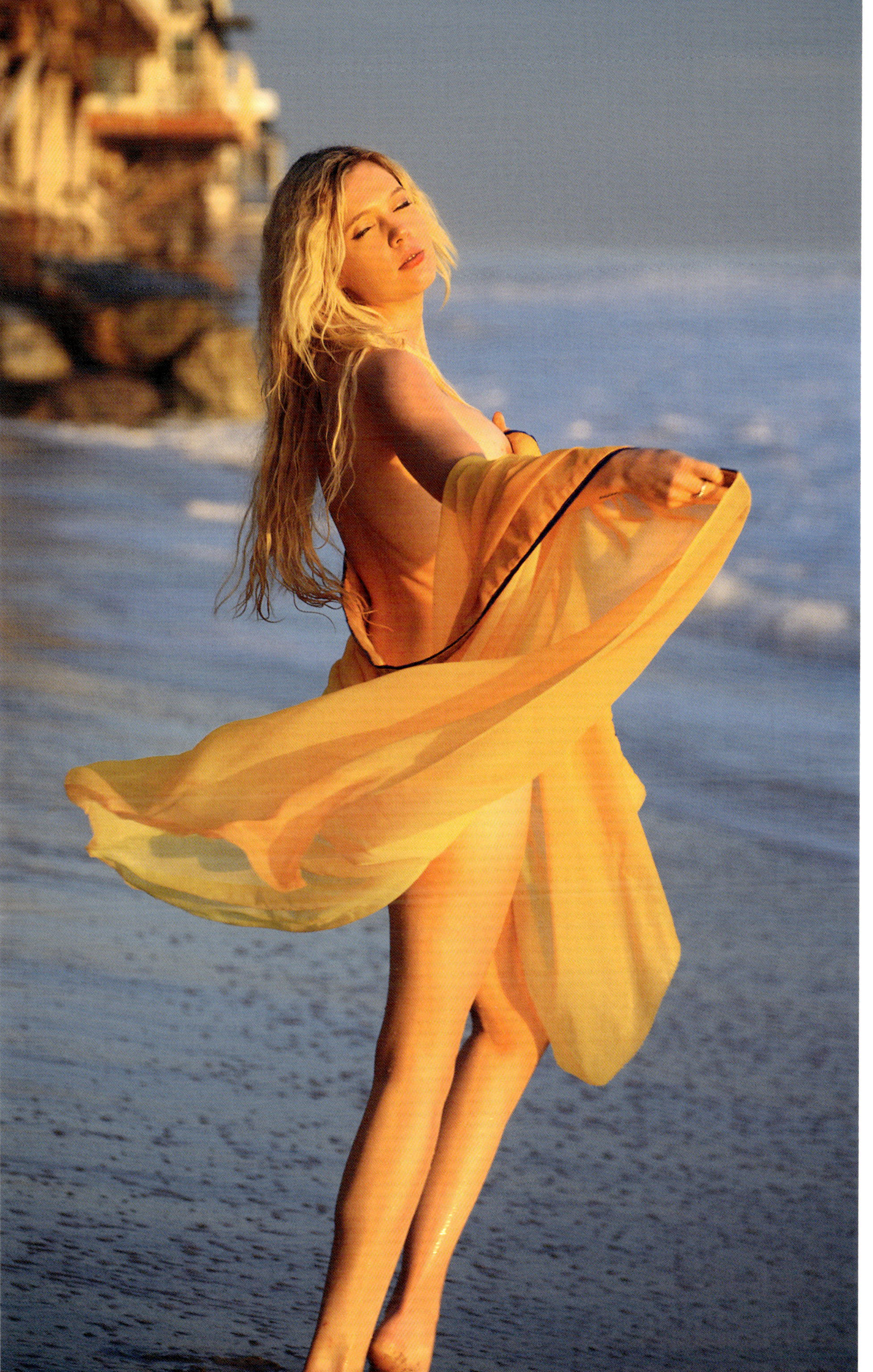

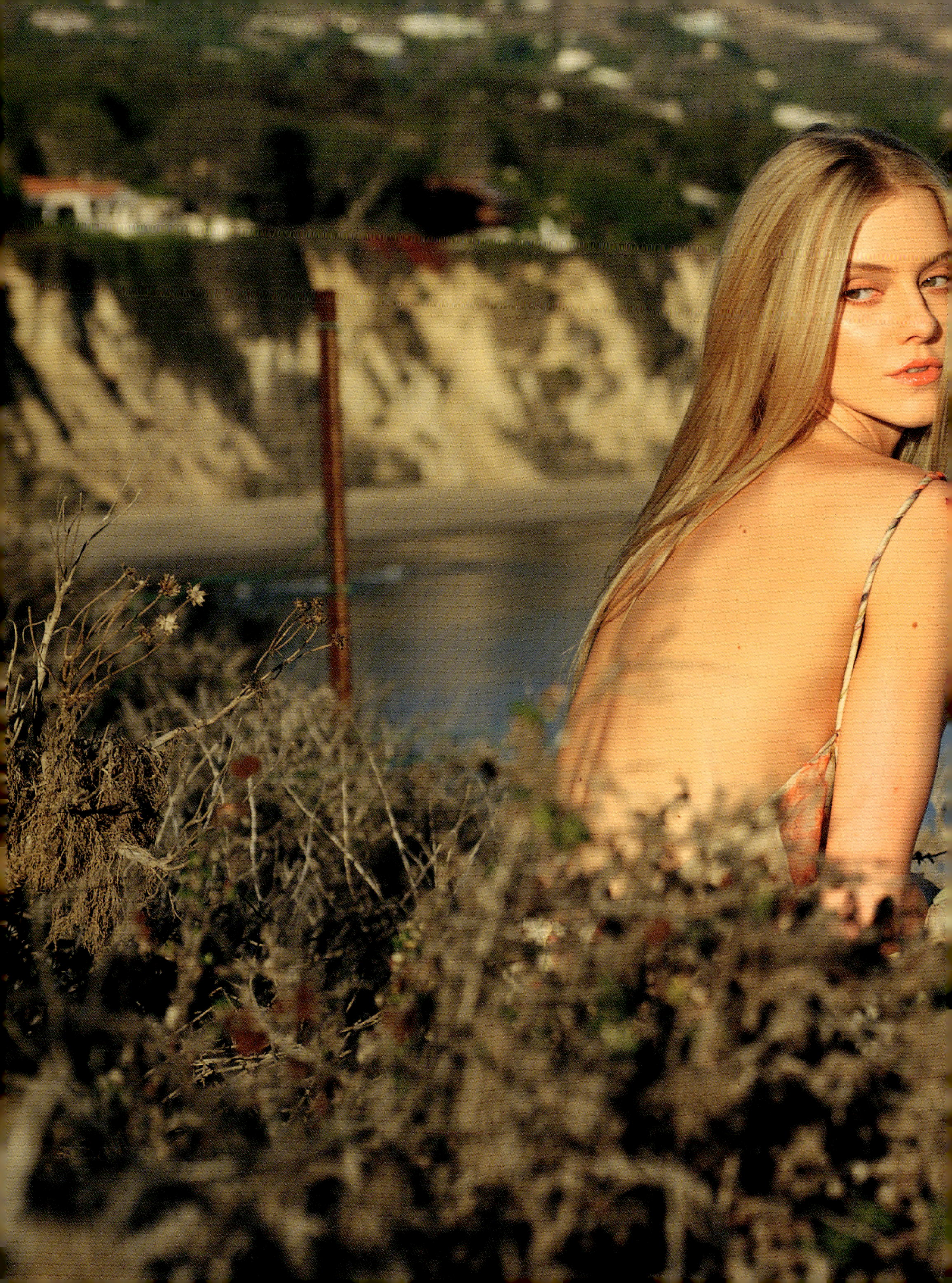

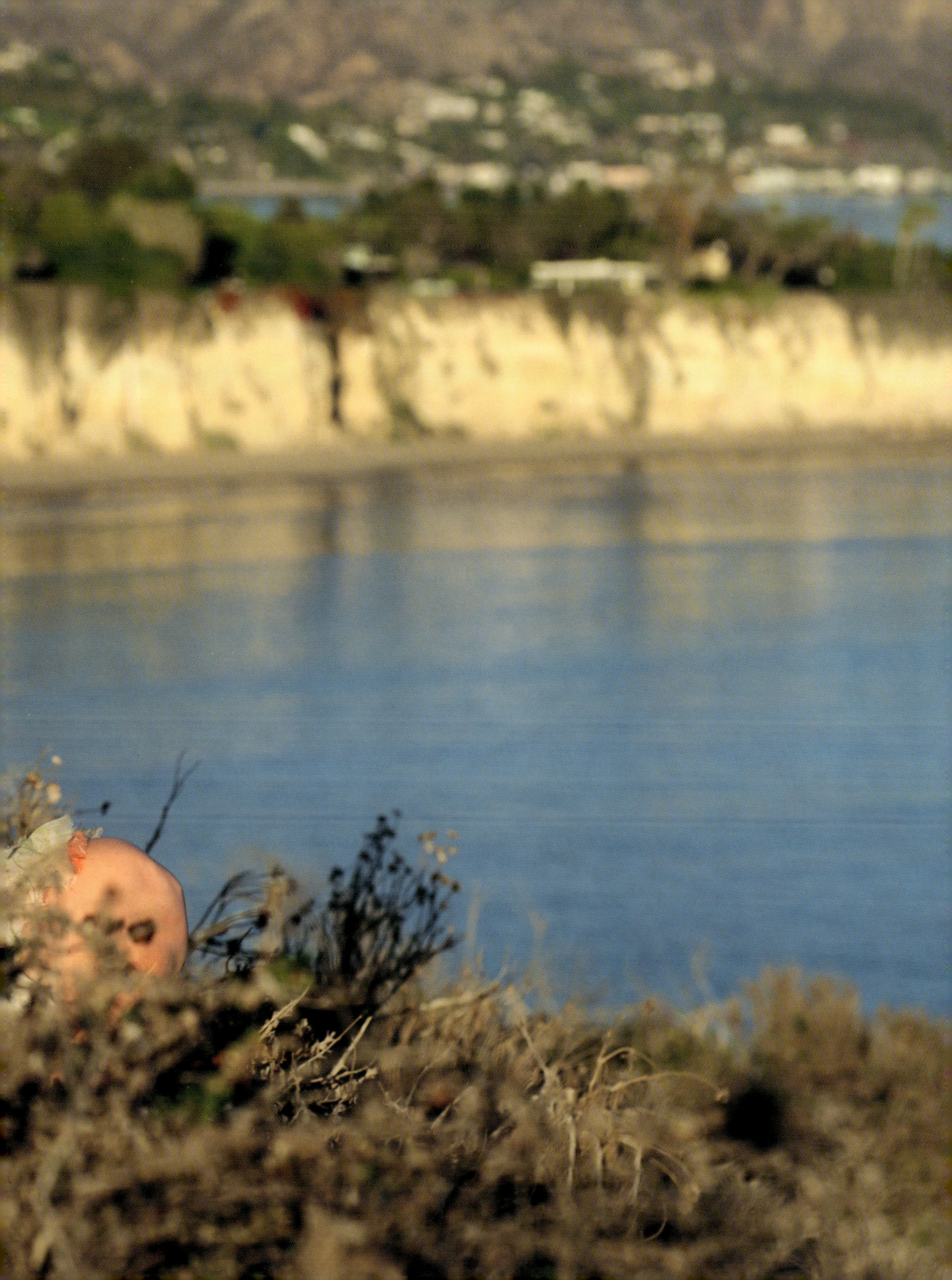

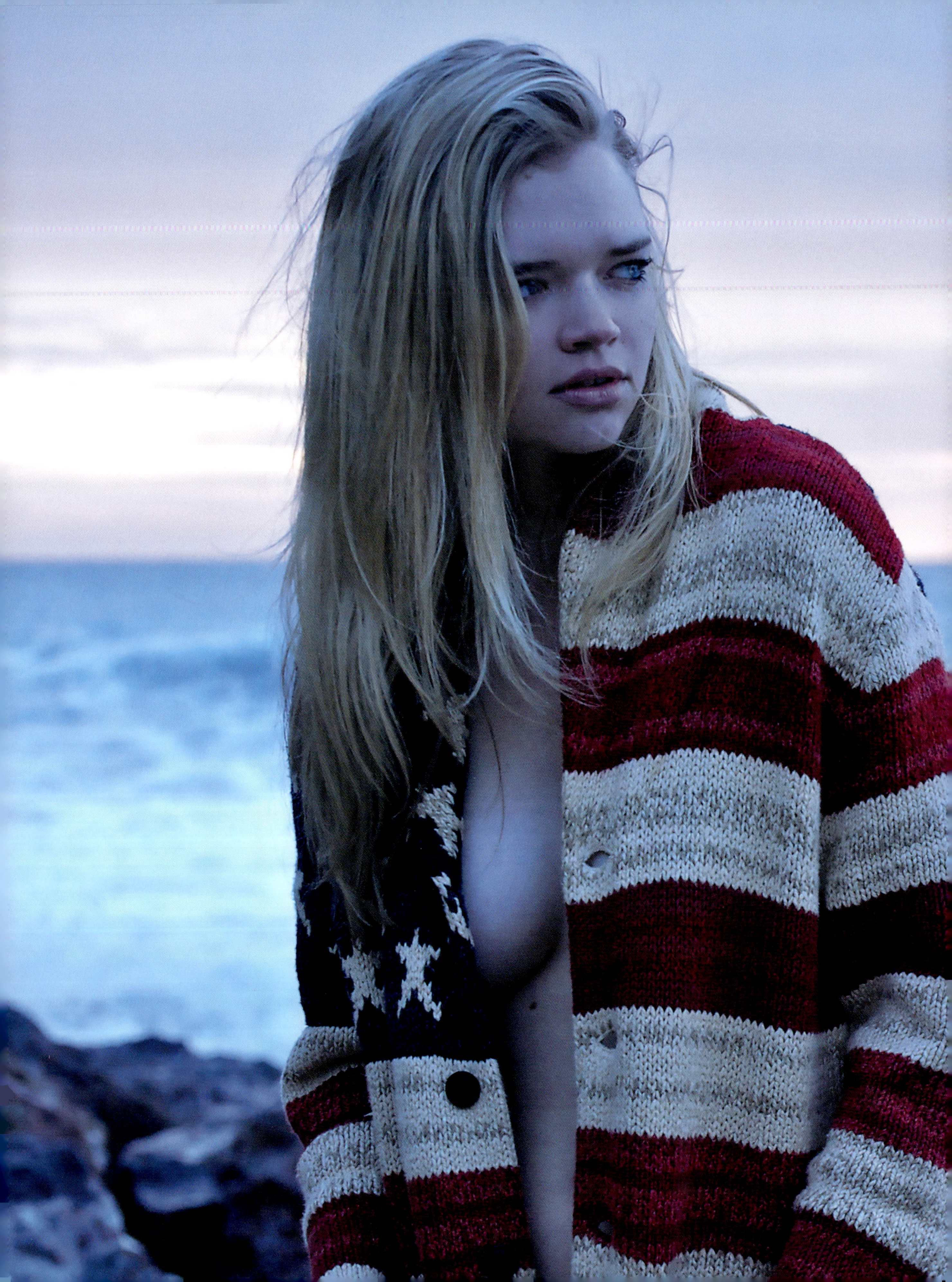

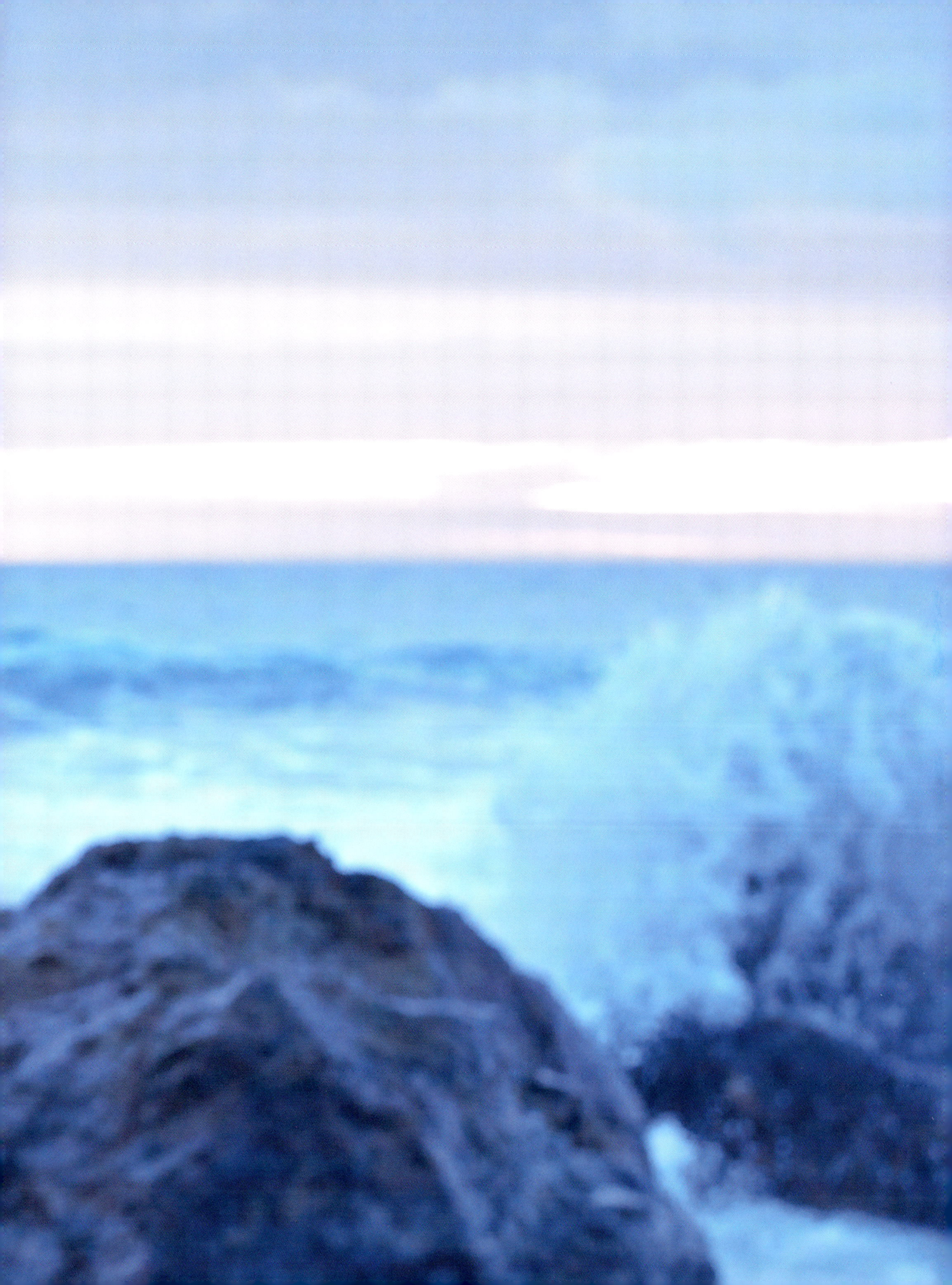

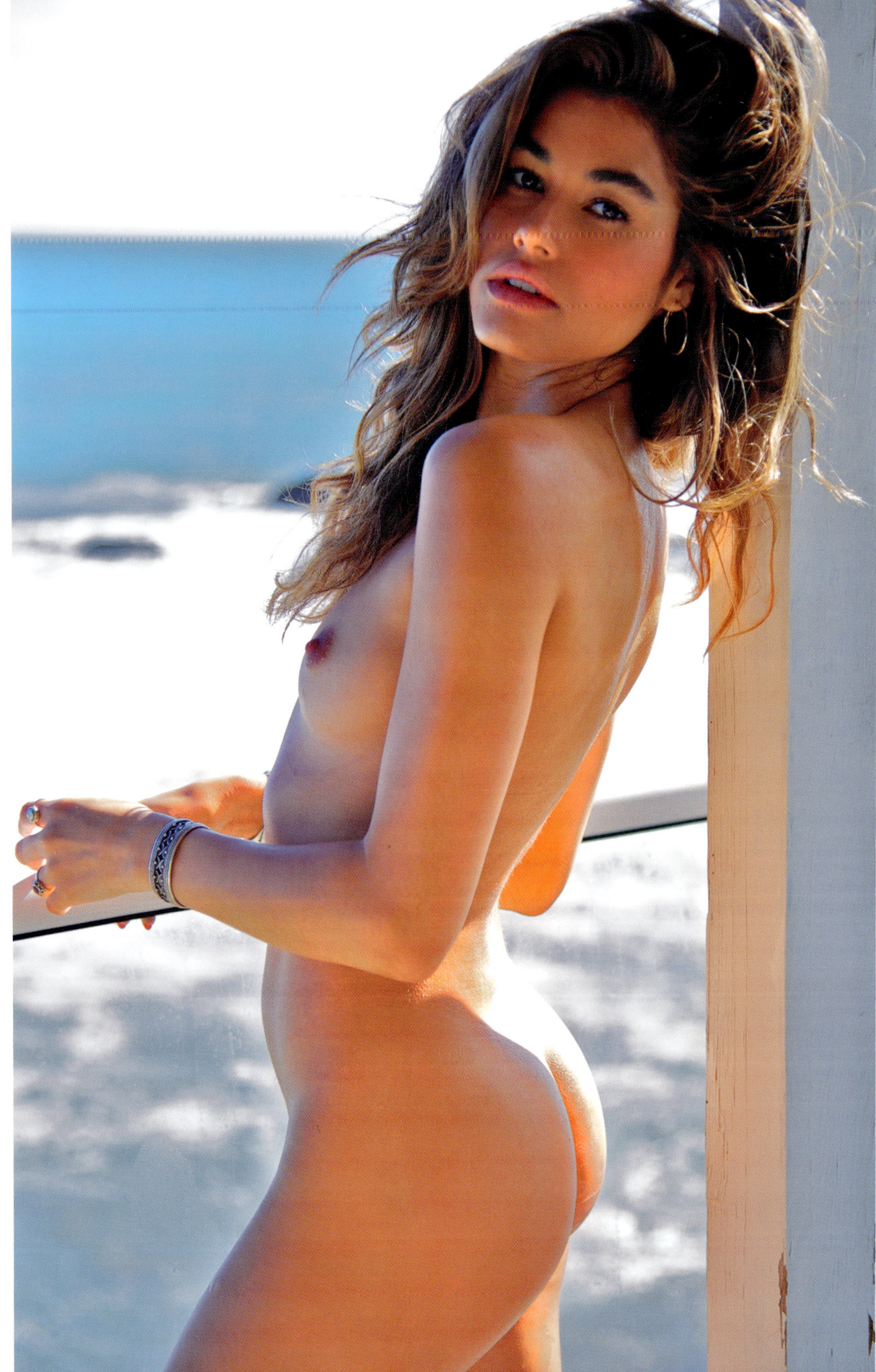

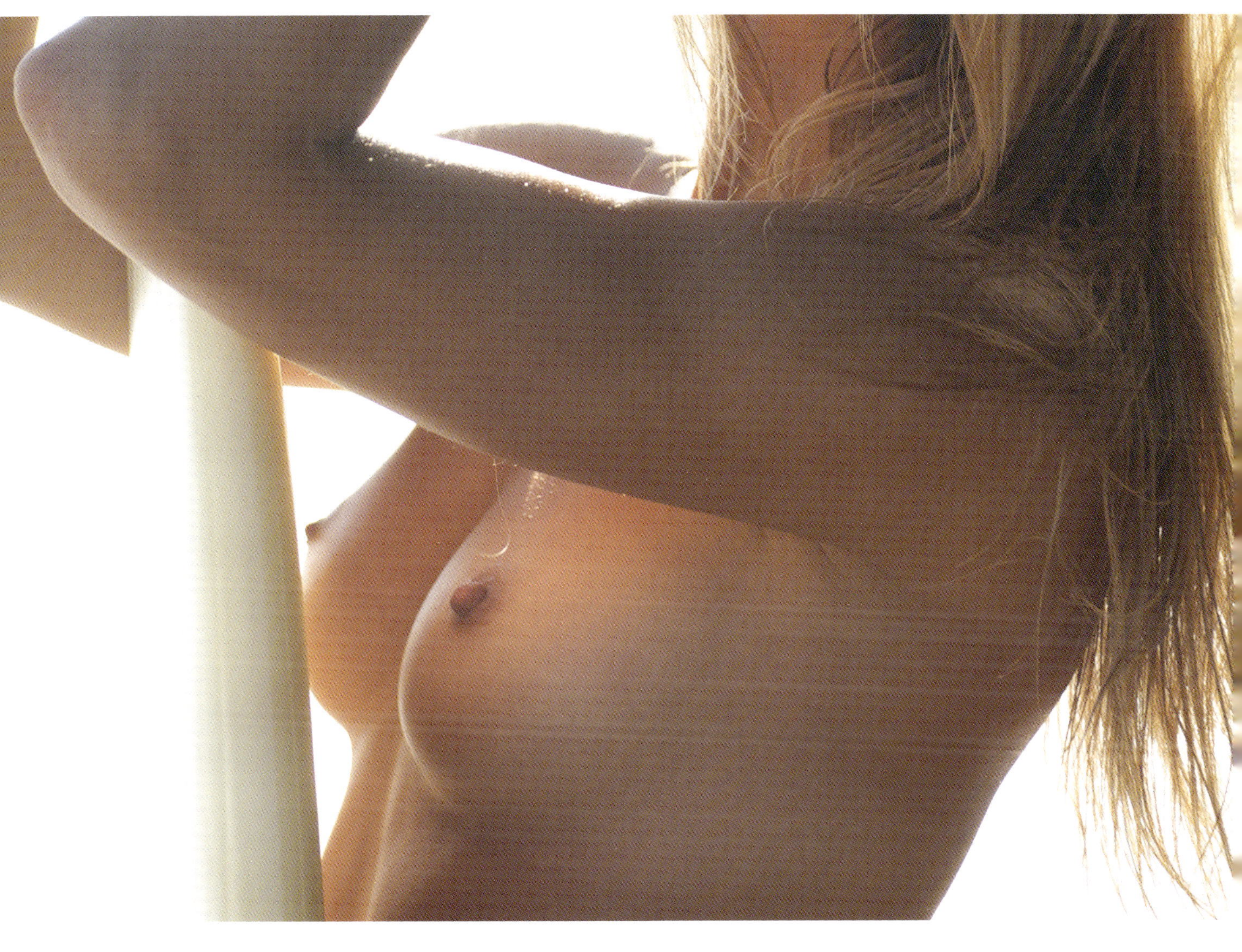

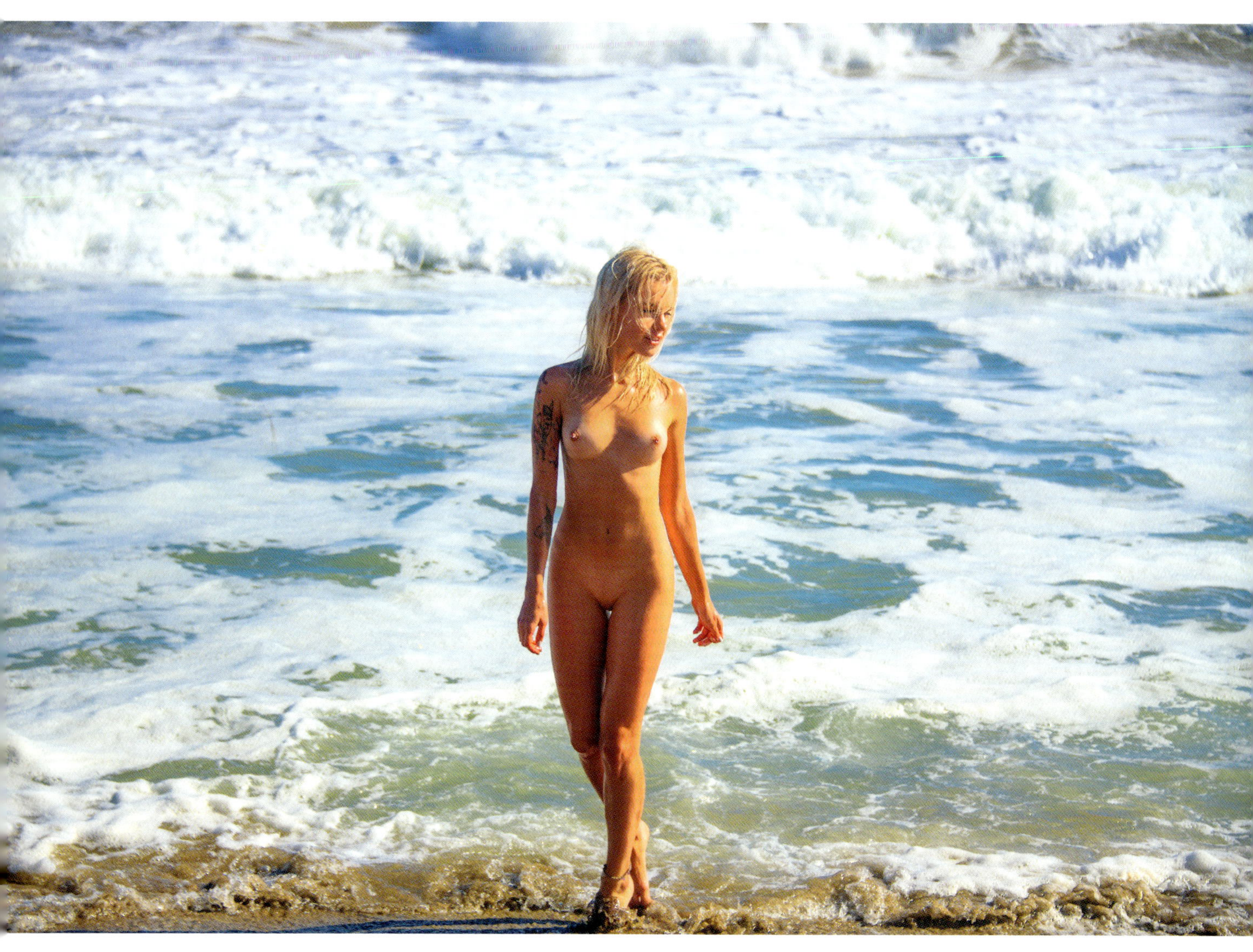

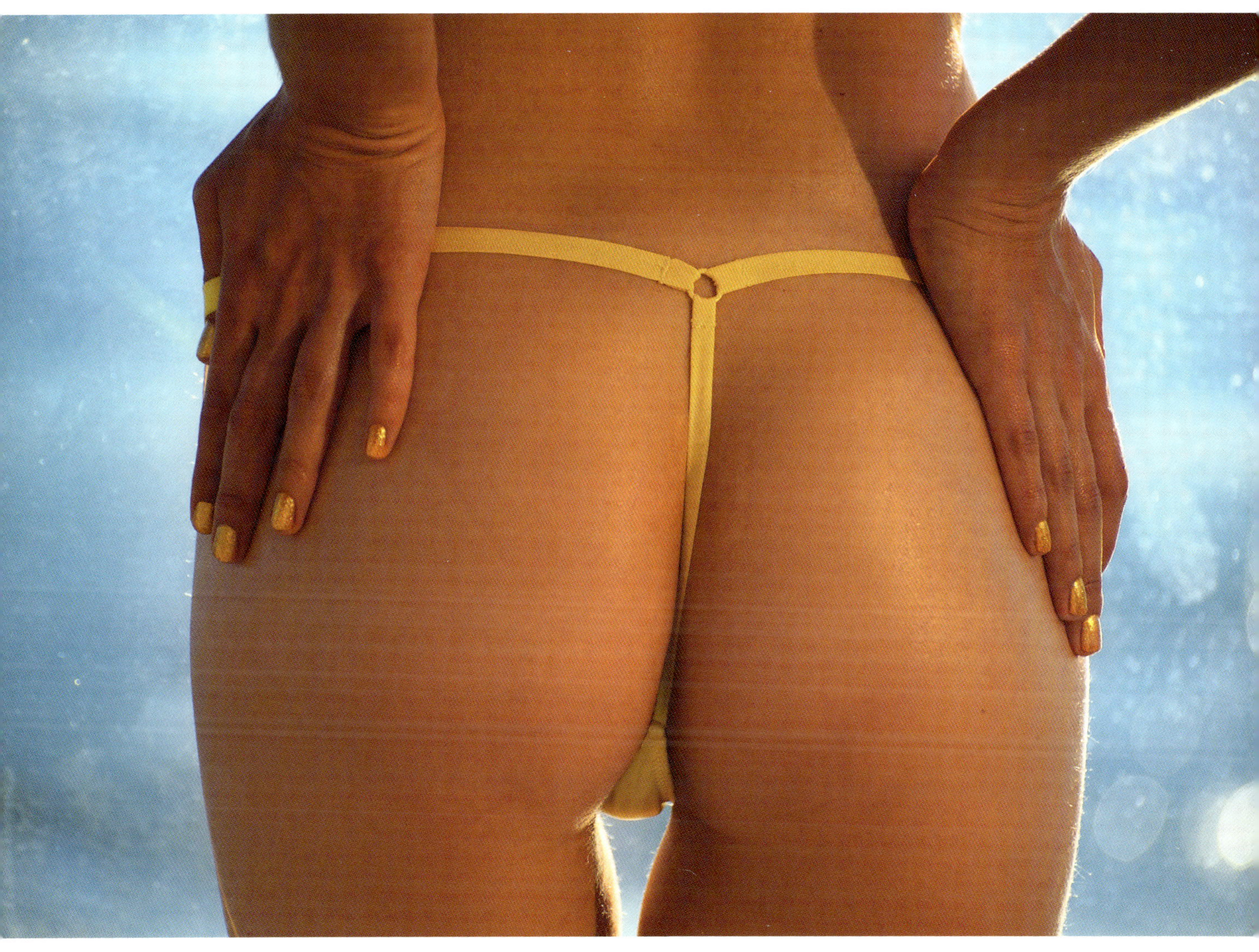

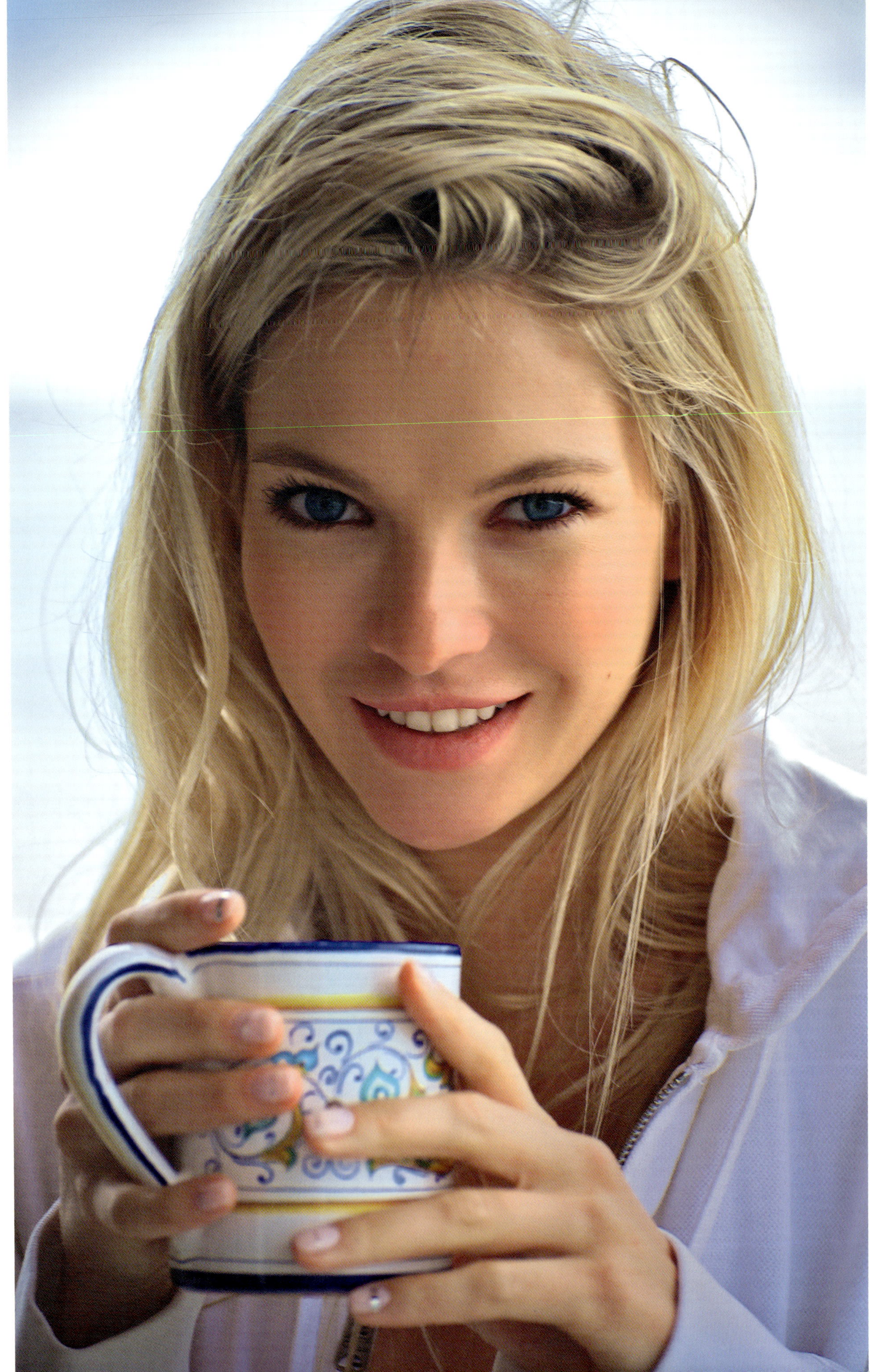

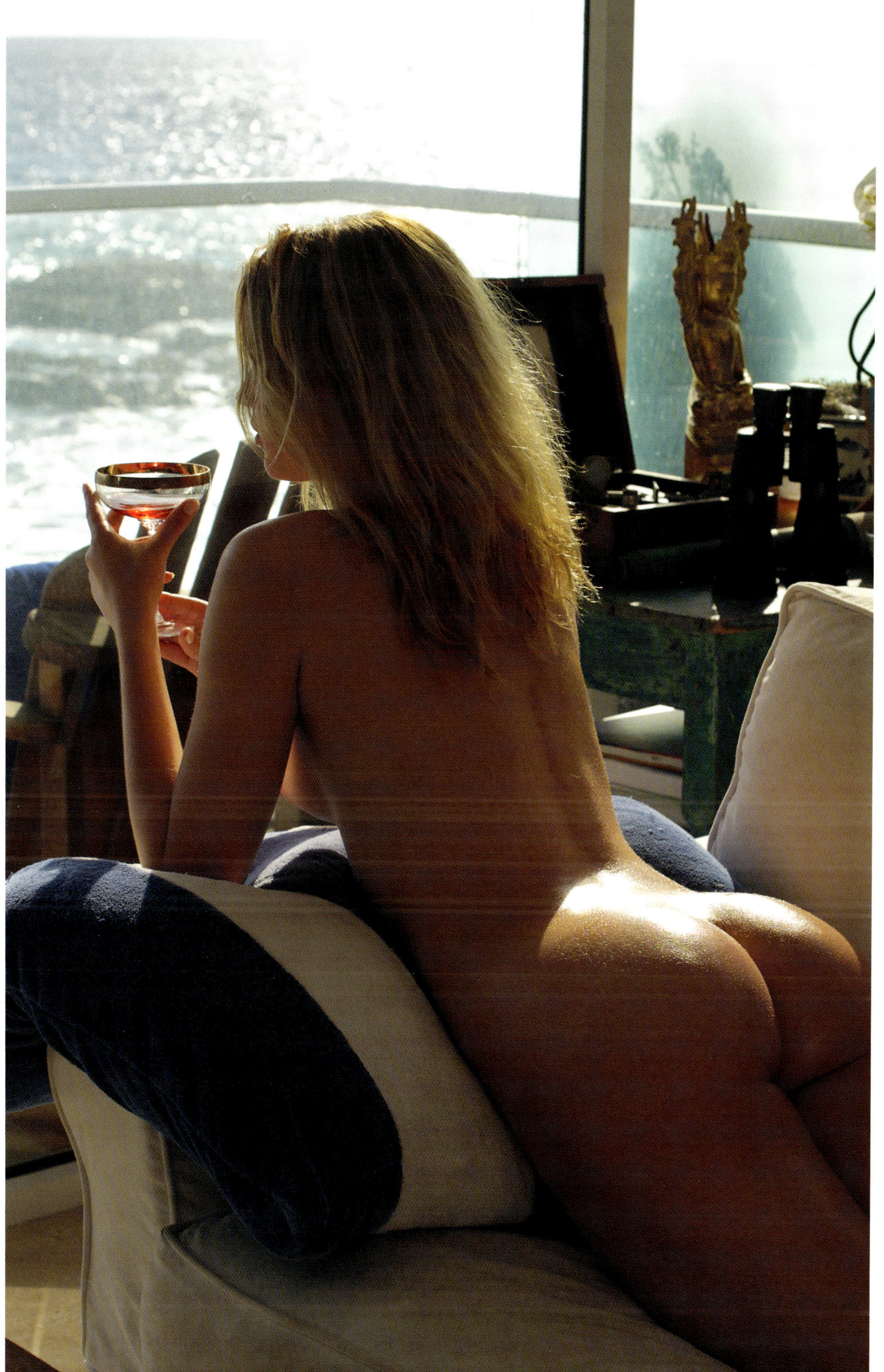

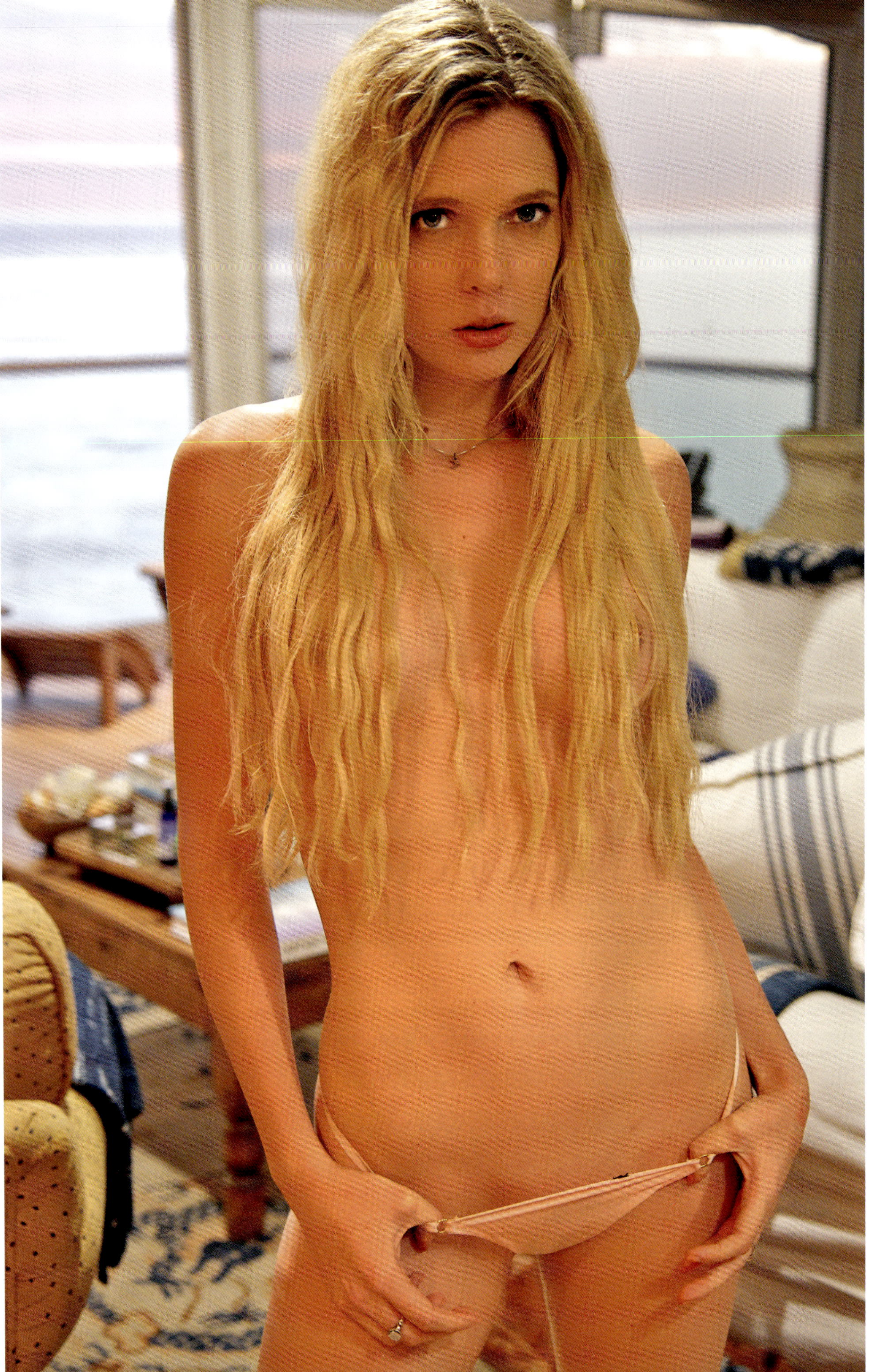

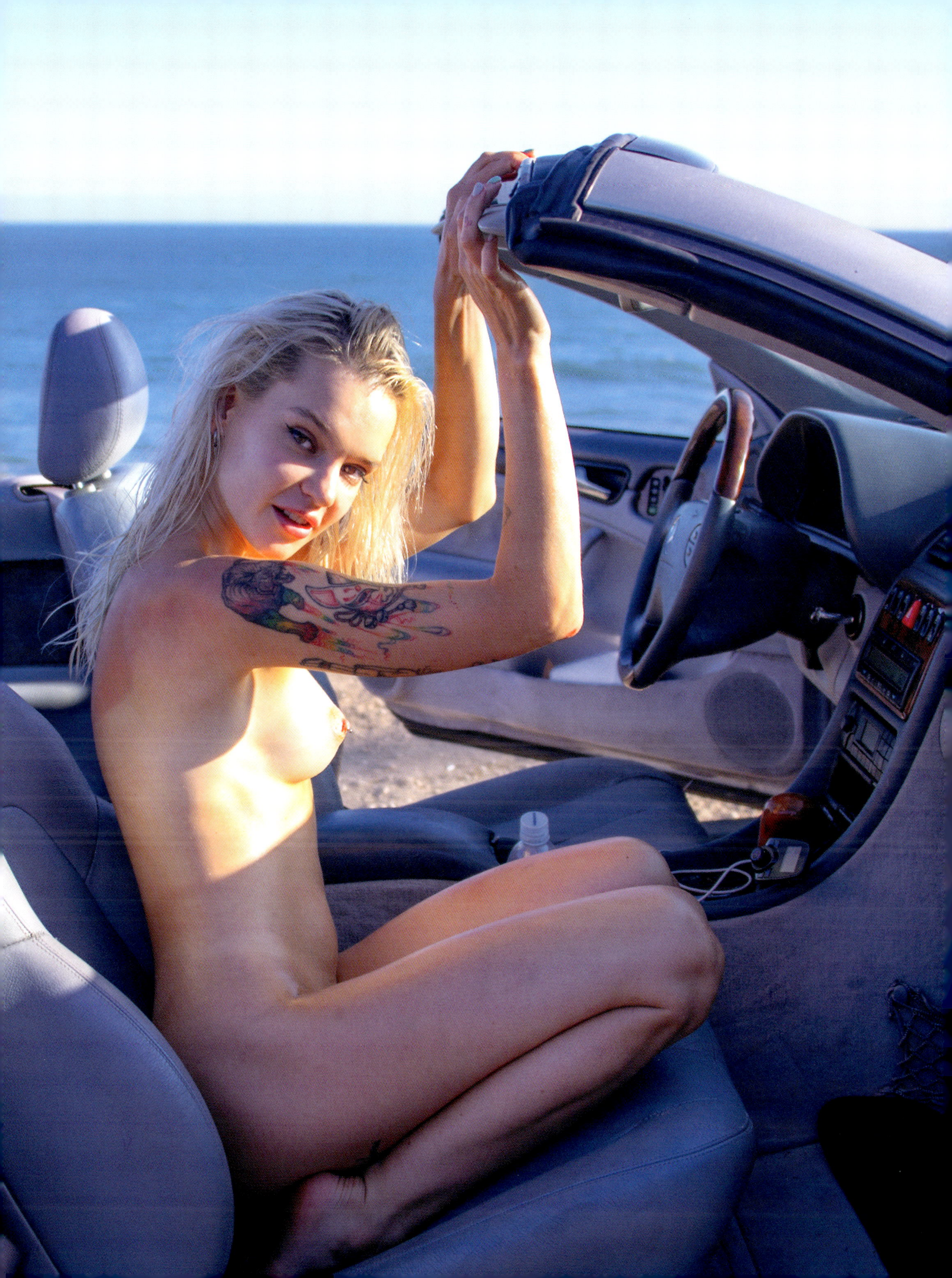

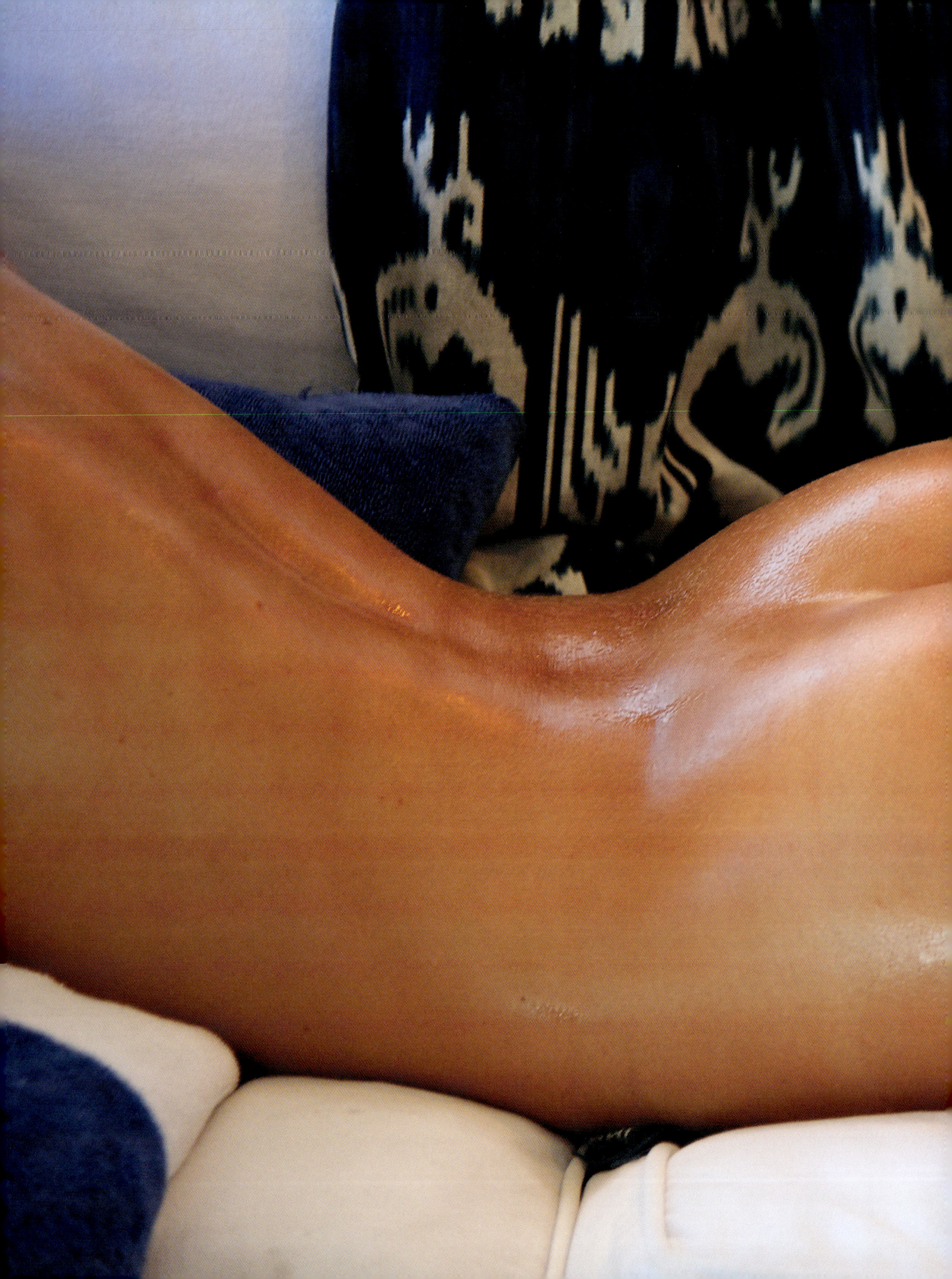

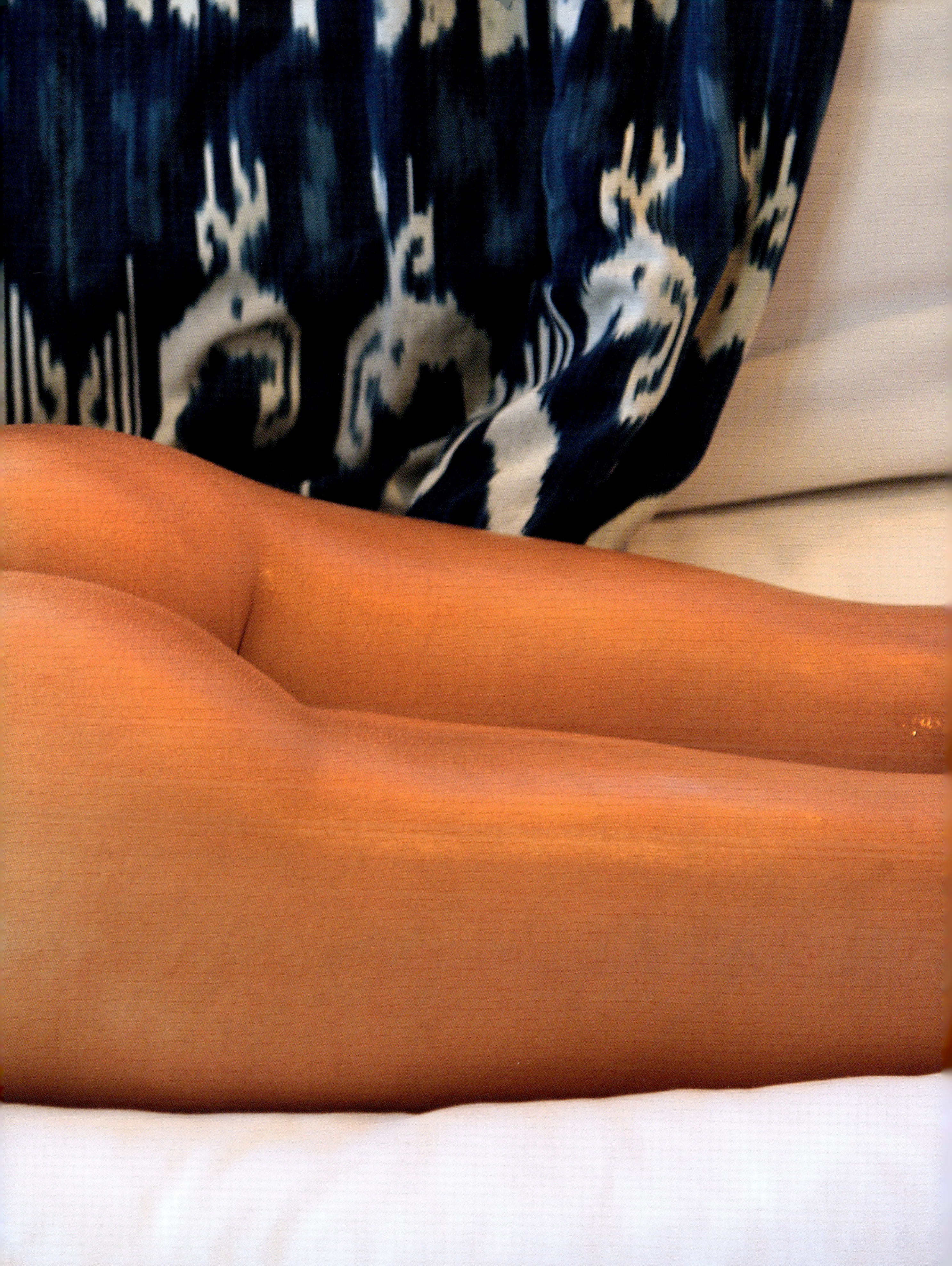

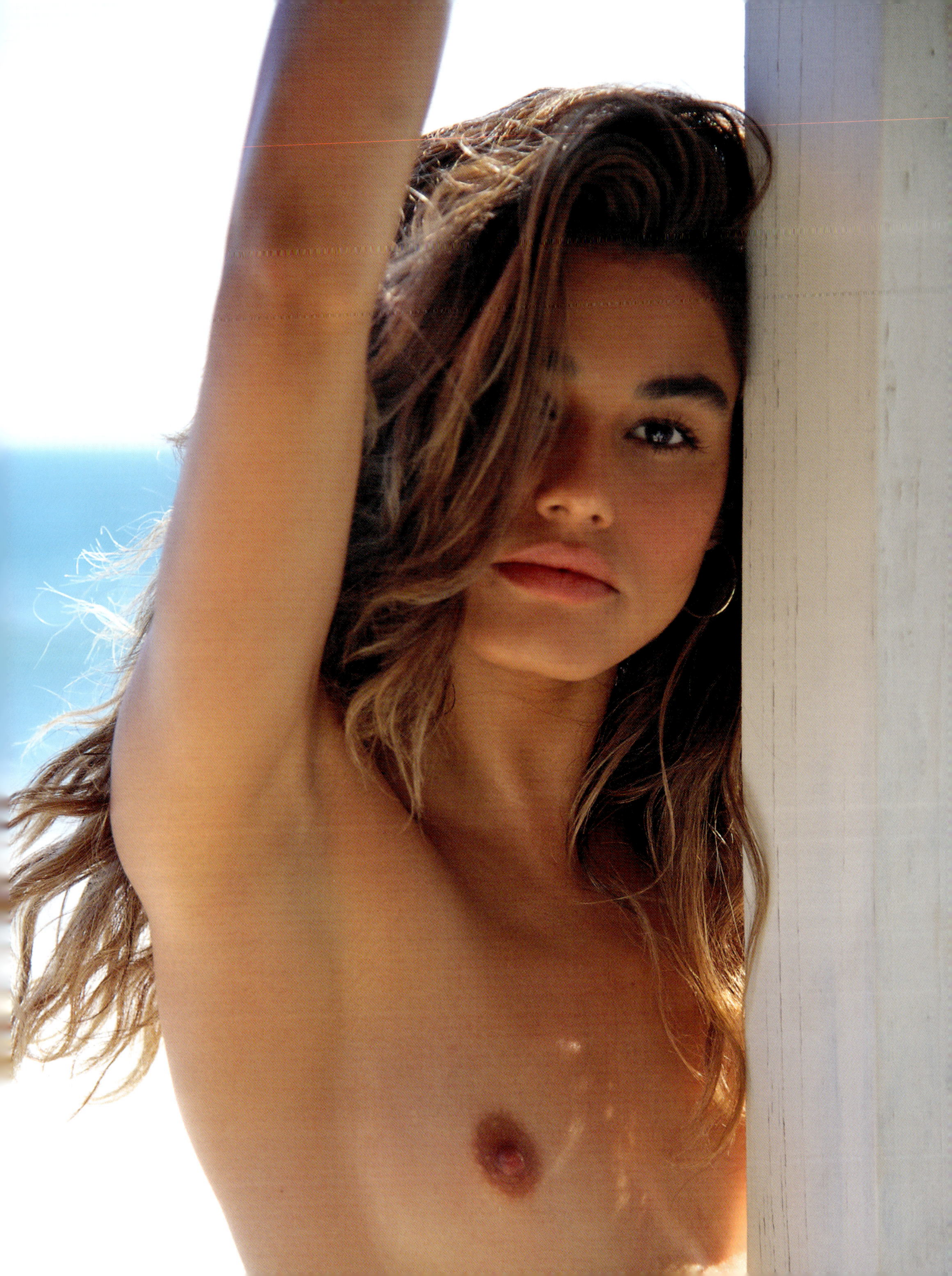

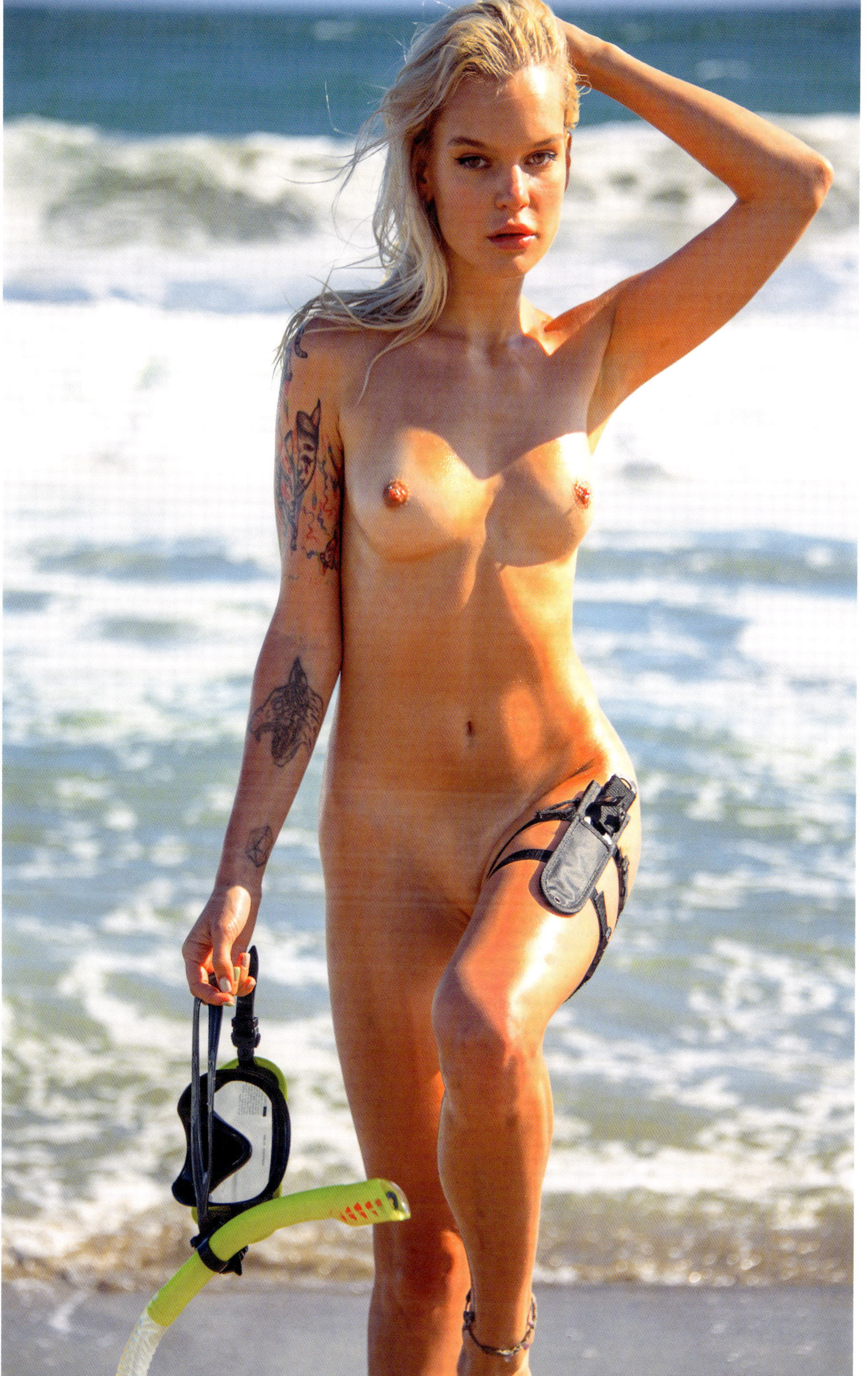

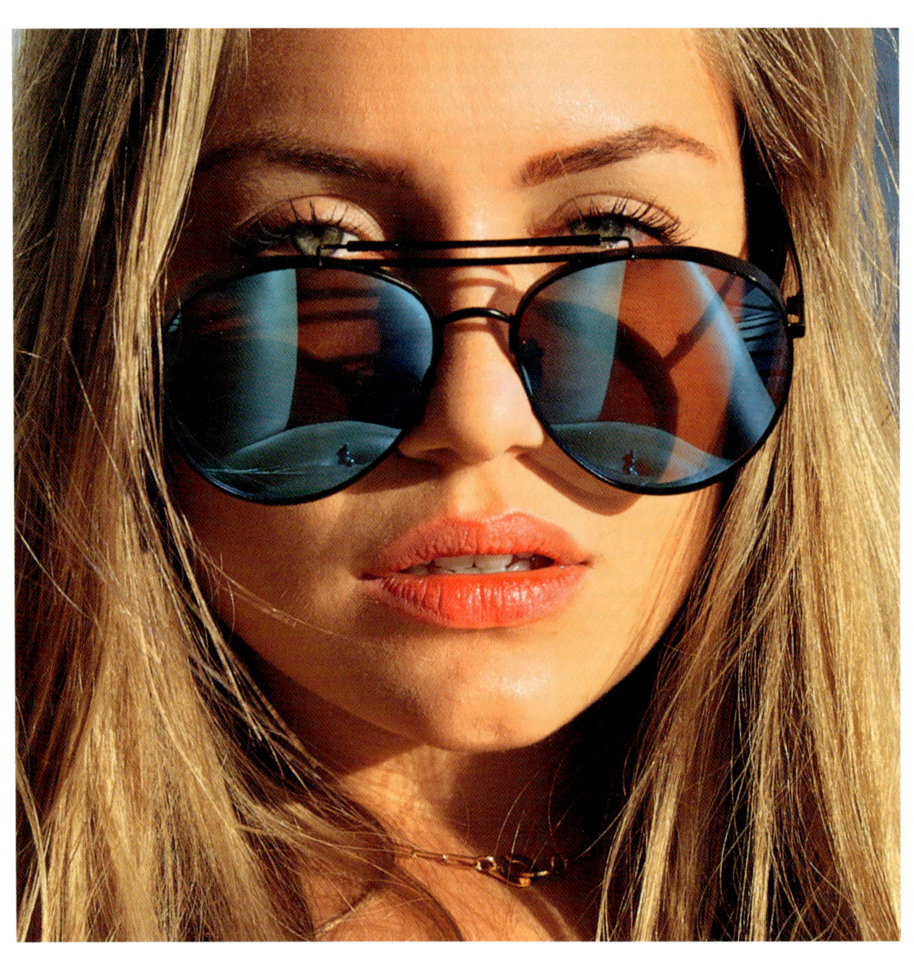

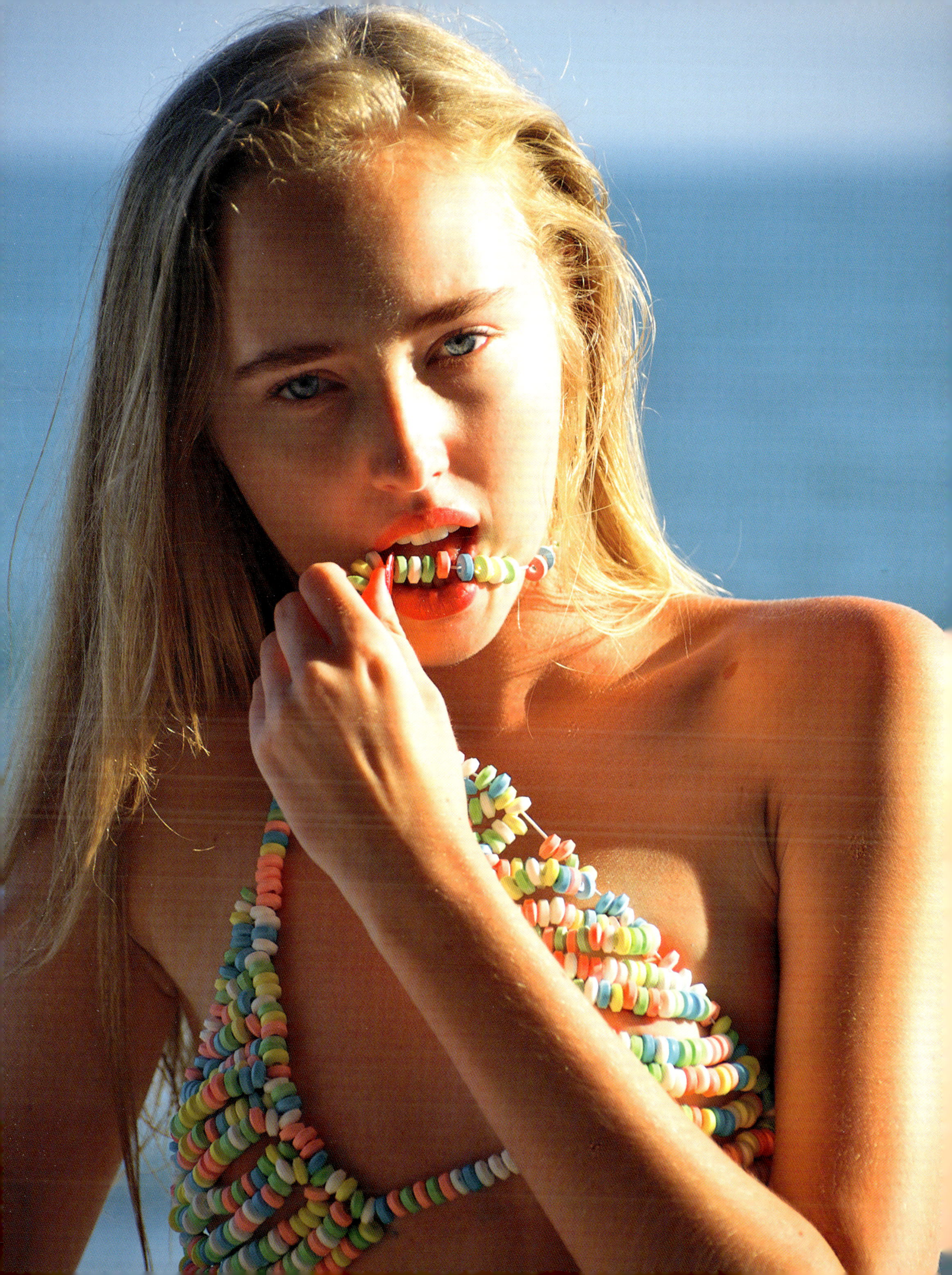

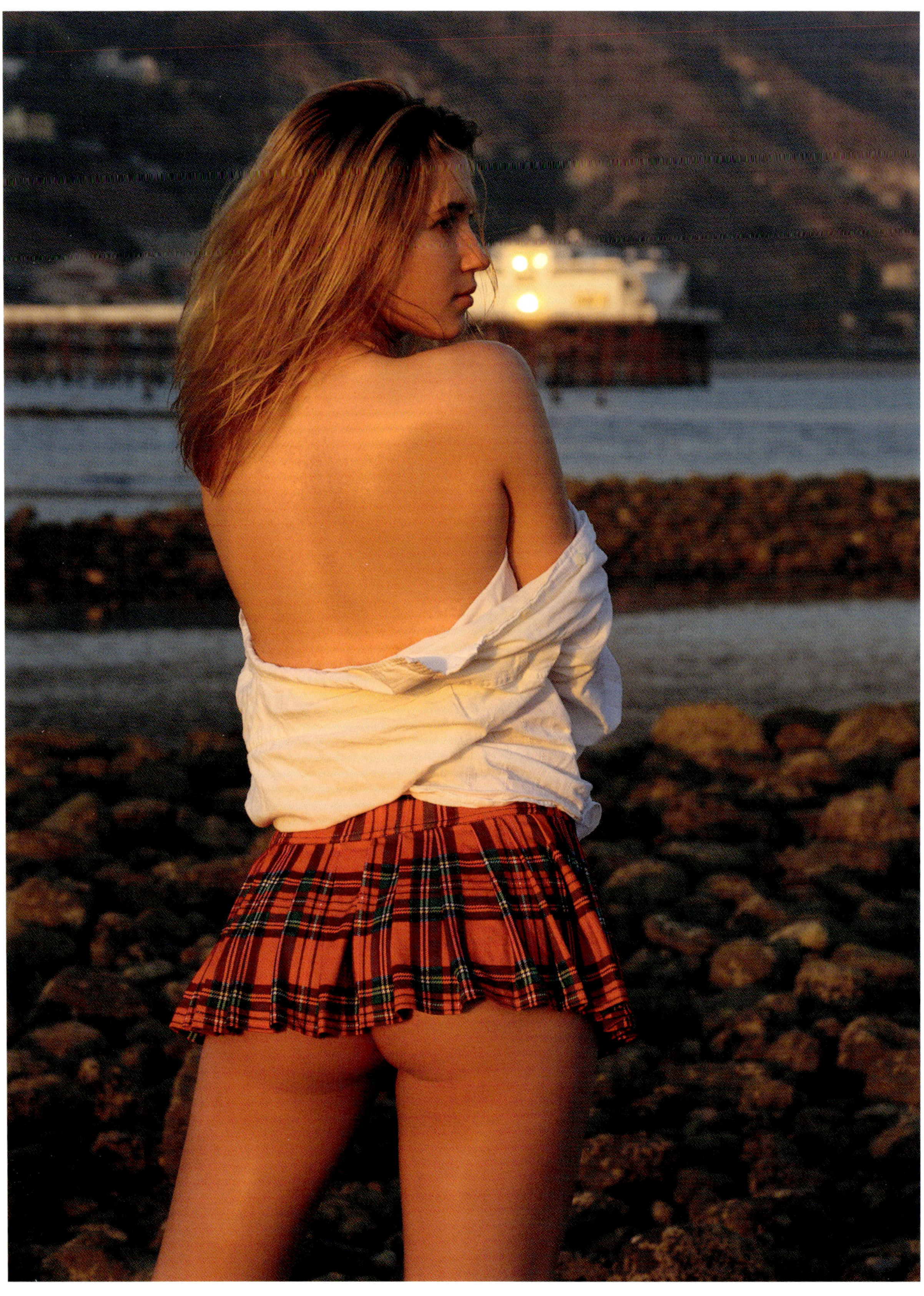

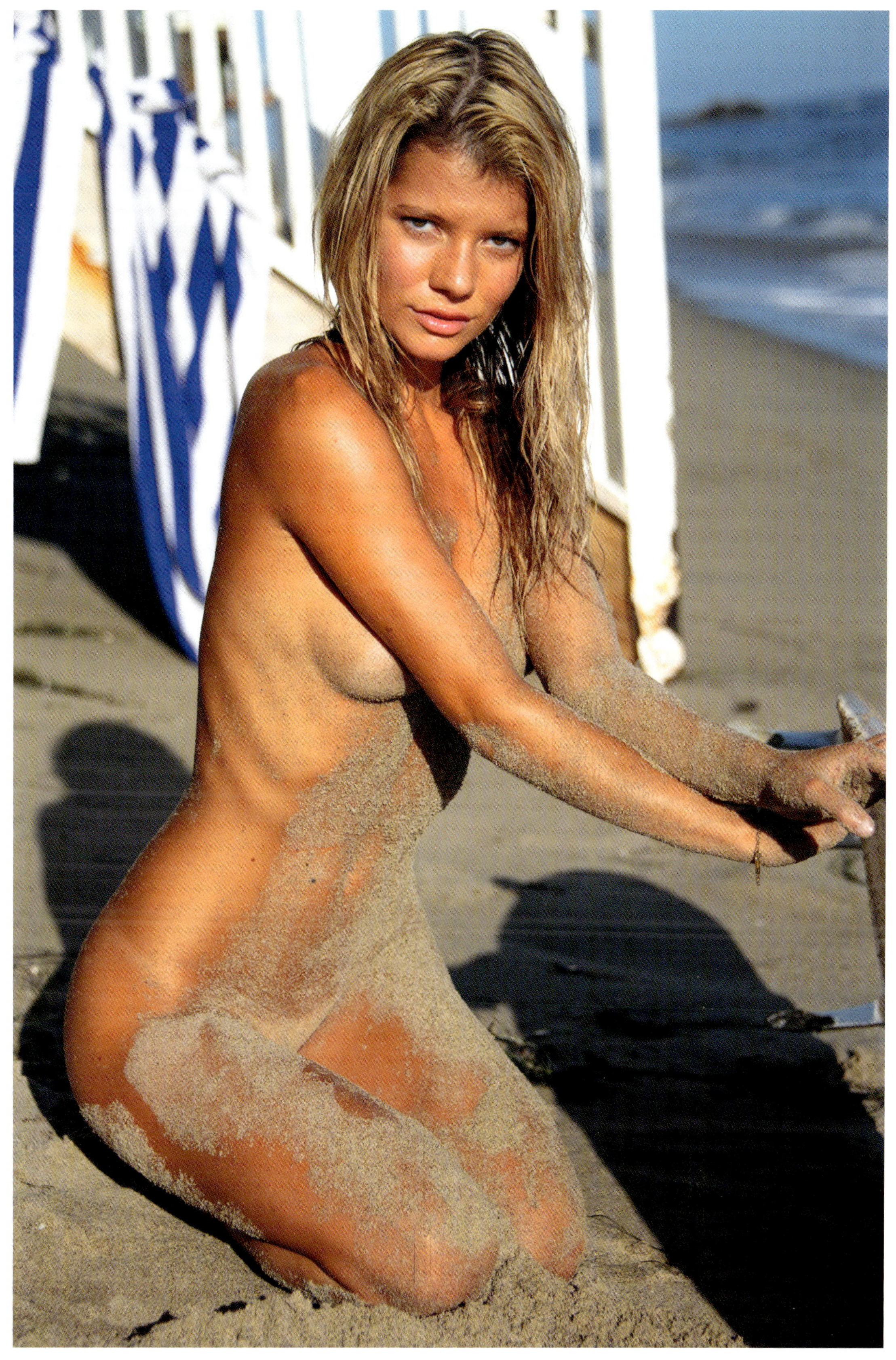

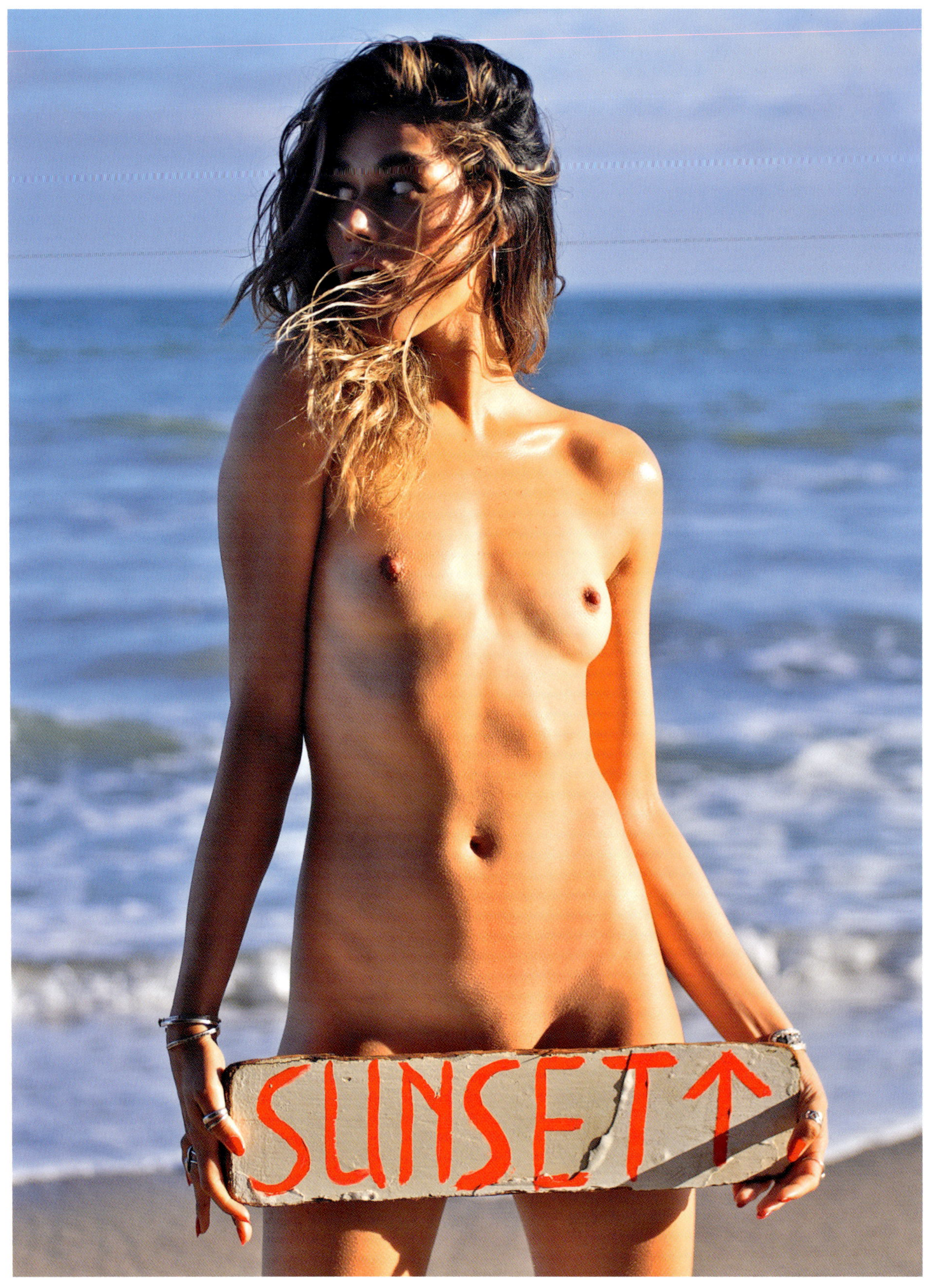
SUNSET ↑

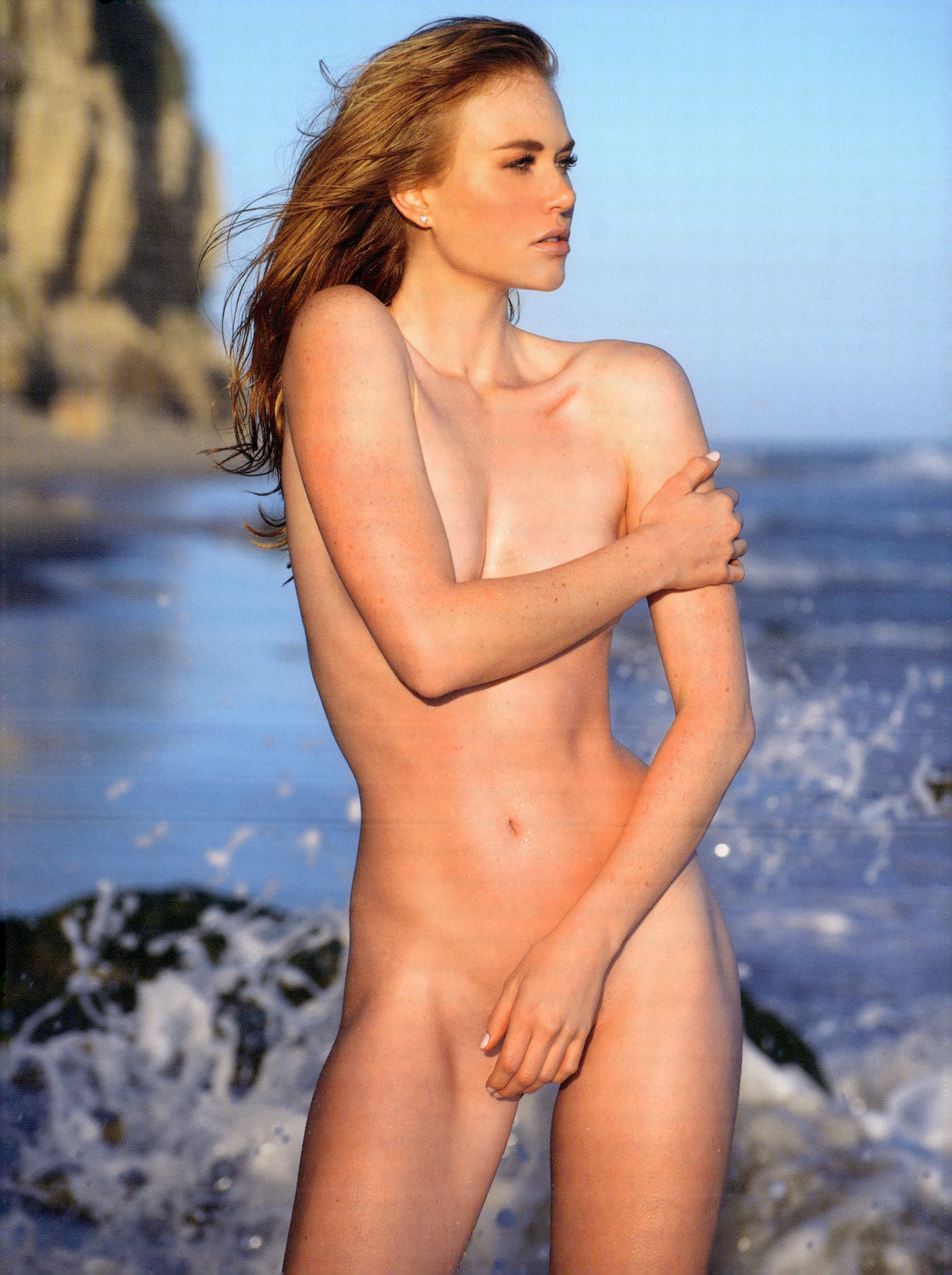

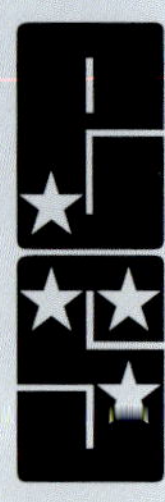

First Edition 2024
Copyright © 2024 by Edition Skylight

EDITION SKYLIGHT
Rosengartenstr. 13B
CH-8608 Bubikon/Zürich
Switzerland
info@edition-skylight.com
www.edition-skylight.com

ISBN 978-3-03766-691-3

Bibliographic information published by Die Deutsche Bibliothek
Die Deutsche Bibliothek lists this publication in the
Deutsche Nationalbibliografie; detailed bibliographic data
are available in the Internet at http://dnb.ddb.de.

Printed in Bosnia and Herzegovina

ALL PICTURES SHOT ON LOCATION IN MALIBU, CALIFORNIA

THE MODELS

Natalia Bardo
2, 90, 91, 144

Chloe Bednorz
82–83, 145, 154

Hailey Beth
20, 22–23, 24, 52, 120–121, 122, 153

Arianna Cardé
134

Eva Crone
7, 86, 87, 152

Elle Evans
6, 40–41, 136–137

Shelby Ferguson
112, 113, 114, 115

Evgeniia Frank
54–55, 56, 57, 126–127, 128, 129, 130, 131, 148–149

Holly Good
138–139

Emma Gradin
84, 85, 123, 124,125

Selma Hadziosmanovic
60, 61, 62, 63, 64–65, 66–67

Andrea Helencikova
32, 33, 34, 35, 36, 99, 100, 101, 141

Chloe Holmes
37, 53

Julia Logacheva
50, 51, 70, 77, 108, 143

Nattida Maneeprapha
15

Lorena Medina
10–11, 16, 17, 18, 19, 58, 59, 102–103, 104–105, 106, 107, 110, 140, 150, 156

Veronika Mudra
111

Pricilla Ochoa
98

Livia Pillmann
12–13, 14, 132, 133

Dallas Rein
1, 5, 71, 72–73, 74, 75, 76, 155

Larissa Schot
68, 69, 109, 118, 119

Aria Skye
96, 97, 135, 146

Makayla Marie Yarbrough
21, 88, 89, 92, 93, 94, 95, 116, 117, 157

Katrina Yehorova
8–9, 26, 27, 28, 29, 30–31, 38, 39, 78–79, 80, 81, 142, 147, 151

Inja Zalta
25, 42–43, 44, 45, 46, 47, 48–49

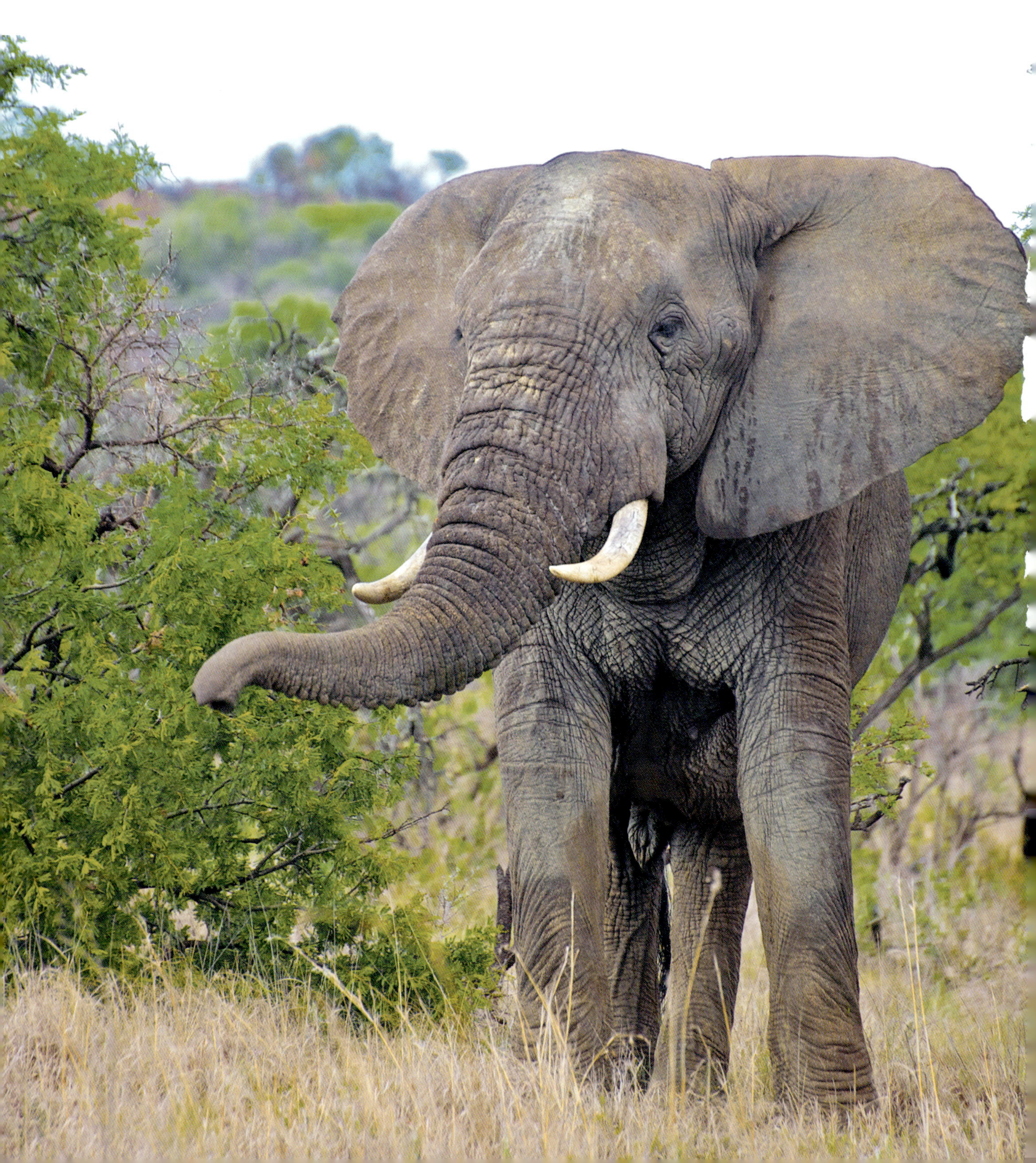